ÉMIGRÉS   The Transformation of Art Publishing in Britain

Anna Nyburg

Preface 7

1
Portraits: The Founders of Phaidon Press, Adprint
and Thames & Hudson 11

2
Roots: Art and Culture in Mitteleuropa and Britain
before World War II 25

3
Flight from Nazi Europe 47

4
Arrival and War: Publishing Émigrés in Britain 65

5
A New Start: Phaidon and Art Publishing after the War 81

6
Between the Pages: Typography, Design and Illustration 99

7
Photography and Printing 125

8
The Rise and Fall of Adprint 149

9
The Birth of Thames & Hudson 163

10
Phaidon Press and Thames & Hudson Come of Age 183

11
Jostling Imitators 195

12
Ripple Effect: The Influence and Legacy of the Émigrés 207

Conclusion 221

Endnotes 225
Appendices 242
Acknowledgements 251
Bibliography 252
Index 267

Preface

In 2013 Sir Mervyn King, governor of the Bank of England, chose E. H. Gombrich's *The Story of Art* as the book that meant the most to him, claiming that it made readers accessible to art, rather than art accessible to readers.[1] *The Story of Art*, first published in 1950 and still in print today, has sold well over six million copies. Its author, art historian Ernst Gombrich, came to England in the mid-1930s and could not return to his native Austria after it was annexed by the Nazis in 1938. The subject of *The Story of Art* was educational, its presentation of ideas was radical – and its publisher was Phaidon.

Phaidon, one of the world's finest publishers of books on the visual arts, was founded in Vienna in 1923 by three former school-mates: Béla Horovitz, Ludwig Goldscheider and Fritz Ungar (who left the enterprise early on). In 1938 Horovitz and Goldscheider fled the Nazis and set up business in London. Thames & Hudson, also a publisher of fine illustrated books, was founded in 1949 by Walter Neurath, an Austrian publisher from Vienna, and his third wife, Eva, a refugee from Berlin. Their aim was, famously, to create 'a museum without walls'. Walter Neurath had also been instrumental in the creation of book packaging, a new approach to publishing pioneered with his friend Harry Fischer in Vienna in the 1930s. Their international co-editions were developed with Wolfgang Foges, who founded Adprint in 1937 to conceive, commission and produce books, many of them lavishly illustrated. It was not long before Adprint was doing business in London, the city to which Foges was forced to emigrate – driven out of Austria, like so many of his compatriots, because, as a Jew, he could no longer work or live there.

This book looks at the influence on the British cultural landscape of German and Austrian refugees from Nazism. Their impact reverberated in the world of British publishing, affecting not only art books but also colour printing, design, photography and illustration. Sales, publicity and marketing were similarly transformed. Adprint was among the earliest book packagers, and the refugee publishers together encouraged a dramatic expansion of co-editions and international sales. They excelled in the skills of integrating text and pictures and produced many books for young people that are considered classics today. Their knowledge and contacts enabled them to publish and sell art books at low prices while maintaining high standards. Their contribution to British art education is also significant. Through their teaching, mentoring and publications, these refugee publishers and book creators left a powerful legacy for future generations.

1   Portraits: The Founders of Phaidon Press, Adprint
     and Thames & Hudson

Béla Horovitz and Ludwig Goldscheider

Phaidon Verlag (German for 'publishing house') was founded in 1923 by three former Viennese schoolmates: Béla Horovitz, Ludwig Goldscheider and Fritz Ungar. The name comes from Phaedo, a pupil of Socrates who was present at the philosopher's death and who discussed with him the immortality of the soul.[1] Ungar left the company in 1926 to set up Saturn Verlag. He stayed in Vienna until 1938, when he emigrated to New York, founding the Frederick Ungar publishing house in 1941. He continued a close, if stormy friendship with Goldscheider, whom he also consulted on publishing matters.

Although Phaidon was set up very much as a cooperative effort, with every partner able to carry out any task, from authors' contracts to layout, Béla Horovitz (fig.1) was initially responsible for the

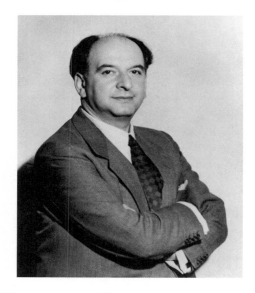

financing of the company and for business matters. Some of the skills he needed for this position can be inferred from a classified advertisement in *Das Börsenblatt*, the influential journal of the book trade: 'To direct an art publishing house ... Only gentlemen who write well, who know the sector and have a talent for organization, are energetic and have a pleasant manner are invited to apply.'[2]

Horovitz was born on 18 April 1898 in Budapest, where his father was a businessman who frequently travelled abroad. The family moved to Vienna, where Béla received his secondary schooling and later went to university. He was enrolled in the faculty of law

1 Béla Horovitz

but also studied philosophy, graduating as Doctor of Law in 1922. In 1925 Horovitz married Lotte Beller (1905–2003), and the couple had three children: Joseph in 1926, Elly in 1928 and Hannah in 1936. Joseph became a composer and professor of music but nevertheless remained involved with Phaidon on a personal basis. Elly Horovitz, with her husband Harvey Miller, took over the firm after her father's death in 1955.

Ludwig Goldscheider (fig. 2) was born in Vienna on 3 June 1896. After serving as an officer in World War I, according to his Imperial Austrian military certificate, he enrolled in 1919 to study art history at the Faculty of Philosophy of Vienna University, graduating in 1923. Although he did not actually receive a doctorate, Goldscheider was nevertheless customarily addressed as 'Herr Doktor' at Phaidon,

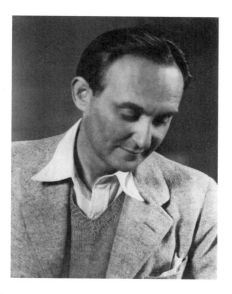

where he acted as the art editor and was himself the author of many major monographs; he translated others from and into English. After a stroke in the 1970s, he relinquished his position as a director and became a consultant to the firm. Goldscheider also had a highly successful freelance career as an authenticator of sculpture and paintings, and as a writer and translator of poetry. In 1924, for example, he produced Die Insel ('The Island'), a German translation of the works of the late nineteenth-century English poet Algernon Swinburne. His greatest love, however, was book design, and he designed books for other publishers as well as Phaidon.

Although Horovitz and Goldscheider were old friends, their relationship was by no means an easy one. Horovitz, despite being the younger by two years, seemed the more mature of the pair. An observant Jew, he was learned in the study of the Torah and Talmud, and his religion was an integral part of his life, and he was devoted to his wife and children. But he was not a conventional businessman: in addition to being very well read, he possessed the famous Viennese wit, the *Wiener Schmäh*, rapier-like and sophisticated.

Jewishness was less important to Goldscheider, and his lifestyle was markedly bohemian. Charming and quarrelsome by turns, he had several relationships with women. In the space of one week he met and married his first wife, Blanka Geiringer, an actress who claimed to have worked with Max Reinhardt; but before the honeymoon was over, they had both already embarked on affairs with others.[3] They maintained an on-off relationship over the next few years, and their daughter Gabriela was born in 1929; she died in 2012. Elly Horovitz, Gaby's closest friend, recalled being envious of Gaby's beautiful white Steiff teddy bear, a gift from parents who both spoiled and neglected her. Their immaturity was perpetuated in their daughter: Gaby (fig. 3) was not an easy person, courting friends but then testing them to the extreme, so that they often rejected her out of sheer frustration. Neither of her Jewish parents was religious, and under the influence of a nanny, Gaby became a Christian.

Ludwig Goldscheider could be vitriolic. More than one friend felt the force of his anger when crossed. Making money came easily to him,

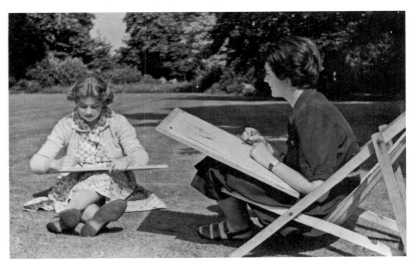

3 Gaby Goldscheider (left) with Lucy Rothenstein, her fellow student at the Ruskin School of Art, *c.*1950s.

but he could not keep it – and he took out his resentment on those around him. Goldscheider had a special gift for art book production: he could visualize books before they were real, and he designed them from the beginning in blank books ('dummies') with real pages so that he could see the layout and proportions clearly. An example of his work, a pasted-up exercise book, can be seen in his archive at the Getty Research Institute in Los Angeles. Despite a career as a respected writer on fine art, as he wrote to Canadian art collector Mr Le Brooay (1 June 1962), he liked designing books much more than writing, and he always designed his own books.[4] He was particularly skilled at choosing details: selecting and highlighting a corner from a painting or sculpture and cropping the photograph, producing a fresh and different image with a technique that was unusual at the time. He was also talented at choosing an appropriate typeface for a particular book, perhaps the new German style of the émigré Wolpe or fonts from the English school of Eric Gill. For the first edition of Gombrich's *The Story of Art*, he used Plantin, a space-saving but easily readable font. Goldscheider's designs, his choice of typography and his own calligraphic skills were characteristic of pre-war book art.

Elly Horovitz has described the way Phaidon operated in Vienna before World War II. The Horovitzes lived on the Parkring, and Elly's maternal grandparents lived next door, in a converted palazzo still occupied by a countess. The Phaidon offices were on the *piano nobile,* and the servants lived upstairs. The offices were impressive, with paintings by Klimt on the walls. After lunch, which the whole family would eat together, Goldscheider and Horovitz would go to the Café Stadtpark to meet friends, smoke and spend time with their children: this was where new publications were planned. Typographers and other specialists in book production also frequented the cafés; Goldscheider, however, took care of these aspects of Phaidon's productions himself. Phaidon's founders knew their authors well, as was usual in publishing in those days, and many were personal friends. They were familiar as well with the *crème de la crème* of Austrian literary society – including such men as Stefan Zweig, Arthur Schnitzler, Joseph Roth and Hugo von Hofmannsthal – and were deeply involved in Viennese music and fine arts.

Indeed, Phaidon's first books were editions of Classical literature and poetry. Ludwig Goldscheider's 'Phaidon Drucke' ('Phaidon Imprints') was a series of seven limited editions comprising complete texts and extracts of works by authors from the Classical world and the Middle Ages (pl.1). Throughout their lives, both

Horovitz and Goldscheider were given to quoting in Greek and Latin, a tribute to their Classical education and a reflection of their humanist schooling.[5] In addition, Phaidon published works by German and English authors of the seventeenth to nineteenth centuries: the Enlightenment, the Neo-Classical period and the Romantic Age.[6] These early books were distinguished by their harmony of text and design, and their rich bindings. The appearance of the book reflected its contents, a design practice for which Phaidon would become famous. Nevertheless, there was little innovative about these early books, which were influenced more by the arts-and-crafts style of the Wiener Werkstätte than the modernizing Bauhaus ethic.

A four-volume German edition of the plays of Shakespeare was brought out at a relatively cheap price in 1923, and the list developed to include history, then cultural history. The latter field demanded photographs and reproductions of paintings, and Phaidon included almost an overabundance of visual examples. In 1930 the firm published Egon Friedell's *Kulturgeschichte der Neuzeit* ('*Cultural History of the Modern Age*') and in 1932 Mommsen's *Römische Geschichte* ('*Roman History*'), both featuring extensive illustrations that brought their epochs to life for the reader. They were offered at very low prices, achieved by long print runs, often more than 20,000 copies.

The books were phenomenally successful, and by 1933, with the publication of Spanish playwright and novelist Miguel de Unamuno's complete works, Phaidon was established as a significant Austrian publisher, simultaneously extending its success to Germany, where the Nazi Party came to power that same year. This success protected the firm for a while as the Nazis introduced their anti-Semitic policies. In Austria, as in Germany, the implementation of Nazi plans to exclude Jews from publishing was complex, and economy was all too often in conflict with culture.[7] Random acts of harassment, such as confiscation of their books, were inflicted on Phaidon as on other Jewish publishers or publishers of émigré literature,[8] and by the late 1930s the threat to all Austrian Jews from German aggression was daily gaining strength.

Wolfgang Foges

Adprint was founded in 1937 by the Viennese publisher Wolfgang Foges (fig. 4), who had been brought up in Schlickplatz 4, near Sigmund Freud's family home, in a middle-class Jewish area of Vienna. Foges' father, a medical doctor, appears in the diaries of Arthur Schnitzler: he was a friend of both Schnitzler and his fellow Austrian

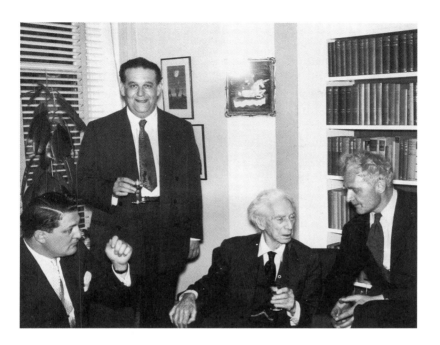

writer Felix Salten. According to Foges' son, Peter, the family later experienced financial difficulties, which was why Wolfgang, unlike his elder brother, did not go to university. Wolfgang's response to this lack was lifelong curiosity and a passion for education. He was especially skilled at bringing people together to work on joint projects, but he often fell out with collaborators in heated arguments. Like Walter Neurath, founder of Thames & Hudson, Foges was given to outbursts of shouting and rage at odds with his cherubic appearance, but he was nevertheless a romantic figure, a completely self-made man who was convinced that people wanted and could be led to higher things.

Foges worked in Vienna as a journalist, and as a 20-year-old was involved in the founding in 1930 of the periodical *Der Neuen Jugend* ('*To New Youth*'), the editorial address of which was Schlickplatz 4; it appeared only twice. Foges was one of three named editors, the others being Paul Lukács and Peter Smolka. Smolka, a Marxist who emigrated to Britain and changed his name to Smollett, headed the Russian section of the Ministry of Information and was later awarded an OBE for his wartime work (some believe he was recruited to spy for the Soviets, and it seems possible that he was a double agent[9]). The two issues of *Der Neuen Jugend* encapsulate the interests and beliefs

4 Wolfgang Foges, standing, with Bertrand Russell, second from right, *c*.1960.
   Foges and Russell worked together in an ultimately unsuccessful attempt
   to publish Nikita Khrushchev's memoirs.

of young Foges and his friends: the journals were dedicated to the youth of Vienna and to all that was new in the arts, social sciences and politics. An editorial in the first issue noted that the magazine was written, published and read by young people. This early project contains the seeds of all Foges' later interests: an enthusiasm for the arts, particularly film and photography, combined with political and social commitment.

The reasons for the demise of the journal were probably financial. Despite the apparent difficulties encountered in the collection of subscriptions, the project nevertheless gave the young Foges a good grounding in editing articles written by himself and others, and in organizing, designing and selling a magazine that was run on a shoe-string with hardly any staff. (Time and time again, refugee publishers would benefit from their prior experience of working for small orga-nizations, where they had to learn the range of skills involved in pro-ducing books from start to finish.) Contributors to *Der Neuen Jugend* included Felix Anselm as well as the editors themselves. The second number was a special edition devoted to the arts. Its strong left-wing bias is clear in, for example, Foges' article 'Aktivität' ('Activity'), which begins: 'Unemployment, social crises, rationalization – all these words come together to give us the underlying melody of our present time.'[10] He comments further on the difficulties for young people in finding suitable employment. Psychosexual issues are the subject of an article entitled 'Problematik', which used the relatively new language of Sigmund Freud.

A review of an avant-garde photographic exhibition in Vienna is enthusiastic, but it is the use of photographs in the journals that is striking. Both issues feature photographs as the back cover, and the second issue has a blue-and-white photographic collage front cover. Articles are illustrated with photos, and there are pages specifically devoted to photographs, probably the editors' own work or that of their young friends. The beginning of a long-term intellectual inter-est in photography and visual reproduction is expressed in an article by 'P. L.' (Paul Lukács) entitled 'The Destruction of the Unique in Art'.

Foges would spend the rest of his professional life dealing with the reproduction and printing of photos and pictures for books. He went on to set up *Neue Welt* ('*New World*'), a colour-illustrated fashion maga-zine financed by textile manufacturers.[11] He was interested in new colour printing, much of which was carried out in Czechoslovakia. According to Peter Foges, his father arranged a deal with a Czech printer but found that his own magazine would not provide enough material to warrant a whole print run. So it was that Wolfgang Foges went to England to look for more printing work. He was successful in persuading department stores such as Bentalls in Kingston-upon-Thames to have their catalogues printed by the state-of-the-art Czech colour printers. He had introductions to bankers and business people who were impressed by the potential of introducing high-class four-colour printing in the UK.[12] His frequent travel between Vienna and London during the early 1930s means it is difficult to establish exactly when he emigrated to Britain.

Walter and Eva Neurath

Walter Neurath (fig. 5) was born in Vienna on 1 October 1903 to Jewish parents. His father, a tea and coffee importer, was conservative; his mother, according to the journalist Matt Seaton, was bohemian: 'She ran an establishment known as the Künstlercafé – the artists' café – and formed a relationship with a "man about town" named Arthur Stemmer, a friend and collector of Egon Schiele. For a while they lived as a *ménage à trois*.'[13] It seems that Walter inherited from his father a shrewd business sense, and from his mother both a disregard for bourgeois standards and a love of art. Herbert Read comments in his obituary of Neurath that 'he was one of those rare entrepreneurs who successfully combine business acumen with idealism'.[14] Neurath was also good at networking. Perhaps his exposure to unconventional living enabled him to adapt easily to different environments

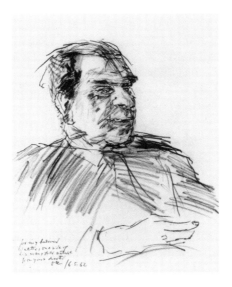

5 Drawing of Walter Neurath by his friend Oskar Kokoschka, 1962.

and lifestyles. He charmed people from different backgrounds and, much married, enjoyed success with women. One picture researcher told how he chased her around the table. However, he also had a tougher side, essential for survival in a competitive business: his temper was legendary, and he could shout for Austria. With his second wife, Marianne, he had two children: Constance, born in 1938, and Thomas in 1940.

Having shone at school, where he matriculated with distinction, Walter studied art history, archaeology and history at Vienna University; his records show that he was also enrolled in the Faculty of Philosophy, a choice of subject he shared with Phaidon's Béla Horovitz.[15] While a young man in Vienna, he was briefly a Communist. Thomas Neurath's view of his father's political development was that he 'deplored orthodoxy of any nature', but he nevertheless later joined the Fabian Society and remained left-of-centre all his life. Indeed, his politics were as integral to what became the Thames & Hudson project as was his love of art and artists.[16] Neurath became involved in the exciting social and cultural revolution of Social Democratic Vienna, including giving lectures on art history 'to the Austrian equivalent of the Workers' Educational Association', the *Kunststelle*.[17] He kept up his contacts with Viennese Social Democrats, sending his son Thomas, aged 14, to stay with the Social Democrat journalist Albert Scheu, who had returned to Vienna shortly after the war.

According to his daughter, Constance, Neurath never completed his degree, like Wolfgang Foges and his own son Thomas; instead, he spent his life creating sources of information for others by publishing books on cultural history, especially art history, for both young people and adults. Thomas says of his father's mission in publishing: 'To his dying day ... he believed that publishing was really about getting authors and academics to write their work for people without university educations.'[18]

After leaving Vienna university in 1925, Walter Neurath ran his father's company while his father was ill, so gaining valuable business experience. Afterwards he worked for at least three publishers active in the field of cultural studies, then for two others: the Verlag für Kulturforschung ('Cultural Research Press') and, later, the Zinnen Verlag, which specialized in publishing literature in translation. There, after six months, he was made production director. From 1935 to 1937, he was an educational publisher with Steyrermühl Verlag, developing new illustration techniques and creating, as general editor, a series of illustrated textbooks for children, designed as an educational counter-influence to the all-pervasive Nazi ideology of the day. The books had a strong democratic and anti-totalitarian bias and were translated into seven foreign languages by like-minded publishers abroad.[19]

Neurath's best-known pre-emigration publication was *Weltgeschichte: Von der Urzeit bis zur Gegenwart* (*History of the World: From the Prehistoric Age to the Present*; pl. 2) with the following credit: 'This series is published and edited by Walter Neurath, Copyright 1936, Steyrermühl Verlag Wien'. The author was Dr Ernst Gombrich, who was to publish his phenomenally successful *The Story of Art* with Phaidon some 14 years later. The genesis of *History of the World* is a curious one. When Gombrich finished his doctorate in 1935, Neurath asked him to translate from English a history of the world for children. Gombrich's answer was perhaps unexpected: 'I looked at the book and I found it so unbelievably awful that I said I would rewrite the book myself rather than translate such a load of rubbish.'[20] The title of the 'awful' original is unknown, but in any case Neurath called Gombrich's bluff and requested a sample chapter. This Gombrich wrote on the subject of chivalry, because, he recalled, 'I knew what I wanted to do because a short while before I had much enjoyed writing long letters to the daughter of some close friends, in which I told the story of my thesis in the form of a fairy story about a prince who built a beautiful palace.' The chapter was accepted, and Gombrich was asked to write the rest of the book within six weeks, a feat he managed by writing a chapter a day with the help of an encyclopaedia. The book was an immediate success, as Gombrich explains: 'I think it owed its merits partly to the way it was written in such a mad rush and also to the conviction that I had (and still have) that it should be possible to explain anything in language that can be understood by a child.'[21] Exactly fifty years later the book was republished in Germany, and it still sells very well. It is ironic that this *History of the World* did not appear in English until 2005. It was Neurath's sense of judgement, when he was still in his early thirties, that was responsible for its success in Europe.

After a creative period at Steyrermühl, Neurath went to work for the publisher and bookseller Wilhelm Frick, who represented the group known as the Buch-, Kunst- und Musikalienverleger ('Book, Art and Music Publishers'). Heinrich (Harry) Fischer, a bookseller who ran the Berger–Fischer bookshop in Vienna's Kohlmarkt, had some work for Frick around the same time. Fischer and Neurath invented the concept of book packaging when they decided to think up subjects for books, find suitable authors, do the design and over-see the book production, and eventually offer the finished product to a publisher for distribution.[22] Together the two packaged first a book on Prague.[23] Fischer also produced, on his own, a volume on the Vienna Philharmonic (referred to by Wolfgang Fischer as 'one of the first coffee table books'), which was then published by Frick.[24]

Frick also published school books, so there would have been a vari-ety of publishing activities in-house for the young Neurath, who was appointed manager of Steyrermühl Verlag in 1937 and continued to commission and publish both illustrated books on the arts and anti-Nazi propaganda. Upon the German occupation of Austria in 1938, however, Neurath was ordered to 'cease his activities immediately'.[25] Frick Verlag was taken over by a Nazi-appointed commissar, and Neurath was forced to flee to England with his second wife, Marianne.

Walter Neurath's third wife, Eva, co-founder with him of Thames & Hudson, was a member of the British publishing establishment for many years and continued to work into her nineties. Her life is well documented, from articles and obituaries in major dailies to an unpublished memoir in the possession of her son, Stephan Feuchtwang, and at least one television documentary.[26] She was born Eva Itzig on 23 August 1908 in Berlin to a Jewish father and an unconventional non-Jewish mother. Two types of upbringing seem to have shaped the lives of the successful art book publishers. They tended to come either from respectable upper-middle-class families on which Kulturdrang (desire for culture) was a major influence, as exemplified by the Horovitz family; or from more bohemian fami-lies, where art played an equally important role but was seen as less of an Establishment activity. This second way of life was exemplified in the families of Ludwig Goldscheider, Walter Neurath and Eva Itzig.

Eva's mother was a socialist, a pacifist and passionate defender of tolerance: in her memoir, Eva called her a 'fighter for freedom from conventionalism'. Like Wolfgang Foges, Eva left school at 14 and never went to university. However, she had a driving curiosity and learned a great deal about art in a work context. She was employed initially by an antiquarian bookseller and at the auction house Graupe, where she catalogued pictures and had them authenticated by scholars at museums. (During the Weimar Republic, many Germans sold paint-ings to Americans to raise money, presumably the result of inflation.) Eva's mother, chronically short of money and with five daughters to support, often on her own, opened an art gallery, Der Parthenon, but it did not provide the hoped-for income.

Eva was by turns tough and charming. Berliners, like the Viennese, are known for their wit (the Berlin version being just as swift but earthier), and this she had in abundance. The drive and energy that kept her working until the end of her life did not stand in the way of her feminine appeal: she had several relationships and was married three times. Eva first married a colleague from Graupe, but divorced him amicably when she fell in love with Wilhelm Feuchtwang, the son of Vienna's Chief Rabbi and a close friend of Arthur Schnitzler. It is ironic that her mother, who had married a second Jewish man when Eva's father died and was a fierce opponent of anti-Semitism, was nevertheless horrified that in order to marry into an Orthodox Jewish family Eva converted to Judaism – an act of convention that flew in the face of all her beliefs. Eva was aware of the risks that she and her new husband would face, having already experienced the anti-Semitism engendered by her name. Nevertheless, they married in November 1934, and their son, Stephan, was born in Berlin.

On the day of the *Anschluss* in March 1938, Eva and Wilhelm Feuchtwang fled Austria for Holland, where Wilhelm had family. There he applied for a permit to go to England, where they moved a few months later.

2   Roots: Art and Culture in Mitteleuropa and
     Britain before World War II

In June 1938 *The Bookseller*, the trade magazine of the UK publishing industry, published the results of an experiment in which a German assistant bookseller, Kurt Adler from Düsseldorf, and his British counterpart, F. J. Sims from Sheffield, exchanged jobs for a number of months.[1] Adler's report, 'What I Found in the English Book Trade', was reproduced in Adler's own English: 'I had an opportunity of being the first German to change my work with an English bookseller, by arrangement of the "Börsenverein der Deutschen Buchhändler" in Leipzig.' Adler was amazed that so many political books were published in Britain, expressing so many diverse opinions; by this time Goebbels' propaganda ministry controlled all German media. But the enviable British freedom of expression was not backed by aggressive marketing: 'What astonished me was that of bookshop propaganda there was as good as none; neither through advertisements nor through dispatch of prospectuses.' Additionally, Adler touched on a lack of rigour in Britain: '... there is no examination for booksellers. To every man is allowed to change the profession and to seek another occupation. During the night any man may become a publisher without professional training or experience.'

The same attitude was underlined in another *Bookseller* article, 'Notes by the Way,' by Hubert Wilson (pen name 'Petrel'):

> In Germany ... the bookseller is a bookseller ... Before he is to
> be considered as qualified to embark upon his real bookselling
> career he will have completed a seven-year apprenticeship
> ... He will have worked six days a week for hours which would
> cause a general strike in England. ... Incidentally, he will,
> I believe, though I am rather vague about this, have attended
> carefully organized courses at Leipzig, with which there is
> nothing in England to compare. At the end of his seven years
> he has been as thoroughly and carefully equipped for his pro-
> fession as a doctor, a barrister or an architect in England.[2]

Petrel also mentions ruefully that in Germany a bookshop was a bookshop, not a store selling a 'shoddy conglomeration of pins, of tea sets, vases...'. It might be a cliché that German-speaking intellectuals were rigourous in their methods, respectful of professional people and tidy-minded, while the British belonged more to the tradition of the bumbling amateur and the clever professor who cannot remember where he has left his bedroom slippers. But an examination of what the émigrés brought to Britain, and what Britain was like in the 1930s, supports at least some of the familiar sterotypes. The Viennese publishers arrived in their host country with much to offer: a familiarity with the Classics, a knowledge of the 'new' subject of art history and, in many cases, a passion for education.

Art and Culture in Vienna before World War II

There had been a unique explosion of creative energy in the arts in Vienna around the turn of the century,[3] as contributed to and chronicled by writers such as Arthur Schnitzler – known for his shocking accounts of sexual freedom in Vienna – the novelist and essayist Stefan Zweig and the poet and librettist Hugo von Hofmannsthal. The Habsburg Empire was nearing its end, barely held together by the ageing Kaiser, Franz Joseph. The cosmopolitan capital, Vienna, had been regenerated and modernized by the building of the Ringstrasse around the inner city. The large working-class population played an important, albeit indirect, role in the development of the city's visual culture. Because of poor housing, many Viennese met in cafés, which, like the parks and other public spaces, provided a potent medium for the cross-pollination of ideas. Stefan Zweig alludes in his autobiography *Die Welt von Gestern* ('*The World of Yesterday*')to the particular importance to young Viennese of the coffee houses, not only as places to meet and exchange ideas but also as a source of international daily newspapers.[4]

Contemporary Vienna was home to several important art galleries. The Kunsthistorisches Museum had the fourth-largest collection of paintings in the world, especially Venetian and Dutch masters. The Belvedere housed seventeenth- and eighteenth-century Austrian paintings, while the Albertina had a major collection of drawings from the fifteenth to the twentieth centuries. Around the turn of the century, however, a reaction against naturalistic painting had resulted in the Sezession, a breakaway group headed by the painter Gustav Klimt, whose work was considered as shocking as Schnitzler's novels. Klimt's flat, decorative style shows his impressions of bourgeois Viennese life. Egon Schiele's raw, erotic paintings contained elements of Expressionism. Vienna seemed to be the location of a heightened interest in sexuality, and it is no coincidence that Sigmund Freud developed his ideas there. The Wiener Werkstätte (workshops) were also part of the city's art landscape. Founded by Josef Hoffmann and Kolomon Moser in 1903, they represented a deliberate attempt to integrate fine arts and crafts and to introduce beauty into the design of everyday objects.

In this creatively dynamic city, Ludwig Goldscheider studied art history at Vienna University, where the subject (as distinct from fine art) was an established academic discipline. The first German chair in art history had been created in Göttingen in 1813, but the subject had been taught in Vienna even earlier. Art historian Gertrud Bing notes 'Vienna's stricter training in textual criticism and the auxiliary historical disciplines, including palaeography and chronology.'[5] In *Goodbye to Berlin* (1931), Christopher Isherwood includes a fictional description of the apartment of Bernhard Landauer, the cultivated nephew of a Jewish store owner, and his volumes of *Kunstgeschichte* (art history). Isherwood had travelled as a young man in pre-war Germany and was doubtless describing something he had seen there, whereas the British at the time were not yet familiar with art history as an academic subject.

The end of World War I, which brutally intersected the lives of Goldscheider and his friends, meant the loss of Austria's empire. The result was shortage and hardship, particularly in Vienna. In response to the poverty they experienced, the Viennese elected the Social Democrats, who created what became 'Red Vienna': a 15-year-long municipal regime characterized by exciting innovations in social welfare. Vienna became an independent province and was able to implement an impressive social programme: housing, education for everyone – including adults – and cultural activities for working people. This revolutionary environment resulted in a mushrooming of ideas and projects, including the Isotype system of pictorial statistics (see pp. 157–59 below), developed by the philosopher Otto Neurath to show the working-class population what the new municipal government was achieving in the new Wirtschafts- und Gesellschaftsmuseum (Museum of the Economy and Society). Isotype could explain in a single panel what would have taken pages of print to demonstrate.

The First Republic, despite being socially and creatively exciting, was politically unstable. The Social Democrats had a two-thirds majority, but the Viennese-born publisher George Weidenfeld remembered that in the inter-war period almost everyone wore a badge on his or her lapel to indicate an allegiance to political groups ranging from Catholic parties through Zionism to Nazism.[6] Vienna's political instability was complicated by increasing urbanization, for large numbers of people had moved to the city from outlying regions of the former Austro-Hungarian Empire. This influx brought a new population of young people to work in the shops and offices. We can see them at play in films such as *Menschen am Sonntag* ('*People on Sunday*'): hedonistic younger workers enjoying the spirit of social and sexual freedom.[7] In their leisure time, they went to the cinema: silent and then sound films, like photography, were part of the Zeitgeist.

'We started Latin at eleven and Greek at twelve, and in the last two years we added philosophy',[8] recalled Martin Esslin, academic and writer, on his years at a German *Gymnasium*. Before World War I the three Phaidon founders – Horovitz, Goldscheider and Ungar – had attended the Sophien-Gymnasium in Vienna's Taborstrasse. Austrian and German *Gymnasien* were run along similar humanistic lines, relating Classical civilization to everyday life to create an integrated, holistic ethos (fig. 6). Joseph Horovitz, the composer son of Béla Horovitz, believed that it was his father's humanist education that enabled him to be comfortable discussing with Goldscheider both the business side of their publishing company and matters of cultural history. An essay dedicated to the memory of Béla Horovitz by a former classmate emphasized how learning Latin and Greek was a means 'to access ... a culture which became ever dearer as he penetrated more deeply into its literature'.[9]

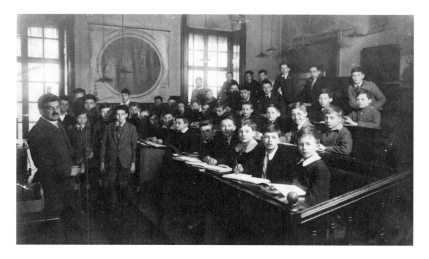

Of course, getting Greek and Latin into the heads of some adolescents was no easier then than today, and the rigorous drilling was tedious to at least some of the émigrés – not all Austrian teenagers were paragons. Stefan Zweig recalled: 'School was a trial to us, boring and bleak, a place where one had to consume measured portions of pointless knowledge.'[10] The fact remains, however, that a Classical education became part of the heritage of all Viennese who attended the city's secondary schools.

Children's homes, kindergartens and play schemes were also created in the new First Republic. Not only did the physical health of

6 Theresianum Gymnasium, 1923; Ernst Gombrich and Theodore Schüller were classmates here.

children become a focus of concern (Ernst Gombrich remembered being sent to Sweden with other Viennese children to build up his strength). Under the influence of the educationalist Franz Cizek, the psychological well-being of the young was also seen as essential, and self-realization through artistic expression was a valuable part of children's upbringing. Cizek oversaw a unique experiment in art education in Vienna when Béla Horovitz was a child. Inspired by the works of Ellen Key, he set up art classes in which children and young people were given free rein. The approach was radical, and Cižek's art education was closely involved in new art movements. In 1906, his classes were integrated into the Wiener Kunstgewerbeschule, an arts and crafts school for older students run along the lines of the British Central School of Arts and Crafts. Cizek's ideas were disseminated throughout Europe and America via exhibitions and lectures.

Not all Austrian and German children learned art in this way; the refugees had different initiations to the world of the visual arts. Claus Moser, now Lord Moser, is well known as a statistician but also made a tremendous impact on British cultural life, especially music. He recalled that, in the Berlin of his childhood, school visits to art galleries and museums were regular affairs. Many Viennese children also got their grounding in high culture from their parents, later realizing this was a 'passport to advantage'. Gombrich recalled that 'nobody was accepted socially or taken seriously if they did not take part in this general culture, in music, literature, in art'.[11]

Later, when the refugees were in Britain, passing on their cultural heritage to their own children was a way for them to keep alive memories of all that was worthwhile in the home country. Constance Kaine, Walter Neurath's daughter, who was carried *in utero* from Vienna and born in England in 1938, can be seen as a literal and metaphorical embodiment of the process of transferring cultural values. For the Neuraths, culture was nurtured through firmly guided reading. *Kultur*, explained Connie, was acquired at home rather than at school – the same was true for the Horovitz children – even though she and her brother Thomas were sent to English boarding schools, as a sign of their father's commitment to their being educated in a 'proper English manner'. The two children were taken by their family as a matter of course to see paintings in Europe's galleries and museums, where they were encouraged to examine how pictures were constructed. At least part of their education took place in Baroque churches. Their maternal grandfather quizzed them with a version of the game *Twenty Questions* based entirely on the arts. Connie also underlined how Viennese children were inculcated with the necessity of distinguishing between art and the despised 'kitsch'. She inherited an acute awareness of the difference, and she was shocked to find that Ernst Gombrich, in whose home she and her brother were looked after following the early death of their mother, had only a few prints on the walls. She was used to the original Egon Schiele drawings brought by her grandfather from Vienna.

Like cultural history, Jewishness is central to the story of the German-speaking refugees. Around 90 per cent of the European refugees who fled to Britain in the 1930s were Jewish; most came from the assimilated middle classes. Many of the refugees themselves were adamant that their heritage was Central European rather than Jewish: Gombrich argued that it was the Nazis who identified as Jews people like himself who had little sense of their Jewish identity. On the other hand, it was the Nazis' very exclusion of Jews from some professions in anti-Semitic Austria and Germany that led to their strong representation in the arts, social sciences, medicine and finance – activities that were still permitted for Jews – and to the creation of new, inter-disciplinary fields. It is possible to argue that there was a distinct German-Jewish identity, common to German-speaking Jews in Austria and Germany.

The Rise of the German–Jewish Publisher

Of the refugee publishers, only Horovitz was an observant Jew, but they all shared the respect for learning incorporated into Judaism. Books were at the heart of the matter: for Horovitz and Neurath, the Austrian publishing scene of their formative years would be the basis for their future lives and livelihoods. In the German-speaking world, Germany dominated. Samuel Fischer Verlag, one of the biggest and most successful publishers in Germany, had by 1918 three dozen successful Austrian authors on its list who were not published in Austria for two reasons: first because Austria had refused to sign the Berne convention on author's copyright, and second because it had a tradition of Catholic censorship, making it difficult for uninhibited writers such as Schnitzler to get their work published.

The situation changed after World War I, when a new generation of Austrian publishers started to establish themselves in the market. They were specialists, unlike publishers of the previous generation who had also dabbled in running bookshops or in the printing trade. For various reasons, the majority of newcomers were Jewish. Phaidon Verlag, founded in 1923, was typical of the trend, being created by Jewish middle-class intellectuals and building up a large market in the German Reich. By 1934, 60 per cent of Phaidon's sales were in Germany, compared with 15 per cent in Austria and 25 per cent elswhere, mainly in Britain and the United States. The early 1920s were characterized by exchange problems: the fall in the value of the Austrian krone relative to the German mark resulted in higher production prices and consequently higher cover prices for books in Austria. In response to the complaints of customers, booksellers argued in 1921 that books had increased by 175 times the original price, whereas chocolate had increased 500-fold.

As a student, Walter Neurath worked for the art book publisher Würthle & Son in Vienna.[12] Founded in 1908, the house was part of a large association of publishers and printing and paper works, all connected through the banker Richard Kola (for commercial purposes the association was known as RIKOLA). The Viennese Chamber of Commerce archives describes RIKOLA's aim as the production and publication of objects from the art trade and works of photography, and all types of artistic and mechanical reproduction.[13] The RIKOLA companies' evolution was complex, as imprints were created and later dissolved.[14] One of the temporary imprints, active from 1920 to 1922, was the Verlag Neuer Graphik which, as its name implies, published new graphic work. The company shared premises with Würthle, and gave the young Neurath his first insight into the publishing of illustrated books. He may well also have benefited from witnessing Neuer Graphik's downfall in 1921, when it published a book of drawings and watercolours from the Austrian National Gallery. A print run of 350 copies was planned, with coloured prints reproduced by Max Jaffé, but the book was huge and unwieldy, and found few customers. With production costs of 300 million kronen, the book was a disaster for the company. The failure may have helped Neurath understand the necessity of shrewd costing, given the high cost of reproduction in art books.

Before the arrival of publishers like Phaidon, heavily illustrated books were usually expensive luxury items. A 1917 Austrian edition of Egon Schiele's drawings published by Richard Lanyi, for example, cost 45 kronen – roughly half of what the printer who may have printed that book earned in a week.[15] Phaidon and other publishers would change this. Milein Cosman, the painter and illustrator, was born in Germany in 1922 and studied at a small art school in Düsseldorf before moving to Britain in her teens. She remembered her parents' support for her chosen career, and how she benefited from the increased availability of art books: 'I was encouraged very much, even [given] art books, so I remember being given *Van Gogh* for Christmas, a big yellow Phaidon book (pl. 4). And I was so overcome ... I didn't go into libraries but we had masses of art books at home.'[16]

The Weimar Republic that began in Germany in 1919 was a time of great social change. While it was an exciting and creative period in the arts, an atmosphere of instability and restlessness was the result of social, political and economic factors. The publishing sector underwent difficult times, having to deal with currency problems in the 1920s as well as adapting to the needs of a new readership: illiteracy had virtually disappeared from Germany, and the white-collar workforce arriving in the big cities from the provinces represented a potential new market. By the time of the republic, publishing houses such as Insel Verlag were successfully selling low-priced, well-designed books. Rowohlt, established in 1911, produced and sold fiction with a solid list of Austrian and German authors. However, other books were not cheap: in a general historical survey of the German book trade, Wittmann notes that the writer Kurt Tucholsky had observed to his publisher in around 1928 that a qualified white-collar worker had to work for about six hours in order to be able to buy a novel priced at 10 marks.[17] Nevertheless, the sales of *Heimatliteratur* (regionalist literature) brought publishing houses a steady income, in addition to literary successes such as Thomas Mann's *Buddenbrooks*. The new white-collar class seeking what Wittmann calls 'comfort for the lost connections and certainties in life'[18] sought solace within the hectic atmosphere of Berlin.

In his study of anti-Semitism in Germany, Amos Elon draws attention to the long-standing tradition of bookselling and publishing among German Jews, noting that, as many other occupations were not open to them, the business offered them intellectual satisfaction. 'As early as 1821, the complaints were heard that too many Jews were in the publishing and bookselling business.'[19] He adds that in some quarters this dominance raised fears that Jews might gain control of the world of ideas,for in the relatively enlightened period of the late nineteenth century, it was possible for Jews to establish publishing companies that were often not only financially successful but also exercised a wide influence on German-speaking culture. In the words of Samuel Fischer, founder of S. Fischer Verlag: 'The publisher's most beautiful and vital mission is to force new values upon an unwilling public.'[20] Fischer's statement goes to the very heart of the often misunderstood role of the publisher in cultural life: good publishers do not simply react passively to public demand, they stimulate and create new demand. Writer Abigail Strubel points out that the ambiguous position of German Jews, as social outsiders yet successful businessmen and pillars of the community, freed them to be unconventional and to take the lead in much of German cultural life. Strubel wrote an account of seven leading Jewish-owned houses: Philo and Schocken,[21] which published books on Jewish subjects, and Mosse, Fischer, Ullstein, Kurt Wolff and Paul Cassirer, which all published a variety of books; the last three produced illustrated and art books.

The German book trade was widely recognized as being the best organized in the world, certainly until World War II. The Börsenverein des Deutschen Buchhandels (German Publishers and Booksellers Association) was founded in 1825 and had no comparable parallel body in Britain.[22] At times *Das Börsenblatt für den deutschen Buchhandel* (*'Journal of the German Book Trade'*), the comprehensive organ of the German book trade, was even issued daily, and books generated many advertisements, trade notices and classified advertisements. One name that featured regularly was the publishing giant Ullstein. The publisher of the famous Propyläen art history series, Ullstein was an enormous enterprise. Between the wars it produced five daily newspapers, four weekly newspapers, three magazines and four technical journals, as well as owning two book publishers and a printing company. Among its other achievements, Ullstein was responsible for the development of the *Berliner Illustrirte*, the model for many modern illustrated magazines and newspapers. It transformed the modest journal it purchased into 'a visual forum of political and cultural events, with original lithographs and biting political cartoons.'[23] By 1926, the paper had a circulation of 1.5 million. *Die Dame*, a magazine for women, was another major success. Strubel notes the parallel between Ullstein and German history: '[Ullstein was] founded near the time of unification, it grew with the nation, survived World War One and flourished culturally during the Weimar Republic. Under governmental control during the Third Reich, it was used for Nazi propaganda before being restored to Rudolf Ullstein after the war.'[24] Almost inevitably, some of Ullstein's many employees made their way to Britain as refugees when Jewish or anti-Nazi staff were forced to leave and the company was 'Aryanized'; they included the picture researcher and book designer Ruth Rosenberg, who worked for many years at Thames & Hudson.

Probably Ullstein's most popular series was the *Propyläen Kunstgeschichte*, which was widely sold in the German-speaking world. The art history imprint had its origins in the purchase of Georg-Müller

Verlag's list, the acquisition of which gave Ullstein the chance to expand its publishing to include luxurious illustrated volumes. (Propyläen and Ullstein were known in-house as the 'wine department' and the 'beer department' respectively.[25]) Around 1922 Propyläen produced 'a remarkably large number of art books'[26] in preparation for its monumental art history project. By 1926, fifteen volumes were already in print in the series, which dedicated a volume to each epoch of art history, with a focus on the images. These authoritative but gloomy tomes graced the shelves of many bourgeois German and Austrian sitting room; some were thought important enough to salvage when flight from the Nazis became inevitable.

To take one example from the series, Paul Schubring's *Die Kunst der Hochrenaissance in Italien* ('*The Art of the High Renaissance in Italy*') is a densely printed, dark volume. The introductory text fills 97 pages, followed by 400 pages of plates, reproduced without comment. It must have been laborious to cross-refer between the descriptions and the images. Other volumes follow the same format. Volume XI, for example, had 114 pages of text and 404 plates (of which only five were in colour), 24 photogravure and 15 offset prints. It was priced at 43 marks bound in half-linen or 48 marks for half-leather, a purchase that would have represented nearly 35 hours' wages for a worker at the time.

The artist Milein Cosman, who was an early Phaidon fan, recalls as a child in Germany owning books by Bruno Cassirer, 'a very famous art publisher.' Cassirer ran a publishing company and art gallery in Berlin with his cousin Paul, specializing in literature and monographs on contemporary artists. One bibliography of the publishing house notes the importance that a publisher could have in the life of an artist, citing sculptor Ernst Barlach as an individual whose works became known thanks largely to Cassirer.[27]

Propyläen author Max Friedländer, one of the more prolific art historians of the period, also wrote many art texts for Cassirer; between 1924 and 1937 he wrote almost a book a year, mainly for the series *Altniederländische Malerei* ('*Old Dutch Painting*'). The respected art critic Max Osborn wrote other Propyläen volumes. Similarly, Georg Dehio was a name well known to those who read art history books in the 1920s; he wrote the second volume of a series on the history of German art published by Walter de Gruyter and Co. Each volume came in two separate books, the first holding the text and the second the plates – an arrangement which allowed for parallel consultation, but which strikes the modern reader as extraordinarily inconvenient. The plates throughout the series were all black and white.

Other houses producing art books at the time included the Munich-based Piper Verlag, founded in 1904 by Richard Piper. From the start, Piper's list was based on three areas: art, music and philosophy, with art proving the most expensive to produce. The ever-resourceful Piper found a solution to the funding of the collected works of the artist Hans von Marées in 1909. The firm could not afford the 40,000 marks to produce the three volumes, so Piper produced 30 copies of the work as a museum edition, with drawings omitted from the cheaper edition and photographs stuck to thin card. At 800 marks each, the edition generated half the total funding for the project.[28] Piper used the same formula to finance other editions, notably the groundbreaking *Der Blaue Reiter Almanach* ('*The Blue Rider Yearbook*') of 1912.

Richard Piper saw good book design as essential. He employed two world-class typographers: Paul Renner and Rudolf Emil Weiss. Piper Verlag was awarded the gold medal for book art at BUGRA (Buchgewerbe and Grafik, or Book Trade and Graphics), the book arts exhibition in Leipzig in 1914 organized by the Deutscher Buch-gewerbeverein.[29] The influence that these early art books exercised on the refugee publishers was twofold: they inspired them to build on the concept of improving on the design and production of such books; and they showed that, being portable, such books were a repository of cultural wealth that the Nazis could not destroy.

Art and Culture in Britain before World War II

While Red Vienna and Weimar Berlin enjoyed a period of creative excitement and innovation, across the English Channel the arts land-scape was rather different. The writer and artist Fred Uhlman admit-ted his absolute ignorance about the culture of the country that was to save his life. Uhlman had trained as a lawyer in his native Stuttgart before moving to Paris to escape the Nazis and discovering through his association with artists his own ability to paint. He recalled rue-fully that the humanist school syllabus in Stuttgart had hardly touched on British history, such were the demands of Greek, Roman and German history.[30] Literature was another matter: he – like other Germans – would not have been surprised to hear that Shakespeare had actually been German, so familiar was he with his works in trans-lation. The French painters also helped inform his artistic knowledge, warning him to avoid English painters. 'When, soon after my arrival, I went to the Tate, I found that my French friends had not exagger-ated: the Pre-Raphaelite pictures were real shockers...'[31] Uhlman continued in a similar vein to disparage Stanley Spencer and William

Blake, before concluding that he agreed with 'nearly everybody in Paris that England had not produced a great artist since Constable and *Turnère*. Somebody had told me about a painter called *Sickère*, but said he was only a weak Vuillard...' He and other refugees who were interested in the arts agreed that Britain on the one hand looked to France for artists to admire and emulate and, on the other, remained a decade behind the continent of Europe with regard to the influence of new movements.

Was Britain in the late 1920s and early 1930s really what the German music critic Oscar Adolf Schmitz called '*ein Land ohne Musik*' ('a land without music')? Of course not, although the music in question was different: the British composers best known in Germany, Delius and Vaughan Williams, were no modernizers. But the sterotype of Britain as a country of philistines and conservatives is a crude one. In the visual arts, music and fiction, there was a wide gap between mass entertainment and the creative output of the few. This gap was most marked in literature: the innovative modernism of D. H. Lawrence, James Joyce and Virginia Woolf reflected the rift with the past opened by World War I; the poetry of W. H. Auden, as the historian A. J. P. Taylor noted, expressed the thoughts of many Englishmen, although few actually read his work.[32] Instead, the wider British public read adventures, such as the works of Agatha Christie or the amusing stories of P. G. Wodehouse. In the visual arts, the only modernists who made their mark were Henry Moore and Ben Nicholson, in sculpture and painting respectively. Generally, the great pre-war European modernists such as Picasso or Stravinsky had little impact on wider British life.

In *Stylistic Cold Wars*, his account of the professional rivalry between the émigré art historian Dr Nikolaus Pevsner (1902–83) and the English poet and historian John Betjeman (1906–84), Timothy Mowl analyzes their distinctive attitudes not only to architecture and cataloguing English buildings but also to lifestyle.[33] From their very gravestones – Pevsner's a starkly square and simple modernist slab, Betjeman's a richly decorated curving stone – the two men epitomized opposing approaches. Betjeman's antipathy to 'der Great Categorist', as he nicknamed his German rival, had much to do with his own dislike of modernism at that time, as well as his personal sense of grievance about Pevsner's dislike of certain florid, nostalgic examples of nineteenth-century churches that were close to Betjeman's heart.

Nevertheless, this crude distinction – between modernism and nostalgia – cannot be taken to symbolize the difference between the two cultures: the truth is more subtle. The German-speaking refugees were by no means all enthusiasts for the Bauhaus; they brought with them a passion for Classical languages and literature and the writing of the Enlightenment. Nevertheless, from Walter Neurath's collections of prints, drawings and other works of art by Oskar Kokoschka to Béla Horovitz's championing of van Gogh, they provided examples of an openness to modern or avant-garde art that was much less common in Britain in the 1930s.

The Englishman's experience of art at that time was based largely on the London art galleries, which were dominated by the National Gallery, the Tate and the Royal Academy.[34] The Royal Academy, as the name implies, was originally an association of artists. Founded in 1876, it became famous for its summer exhibitions by living artists. The Tate Gallery, which was commissioned in 1894 to be the national gallery of British art and opened to the public in 1897, was based on the collection of contemporary British paintings donated by Sir Henry Tate, the Victorian sugar magnate. The National Art Library at the Victoria and Albert Museum was founded in 1837 as part of the Schools of Design at Somerset House, and in 1852 joined the Victoria and Albert Museum at Marlborough House.[35] The National Gallery building in Trafalgar Square was completed in 1836. More private donations followed, including some important Canalettos. The gallery was much visited by the Victorian public, whom Ruskin described tellingly as 'the idle and unwashed'. The British Museum at the same time required a written application and a character reference before it admitted visitors, a policy that inspired Sir Henry Cole to turn the Victoria and Albert Museum into a gallery welcoming to families. After further expansion, the National Gallery's collections comprised largely Italian paintings, with the Dutch and Flemish schools also well represented. British painting was augmented by Turner's bequest of works in 1851, while French eighteenth- and nineteenth-century painting was better represented in the Tate, with the notable exception of works by Poussin and Claude.

It is a reflection of the essentially snobbish attitudes towards art in Britian before World War II that the histories of all three major London galleries feature episodes of indifference, if not actual hostility, to public visitors. Before the war there was no policy of regular exhibitions at either the National Gallery or the Tate, although the Royal Academy held its summer and major winter exhibitions. Displaying and promoting modern art fell to smaller private galleries, such as the Leicester Gallery and, from 1929, Zwemmer's Gallery.[36]

For those with a more developed interest there were also art journals. *The Studio* and *The Burlington Magazine* reviewed the arts scene
from differing perspectives. The former, founded in 1893, had a more
contemporary focus and covered design as well as art. Typical coverage in 1938 included articles on textiles and ceramics, as well as on
architecture by the rivals Betjeman and Pevsner, and reviews of current exhibitions. The review of the famous 'Modern German Art'
exhibition by an unnamed writer made no mention of exiled painters, other than a coy reference to the German state establishing a new
criterion for art.[37] Unlike *The Studio*, in which virtually every page was
illustrated, *The Burlington Magazine* was more text-based, with fewer
reproductions. The articles were more academic, some written by
Warburg Institute scholars, and dealt typically with the Renaissance
and Flemish periods. The journal also covered art sales, in keeping
with its full title '... *for Connoisseurs*'. As well as informing British readers, both journals were widely read outside Britain. Stefan Zweig read
them in Viennese cafés.[38]

A small number of Englishmen played a pivotal role in creating
links between the European and British cultural scenes. They had particular links with German-speaking Europe at a time when French
art was more highly thought of and when anti-German feelings still
ran high after World War I. These same influential individuals provided direct or indirect support to the refugees after their arrival in
Britain. An ability to speak German was a contributory factor, notably
in the success of the bookseller and publisher Anton Zwemmer. This
Dutchman, whose art bookshop on London's Charing Cross Road is
still known to many British readers, ran the shop from 1916. The art
historian Anthony Blunt is another such individual, whose long face
and gloomy expression gave no hint of his other life as a Soviet spy.
The art historians Herbert Read and Kenneth Clark are further examples of these crucial links between British and Germanic culture.

Kenneth Clark (1903–83) is known to many British viewers as the
presenter of the BBC television series *Civilisation*, as well as the author
of a number of books on the arts. He was made director of the National
Gallery in 1934 and was 'determined that the public should stop
thinking of a gallery as a mausoleum for masterpieces but rather consider it as somewhere one might be accosted by new ideas, however
curious.'[39] There was much need for innovation: visits to the gallery
had fallen from 670,000 a year in 1928 to 531,000 by 1934. In the early
1920s, the prevailing attitude towards such visitors was reflected in
the practice of having four days of paid admission each week, which

'were actually instituted to keep people out, in order that copyists might work without interruptions from the common herd.'[40]

While a scholar such as Anthony Blunt helped disseminate the ideas of the German émigré art scholars, Kenneth Clark intervened more directly. Clark's childhood had been deprived of emotional warmth, which was perhaps why he had a heightened response to the sensual pleasure of shapes and colours. Art books had played a pivotal role in shaping his life, particularly one he was given in 1910 on the paintings of the Louvre. Although the 54 colour plates were poor reproductions, they gave the young Clark an idea of European painting. 'At the age of seventy, he could close his eyes and reel off the names of paintings he had first seen in the Louvre book some sixty-three years earlier.'[41]

Having met and worked with the collector and connoisseur Bernard Berenson, Clark came under the influence of the art critic Roger Fry. Previously enamoured of the ideas of John Ruskin, in particular his thoughts on art, moral values and subject matter, Clark now embraced Fry's contrasting championing of the importance of purely aesthetic considerations in art: iconography and pictorial content. In 1926 Clark went to Germany to 'perfect his German' and researched German art and architecture. While there he heard a lecture by Aby Warburg that was to prove a revelation. For Warburg, 'paintings spoke in symbols, and the purpose of art historical research should be to unravel the riddles and put them in their historical perspective'.[42]

As director of the National Gallery, no doubt partly because he was an ardent admirer of German art and art historical scholarship, Clark took on the task of raising the profile of German-speaking refugees in Britain. As his biographer notes, 'When there were refugee artists who had made their escape from Germany and elsewhere, their logical mentor was Kenneth Clark.'[43] Clark not only supported refugees when he could; he also championed the refugee publishers in general, and Phaidon in particular: 'He turned from a series of lectures on Rembrandt to a book on Piero della Francesca commissioned by Dr Béla Horovitz, the enterprising director of the Phaidon Press.' In Clark's book, which was published in 1951, 'his patron at the Phaidon Press spared no expense in commissioning photographs of exemplary clarity and fidelity, and the resulting book was declared a masterpiece.'[44] One can imagine Béla Horovitz and the art historian Ludwig Goldscheider appreciating both Clark's scholarship and his excitement at the project: not many scholars could combine intellect and visual sensibility to the same degree. Other books followed for Phaidon, for Thames & Hudson and for Cambridge University Press.

Clark also employed less high-profile refugees in the production of his books. The art historian Hilde Kurz, cousin of Oxford University Press editor Theodore Schüller, mentioned in a letter to her sister Ilse in June 1938 that Clark had asked her to compile the index for his book on Leonardo da Vinci. She was not paid for the job until 6 May 1939, and wrote bitterly to her sister: 'The first index brought in £12, it arrived today with the excuse that it had taken Sir Kenneth so long to find out "the correct amount".'[45] Explaining that he had asked several people for their advice, she added: 'And this is one of the richest men in England and is supposed to be as elegant as he is distinguished!' The eminent art historian had little idea what it was like to worry about money.

The strongly held opinions of such prominent figures on the art scene led to the formation of both alliances and rivalries. One example of this animosity was to be found between Kenneth Clark and the critic Herbert Read (1893–1968) who, like Clark, was what his biographer called both a 'taste-maker' and 'cultural impresario', and an active supporter of the German-speaking refugees, publicly and privately.[46] During his career, Read held a post at the Victoria and Albert Museum, wrote and broadcast on the arts, editing for a time from 1933 the *Burlington Magazine* (for which refugee scholars including Erwin Panofsky and Friedrich Antal also wrote), and was partly responsible for the creation of the Institute for the Contemporary Arts (ICA) in 1946. Read's own discovery of avant-garde European art came about by chance because Leeds, where he went to study, was one of the very few places in England at the time where one could see contemporary European art. The avant-garde Ukrainian-born sculptor Jakob Kramer lived there and was a member of the Leeds Arts Club. In 1912, Read was invited by the Vice-Chancellor of Leeds University, Michael Sadler, to view his collection of the works of Wassily Kandinsky. Read firmly believed that art should be accessible to everyone. His quarrel with Kenneth Clark was based on his belief that 'advanced art' was elitist.

The Warburg Institute is in many ways the embodiment of the successful transplantation of German art history to Britain, although in some ways isolated: in Britain, but not integrated into it.[47] It was originally a private collection of books relating to the Renaissance established by Aby Warburg, born in 1866 to a wealthy Jewish banking family in Hamburg. The Kulturwissenschaftliche Bibliothek Warburg acquired its own specially constructed library from 1925 and was opened to scholars. Dedicated to '*das Nachleben der Antike*' ('the afterlife of Classical antiquity'), it was arranged in a highly innovative way, covering such diverse subjects as astrology, religion and philosophy.

After Warburg's death in 1929, his Austrian assistant Fritz Saxl took over the running of the library. In 1933, Saxl realized that the Jewish-owned collection was in jeopardy under the new Nazi regime. Although offers to house the books came from all over Europe, only London could offer safe accommodation to the library and staff. Accordingly, about 55,000 books, the photographic archive and the library's furniture were shipped in December 1933 to the city's Imperial Institute (now Imperial College London). The German and Austrian refugee staff was soon augmented by more scholars fleeing the Nazis, including Gertrud Bing, Otto Kurz and Edgar Wind. For Kenneth Clark, whose life had been changed by hearing Aby Warburg lecture in the 1920s, it must have been an exciting development, especially since Clark had concluded that philistinism ruled in pre-war Britain, that people did not understand art, old or new, and did not want to understand it. Here was a chance to change things.

The first truly British art historical institution was the Courtauld Institute, which became the first university art history department, part of the University of London, in 1932. It was founded as the result of the donation by Sir Robert Witt of a collection of paintings, and was then turned into a centre for research by Samuel Courtauld. After the arrival of the Warburg library, the two institutes continued to thrive side by side, without much rivalry. Researchers moved from one to the other, but it was at the Warburg that Anthony Blunt and other scholars learned rigorous research techniques in the new field of art history, particularly under the tutelage of Fritz Saxl. Refugee scholars were also employed by the Courtauld, one of the most celebrated being Nikolaus Pevsner, who had a profound influence on a generation of Englishmen less as a teacher of art history than as the author of the series 'The Buildings of England'.[47]

Anthony Blunt (1907–83) played a significant role in disseminating ideas about German art historical scholarship in Britain, having spent his career at both the Courtauld and the Warburg Institute. Although, unlike Kenneth Clark and Herbert Read, he cannot be said to have assisted the refugees personally, he nevertheless had connections with refugee art historians, many of whom remarked on his warmth. Blunt was fluent in German, French and Italian, which distinguished him from other Englishmen in the field. As his biographer notes, 'he seemed to identify with [refugees'] outsider status, and was comfortable with their foreignness.'[49] However, he was not always sensitive to the refugee experience; for example, he criticized a German artist's drawings of his persecution at the hands of the Nazis for being too 'close' to the experiences that had produced it. In his review, Blunt does at least acknowledge the nightmares from which the artist is suffering, his political persecution and 'the horrors of a concentration camp'.[50]

Blunt was born into an upper middle-class family, distantly related to the British royal family. His childhood was marked by privilege, typified by his schooling at Marlborough and, perhaps, by emotional remoteness within the family. After studying at Cambridge, where he was reputedly recruited as a Soviet agent, Blunt visited Vienna and Munich to view art treasures *in situ*. Although he remarked that he had no training in '*Kunstgeschichte*',[51] he had his first encounter with German art historical scholarship in the form of Walter Friedländer. Blunt was also friends with the refugee art historians Rudolf and Margot Wittkower, who introduced him to the Warburg in London.[51] Early in his career, Blunt was engaged by the Warburg to edit its publications, an enterprise that illustrates the mutual advantage that the refugees and their British counterparts sometimes offered each other: Blunt could improve the German speakers' imperfect English, while they helped him refine his research methods along German lines. The Warburg's publications soon joined forces with those of the Courtauld, becoming the *Journal of the Warburg and Courtauld Institutes*. While Blunt is not usually considered as a modernizer, unlike Herbert Read, in fact he championed Picasso, encouraging the Tate to make its first purchase of a Picasso painting.[53]

It is not impossible that Blunt became persuaded of the merits of such avant-garde painting through his relationship with German scholars who were more interested in the contemporary art scene than their British peers. He could justly call himself one of the first British art historians, along with Clark and Read, all of whom were influenced by the Germanic tradition. Blunt was himself able to spread art historical theories, including those inspired by his refugee teachers and colleagues, in his position as the art editor of the *Spectator* from 1932.

World War I had impacted on the British publishing industry as it had on all others: there were terrible losses of staff and shortages, particularly of paper, that resulted in difficulties for British publishers competing in the book market. After the war, according to Ian Norrie's account of twentieth-century British publishing, the General Strike of 1926 affected books less than other trades, as workers in the industry were not unionized. Printers, however, were a different-ent matter, and the 1920s saw high printing costs as well as expensive and scarce paper.[54] In 1928, inspired by the German *Börsenblatt*, the Publishers' Association persuaded Whitaker's to set up what was the first version of *The Bookseller*. Whitaker is also a source for that decade of statistics on publishers, firms that were largely family-owned in Britain until after the 1960s. Whereas in 1920 there were 11,004 titles published (including new ones), in 1930 there were 15,494, rising to 17,137 in the pre-war record year 1937.[55] Of these last, 230 were categorized as 'Art and Architecture', compared to 591 in that category in 1955 (and only 67 during 1943).

The late 1930s were characterized by lively publishing. As in Germany, there was a strong trend towards urbanization and the creation of new suburbs, and leisure time increased, with the average working week falling from 54 hours in 1914 to 48 in the inter-war period. New products were aimed at a mass market with more free time. For example, 1935 saw the arrival of Penguin Books, which owed its origin to more than one German connection and was an immediate success. However, Britain was a nation of book borrowers rather than buyers, with a robust network of private and public libraries. Book clubs, another feature of the 1930s, were to add to the pressure on publishers' profits.[56]

Among the general publishing houses that dominated the scene between the wars were John Murray, Longmans, Constable, Nonesuch, Hutchinson and the great university presses: Oxford and Cambridge, including the Oxford University Press imprint, Clarendon Press. These were joined by political publishers such as Victor Gollancz, who took on the task of warning the British of the menace of Fascism, creating the 'Left Book Club' series. The publishing house of Batsford, established in 1874 by Thomas Batsford and his three sons, specialized in books on architecture and topography.

The difficulty Batsford faced in reproducing photographs to illustrate their publications is referred to in the house's history. By 1908 Bradley Batsford had begun publishing big books of photographic plates reproduced in collotype, a 'delicate and fickle process'.[57] The author goes on to explain that the architectural books, typically priced at around £6.6s., held plates 'photographed by Charles Latham on 15 in×12 in plates at £3.10s. an exposure, plus heavy expenses. The enlargement now universally employed was anathema.'

The slump of the early 1930s was an anxious time for Batsford, as for other publishers, but as the history records, 'the only way to weather the storm was to adapt to attract a different public and to offer attractive books at a lower price'. It was at this time that the firm was joined fortuitously by Harry Batsford's nephew Brian Cook, 'a young man with a unique talent for design and painting highly coloured book jackets'. Batsford decided to embark on an ambitious series of books about Britain, 'The British Heritage Series', which was intended to show British readers the splendour of their own architectural landscape.[58] The series was followed by another, 'The Face of Britain', which concentrated more on the natural than the geographical divisions of the country. Each book in the first series was to contain some 40,000 words of text, accompanied by good photographs, one or more colour plates, numerous line drawings, picture endpapers and one of Brian Cook's iconic colour jackets. The first print run would have to be 10,000 to make the project viable. It was a huge gamble for the house, but the series sold extremely well. Two directors, Harry Batsford and Charles Fry, joined the team of authors, travelling round the country with fellow director Brian Cook, who continued to illustrate the series with his striking watercolours.[59]

So the British publishing scene awaiting the refugees was not visually unsophisticated: books with photographic illustrations were commonplace and their value recognized. In the significant year of 1938, Cambridge University Press was praised on more than one occasion by reviewers in *The Bookseller* for its good practice in this area. In an article on publicity for publishers, the author John Baker commented on a new trend. Having pointed out the growing significance of the camera, he referred to the Cambridge prospectus of *Men Without Work*. 'I said that here was a picture worth a million words; it would have been better said that the camera–pen combination can many times reinforce what words alone can say.'[60] Perhaps the refugee art publishers Phaidon and Thames & Hudson would have found less of a market if Batsford, with their attractive, colourful and cheap volumes illustrating the British landscape and buildings, had instead produced art books.

3   Flight from Nazi Europe

Josephs Klage

Was hat es euch eingebracht, o meine Brüder?
Ihr habt mich verkauft, weil mein Kleid nicht wie eures war,
Anders meine Augen, anders mein Haar
Und weil ich nie zu euren Scherzen gelacht,
O meine Brüder.

Joseph's Coat

What has it gained you, oh my brothers?
You sold me, because my robe was different from yours
Different my eyes, different my hair
And because I never laughed at your jokes
Oh my brothers.

L. Goldscheider[1]

Refugee, émigré or exile? These terms have different connotations.
Ernst Gombrich (fig. 7) was adamant, for example, that he was not a
refugee, since he left Austria before the *Anschluss*. Likewise, he refused
to see himself as a Jew, arguing that this was something that only the
Gestapo were interested in; yet, of course, his family was Jewish, which

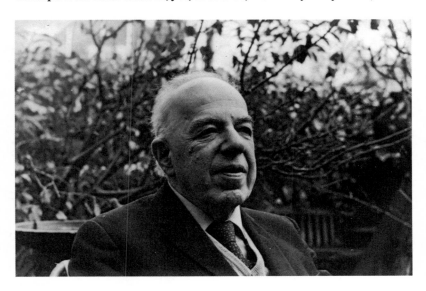

7 E. H. Gombrich in his garden in Hampstead, London, *c*.1986.

meant that he would not have survived in Vienna had he stayed. Exile implies a longing for a homeland, and Béla Horovitz, for one, does not fit this classification, refusing ever to return to Austria after the war.

Whatever the label, some 80,000 Austrians, Germans and Czechs were in Britain by the time war broke out in September 1939.[2] Around 90 per cent of those who arrived in the 1930s were Jewish and came from the assimilated middle classes, whether German or Austrian. Jews who did not have the business and family contacts typical of middle-class professionals were more likely to run up against the barriers that could make the emigration process difficult. Many Jews with less money or influence failed to escape, and many poorer families were murdered in the Holocaust. But Adolf Hitler did not invent anti-Semitism, which was a constant in both Austria and Germany.

The Plight of Jewish Publishers in 1930s Germany and Austria

In Austria, Jews began, in 1781, to be released from the ghettos to which they had been banished in the Middle Ages; they were encouraged to assimilate, and in particular to convert to Christianity. Jews were also admitted to universities. After the political revolutions of 1848, which occurred in both Germany and Austria, Jews were granted complete legal equality. However, legal rights and reality were not the same thing. Viennese anti-Semitism expressed itself in the higher bureaucracy: professing Jews were more or less banned from both the army and the diplomatic service.[3] In Germany in 1871, during a period of large-scale assimilation of middle-class Jews into German social and cultural life, a new emancipation law theoretically abolished all restrictions on civil and political rights. However, restrictive practices continued unchallenged. Professions that excluded Jews in late nineteenth-century Germany included the law, university teaching and most secondary-school teaching.[4] Germany before World War I also discriminated against Jews in the army, the bureaucracy, the diplomatic service and the universities. Nevertheless, life in *fin-de-siècle* Vienna was, for those who could afford it, predicated on leisure and the arts. Perhaps only Paris and Berlin equalled Vienna in the liveliness of their café society and cultural scenes. Stefan Zweig underlined the priorities of his fellow citizens: dancing, but above all music and the theatre.

The vexed question of Jewish culture is still debated today: was there a uniquely Jewish quality in the culture of even those pre-war Austrian or German Jews who were virtually non-observant? Perhaps it was the official and unofficial exclusion of Jews from some professions that led to their strong representation in the arts, social sciences, medicine and finance – all activities permitted for Jews – and also to their creation of new, interdisciplinary fields. A man such as Gombrich, with his arts background, mixed with academics from the new fields of psychology and sociology (where Jewish scholars were well represented) and thus enriched his own view of art history. Another theory that seeks common ground in establishing a Jewish cultural identity focuses on the Jews' long history as a border people, always on the interface between different cultures, in them but not of them, borrowing from them all.

The relationship between religion and Jewish identity is part of a wider debate on Jewish culture. Only one of the émigré publishers discussed in this book, Béla Horovitz, was an observant Jew, but the Jewish tradition of learning was often continued in secular life. Even in poor rural *shtetls* in the Austro-Hungarian Empire, Jewish children would routinely be taught to read Hebrew at the age of three, while their Catholic peers were not taught to read their own language until the age of six or seven. 'When ... the Haskalah proclaimed that Jews should adopt the culture of the Enlightenment and study nature as well as Holy Law, there were many Jews who were ready to listen.'[5] This wider approach was to be central to the Jews' attitude to learning. Wilhelm Neurath (no relation to Walter), to take one example, was the child of very religious rural Jews. Born in the middle of the nineteenth century, he turned towards empirical science rather than religion, but he adopted his father's habit of religious questioning. Eventually he became professor of economics at the Hochschule für Bodenkultur in Vienna. Wilhelm was the father of Otto Neurath, the founder of Isotype (see pp. 157–59 below).

In 1933 there were approximately 680,000 citizens of Jewish origin living in Germany and Austria, amounting to less than 1 per cent of the population,[6] mostly living in large conurbations. A large number of Jews had volunteered for active service in World War I, but even this display of patriotic loyalty had not mitigated the anti-Semitism deeply ingrained in German society. Instead, Jews were blamed in the press and elsewhere for Germany's defeat, and accused of cowardice and profiteering. So it was that Hitler's virulent attacks on Jewish citizens were accepted, and protests against them were put down by the new National Socialist forces created for such tasks, the SA and SS.

After Hitler was appointed chancellor of Germany in January 1933, the Nazis began a programme of restrictions and punitive measures against Jews. The first targets of *Gleichschaltung*, the euphemistic term meaning 'coordination', were Communists and Social Democrats; their exclusion was made easier after the Reichstag fire on 28 February 1933, for which Communists were blamed. Next came moves to push Jewish citizens out of the Reich.[7] The authorities designated as 'non-Aryan' anyone who had a Jewish parent or grandparent. Restrictions on civil servants, including university teachers, were among the first to be implemented: it was central to the Nazis' authority that they tried to control what people thought. Staff who were 'non-Aryan' were dismissed from their posts in 1933; the same year saw the fateful book burning in Berlin on 10 May, instigated largely by right-wing students.[8] Thrown into the flames were books by a range of writers deemed undesirable because they were Jewish, left-wing or 'decadent', including Karl Marx, Sigmund Freud, Kurt Tucholsky and many others. This symbolic act sent a shudder through all Jewish writers, publishers and book artists – and many non-Jews – and signalled to many the need to prepare for flight. Others, perhaps understandably, believed that such barbarism must soon pass and assumed a passive attitude, adopting the line of least resistance.

Increasing ghettoization of Jewish life led to the exclusion of Jews from German cultural activities. The Reichskulturkammer (RKK) was set up in 1933 to impose *Gleichschaltung* in all areas of culture: the fine and performing arts, the press and publishing. In 1933 the Jewish Cultural League was created as essentially a parallel association with exclusively Jewish membership, but Jews were formally excluded from membership of the RKK the following year and were deprived of their right to work in their professions, with the resulting loss of employment and income. 'Aryanization' of Jewish-owned companies followed, coinciding with attacks on the premises of Jewish-owned businesses, their owners and employees. Although the Nazi state bodies were often talked of in terms of 'machinery', there were inconsistencies and exceptions throughout their regime. Individuals also took up the cause: the journalist Will Vesper embarked on a witchhunt against Jews in publishing through articles in his magazine *Die Neue Literatur* and elsewhere, attacking booksellers who continued to flout the ban on Jewish authors and publishers.

The Nazis applied the term 'cultural bolshevist' to many of those working or studying at the modernizing Bauhaus art school, implying both political opposition and degeneracy. Moreover, they associated Marxism with Jewishness, a crude link that may have originated in the high numbers of Jews involved in left-wing politics. This was a useful tool in helping Nazi propaganda exaggerate the likelihood

51

of a bolshevist revolution. In 1933 the typographer Jan Tschichold was labelled a 'cultural bolshevist' and served with a ban on exercising his profession. He was arrested by the Gestapo and spent six weeks in prison. He and his wife fled to Switzerland, where he managed to have a successful career before moving to England to work at Penguin from 1947 to 1949.[9]

Publishers, authors and booksellers were identified immediately as purveyors of cultural values, and Jews in these fields were served with notices that designated them as individuals who lacked 'the necessary reliability to carry out a cultural activity in the new Germany',[10] vague phraseology that made it easy to dismiss them. An early victim was the Berlin publishing giant Ullstein,[11] which by 1933 employed some 10,000 people. The vast enterprise not only possessed its own printing works, radio station and fleet of planes, it also produced several national and regional newspapers, some of which had circulation figures in the millions. As such, Ullstein was in a position to influence all Germans who read newspapers, illustrated or literary journals, women's magazines or books – and the Nazis were quick to take control.

Herman Ullstein recalls that the first threat from the Nazis occurred on the day of the boycott of Jewish businesses on 1 April 1933, when a group of party members marched ostentatiously through the vast Ullstein buildings from the editorial offices through to the printing works, chanting anti-Semitic slogans. It became clear that there were Nazi supporters within the Ullstein staff, so introducing *Gleichschaltung* into the editorial team once the company was in Nazi hands was relatively easy. Nevertheless, the five Ullstein brothers continued to publish their papers under increasing censorship until 1934, when the Nazi authorities made it impossible for them to continue.[12] They were forced to sell off their empire for around six million marks (plus bonds for a further six million), instead of its real value of 60 million. Herman Ullstein fled to Britain with only ten marks. Many Ullstein authors and other collaborators, notably Vicki Baum, had already emigrated to the United States. The editor of the Propyläen art imprint, Dr Franz Leppmann, moved to London, leaving his non-Jewish wife behind.

The new Nazi owners kept Ullstein going, wrestling with the dilemma of keeping the successful brand name alive while also demonstrating the company's new non-Jewish identity. Ruth Rosenberg, later to work at both Adprint and Thames & Hudson, recalls the terrifying Nazi regime at Ullstein just before her emigration. She notes that the Berlin publishing house had published an anti-Nazi book by the celebrated writer Kurt Tucholsky, for which she had sourced the photographs. She 'mislaid' the images in the picture archive, hoping to avoid being associated with them.[13]

Jewish publishers were affected from the very start of the regime, not only because of their 'racial' origins but also because they published authors who were inimical to the Nazi cause.[14] Two directors of the publishing house Gustav Kiepenheuer, Fritz Landshoff and Walter Landauer, left Germany because they published such authors as Joseph Roth, Heinrich Mann and Anna Seghers. The pair went to Holland to run the German section for two Dutch publishers: Querido and Allert de Lange, respectively.

Bermann Fischer was the head of one of Germany's biggest publishers of fiction, Fischer Verlag. He agonized over the right decision: if he fled, would his authors remain with the house? In only one of many cases of pressure being put on the company, the author Heinrich Hauser demanded that a dedication to Göring be printed at the front of his book, due to appear the following month and already at the printers. Bermann Fischer, as a Jewish publisher, said that he would have to ask Göring for permission to print the dedication, hoping to have the request refused. It was not, and Fischer had the humiliating task of including a dedication to his 'arch-enemy and persecutor' in the book.[15]

Eventually flight became inevitable. Having considered moving to either Switzerland or England, Bermann Fischer moved to Vienna in 1936, after transferring the continuing publication of those authors who were not unacceptable to the Nazis to Peter Suhrkamp, an editor on the Ullstein magazine *Uhu* to whom Fischer had offered the editorship of its own *Neue Rundschau*. From Austria, which was annexed not long after, Bermann Fischer would flee to Stockholm and thence to the United States, where he continued to publish despite major obstacles. He returned to Germany after the war.

Although Austria was not formally annexed until 1938, there had been moves since 1933 to bring Germany and Austria together culturally, such as the 'gentlemen's agreement' of 1936, which amounted to Germany agreeing to honour Austria's sovereignty in exchange for Austria agreeing not to damage Germany's reputation in the press and elsewhere.[16] The National Socialist German Workers Party had been banned in Austria in 1933, but although there was no equivalent of the Reich Publishing Chamber (RSK) in Austria, a programme of censorship was introduced in the mid-1930s. In addition, Germany attempted to control Austrian publishing, 70 per cent of the sales of which were made in the German Reich. In 1935 the Germans introduced what was known as 'book dumping', slashing the prices of German books on sale in Austria by 25 per cent so they could compete against home-grown Austrian books, despite Germany's straitened economic circumstances and shortages of raw materials, notably paper. Although Austrian publishers were exempted as foreigners from being forced to join the RSK, pressure was still brought to bear on them, often by unofficial means. They were not able to sell any books that were unacceptable to the Nazi regime, although German domination was still unofficial. On 21 April 1936, for example, in response to a challenge from Béla Horovitz of Phaidon, the German Foreign Office wrote to the Austrian Legation in Berlin that Germany had nothing to do with a boycott of Phaidon's books.[17] The German authorities faced a dilemma: on the one hand, Phaidon was an enviably successful Jewish-owned company; on the other, the Viennese company provided much revenue for suppliers and booksellers inside the Reich.

One way in which the Reich was able to damage Austrian publishing was by excluding publishers from advertising in *Das Börsenblatt*, the book trade journal, a tactic employed against the Viennese Jewish publisher E. P. Tal. When Tal complained through the Austrian representative in Leipzig, Wilhelm Frick, he was told that the exclusion was the result of his dealings with the émigré press, which was anathema to the Nazis. Typical of the random way in which these affairs were treated, Tal was eventually allowed to advertise again in the *Börsenblatt*. As an example of the rapprochement between the two countries, in 1937 Austria lifted a ban on Hitler's *Mein Kampf*, which could now be sold freely there. Yet in that same year, Germany cut the Austrian quota of imports to the Reich, a measure that damaged Austrian publishers and writers.

On 12 March 1938, Germany annexed Austria, and German troops marched into Vienna to cheering crowds and little opposition from the population. At once the Gestapo began arresting large numbers of people opposed to the regime and launched a vicious campaign of persecution against Austrian Jews, including random beatings and the confiscation of Jewish businesses, of which there were some 50–60,000 in Vienna alone. In the following weeks some 20–30,000 self-appointed 'rogue commissaries' (they might also have been termed 'robbers' [18]) used threats or physical abuse to take over Jewish businesses they were largely ill-qualified to run,[19] or bought them for well under the market value in what was a buyers' market. Some 30 publishers were 'Aryanized' after the *Anschluss*, resulting in 'immeasurable personal suffering, personal tragedy, loss of rights and property and humiliation'.[20]

Although staying on in the Reich was untenable for the targets of the Nazi authorities, the decision to emigrate remained difficult for several reasons. Since 1931 a substantial flight tax – 25 per cent of the emigrant's total property – was payable on monies being transferred out of the Reich. There were also restrictions on what assets could be taken out of the country. Until 1935 Jewish emigrants exchanged their marks at 50 per cent of their value, then at 30 per cent and finally, just before war broke out, at 4 per cent,[21] by which time refugees leaving the Reich found themselves stripped of virtually all their funds.[22] Their dependent state in turn made it increasingly difficult to find a host country to accept them.

There was no single obvious country of refuge. In the first instance some émigrés, particularly writers, moved the relatively short distance to Paris or to cities in the Netherlands, which seemed safe havens at the time, or to nearby German-speaking Vienna or Prague. Although the United States was a long-standing refuge for the oppressed, the Americans operated a strict quota system for refugees from each country, with no expansion of the number from Germany made after the Nazis came to power in 1933. Because of this restriction, many refugees travelled to Britain first to wait for permission to move on to the United States. Some, like Ludwig Goldscheider of Phaidon, applied successfully for visas to the USA as a backup plan in case their British immigration ran into difficulties.

Palestine may have seemed an obvious destination for those Jewish Germans and Austrians who had embraced the Zionist ideal of a separate homeland for the Jews. Britain administered immigration to Palestine through its mandate from the League of Nations. Since Theodor Herzl (1860–1904) had published his revolutionary idea in *Der Judenstaat* ('*The Jewish State*'),[23] Jews had been divided about whether they should continue to try to assimilate into German society or abandon the struggle and create a new society. For many German Jews, however, Zionism was a shameful anathema that created a separate identity rather than promoting integration. Moreover, the idea of emigrating as pioneers to an undeveloped land was unacceptable to some who, as professionals, found it hard to commit themselves to a life of hard labour in a harsh climate. Others embraced the pioneering spirit, such as the Berlin publisher Salman Schocken, who transferred his successful publishing house to Palestine, only to emigrate again to the United States.[24] By 1936 Palestine's Arab population was objecting to the large influx of European Jews. As a result of the White Paper of 1939, Jewish immigration would be permitted only with Arab consent.'[25]

German and Austrian Publishers Turn to Britain

Before the arrival of refugees from Nazi-occupied Europe, British immigration policy was governed by the Aliens Acts of 1905, 1914 and 1919, which had been enacted largely to control the influx of Russian and Polish Jews, victims of pogroms, who came to find asylum in London's East End.[26] The 1919 act, which 'continued and extended' the two previous versions, stipulated that no alien could land in Britain if he could not support himself and his dependants; even if he could show proof of employment in Britain, he must satisfy the Ministry of Labour that he was not depriving a British worker of employment. The act also allowed for the Home Office to deport aliens and for the Secretary of State to make further restrictions if necessary.

The arrival of the refugees from Nazism was marked by a tension between, on the one hand, respect for the British tradition of offering refuge to the persecuted and, on the other, serious concerns about the cost of sustaining unlimited numbers of new arrivals. British officials were also reluctant to allow entry because they feared a possible backlash against refugees owing to domestic concern about unemployment or potential anti-Semitism.[27] It is difficult accurately to assess the number of Jewish refugees who arrived in Britain, because of the large movements of people in and out of the country at the time and the difficulty of categorizing incoming immigrants.

On 12 April 1933 the British cabinet agreed that certain 'prominent Jews' from the sciences, medicine, technology, music or art should be allowed entry.[28] An element of self-interest was at play: Britain would take in migrants who would be useful to its economy or its reputation, especially if they brought funds with them or had a guarantor in Britain. The very first arrivals were generally more fortunate members of society who were not stripped of their assets before fleeing the Reich; they numbered between 1,000 and 2,000 by April 1934.[29]

Thereafter, each new aggressive act by Hitler's Nazi government – the Nuremberg Laws, the annexation of Austria and Kristallnacht – was followed by an increase in emigration. Once it became evident that there would be a significant influx of refugees into Britain,

Anglo–Jewish charities stepped in to assume the financial burden. Otto Schiff, a banker who had worked with refugees after the World War I, acted closely with the Home Office to set up the Jewish Refugees' Committee (later the German Jewish Aid Committee), which undertook to bear all the expense of incoming German refugees. At first, British policy was to forbid refugees to work, in view of high unemployment and fear of reaction from the British working population. However, many exceptions were made, and work permits were issued for categories such as agricultural workers and nursing trainees.[30]

After the *Anschluss*, the British government introduced a visa system to cope with the sudden increase in numbers, meaning a pre-selection of suitable immigrants.[31] Among those awarded visas were refugees with an international reputation in the sciences, medicine, the arts and so on, whose entry again typified the ambivalent British attitude of sympathy mixed with opportunism.[32] Visas were also issued for domestic servants, which led to large numbers of professional Austrians coming to Britain to work as domestics.[33] Others, who entered Britain as visitors, were able to work as academics, aided by the Academic Assistance Council, which in 1936 became the Society for the Protection of Science and Learning (SPSL). Although academics as a rule were not supposed to stay permanently in Britain, again the policy was applied selectively.[34] (In November 1939, after the outbreak of war, the ban on refugee work permits was gradually lifted, except in certain sectors deemed sensitive, such as armament industries.) A record of employment taken up by German-speaking refugees shows that female domestics accounted for by far the highest number, nearly 10,000.[35]

The champions of the German-speaking refugees were few but tenacious: MPs Josiah Wedgwood and Eleanor Rathbone pleaded repeatedly in the House of Commons for mercy to be extended to the victims of Nazism. The Religious Society of Friends, or Quakers, were also active in supporting the refugees, both sponsoring them personally and working with other relevant organizations. Individual Liberal party intellectuals, such as Victor Bonham-Carter, were also outspoken in their support. The British popular press, especially *The Daily Mail* (a newspaper the owners of which were sympathizers with Oswald Mosley's British fascism) and *The Daily Express*, were on the whole hostile to the immigration,[36] seeing the refugees as a potential cause of unemployment. The *Manchester Guardian* was alone among the serious dailies in consistently supporting the refugee cause. Following the outbreak of war, and particularly after the fall of

France in June 1940, public hostility to the refugees increased, fuelled by the popular press. After the introduction of mass internment of enemy aliens in 1940, the British government took the step of deporting some refugees to Canada and Australia, with tragic consequences: the *Arandora Star*, headed for Canada, was torpedoed and sunk, resulting in many deaths. The British public's attitude changed in general to one of greater sympathy to the immigrants following the tragedy.

Those refugees who had read the signs early and left Austria well before the *Anschluss* had the advantage of bringing money and possessions with them. This was not possible after 1938, when for most people emigration was simply a question of obtaining a sponsor or a visa to enter Britain as quickly as possible. Inevitably, well-connected, middle-class professionals fared better when it came to finding a sponsor, although an element of chance was often involved. Those who worked in publishing or the book arts had fewer difficulties than most in both gaining entry to Britain and finding work, largely thanks to their prior connections in the multi-national world of books.

Walter Neurath, who was not only Jewish but had also been involved in the publication of anti-Nazi books, was particularly fortunate. A friend of his, Alfred Geiringer, had been in Britain since 1936 and had got to know Frank Margesson, the son of the First Viscount Margesson of Rugby, later Secretary of State for War. Geiringer asked Margesson to persuade his father to sponsor Walter. According to Neurath's daughter, Constance, the family received a letter from Viscount Margesson, asking them to 'visit' England and suggesting May or June, 'when the countryside is at its best'. No doubt Margesson knew that he had to give the impression that the Neuraths would be visiting, not emigrating. Neurath and his wife arrived on 1 June 1938, and stayed with the Margessons for some five years.[37] Neurath was also lucky enough to know and have as another sponsor Martin Charteris, later Private Secretary to the Queen. This connection was instrumental in allowing the family to bring their belongings from Vienna, including valuable furniture and their Schiele drawings.

Despite a short-term reprieve from Nazi measures against Phaidon, it became obvious that life in Austria was no longer possible for Jews, and the Horovitzes and the Goldscheiders and their immediate families also left Vienna. Elly Horovitz does not remember specific incidents of anti-Semitism at school before the *Anschluss*, although her brother suffered from the prevailing anti-Jewish feeling there and on the streets. However, the family did have a nanny who was a Nazi, to whom they had to entrust the youngest daughter,

Hannah, until she could follow them from Austria. Elly recalls that she had her tenth birthday days before the *Anschluss*. A few days later, many of the schoolmates who had come to her birthday party would no longer speak to her. Gaby Goldscheider did not remember anti-Semitism in Vienna prior to the *Anschluss*, but after 1938 she was no longer allowed to attend school.

According to Elly, Béla Horovitz had had the foresight to obtain passports for the whole family after the assassination of the Austrian chancellor Engelbert Dollfuss by Nazi agents in 1934. This was not common at the time, and indicates that the Horovitzes were already particularly aware of the threat to Jews from Hitler's rise to power. The family moved briefly to Marienbad after the assassination, but returned to Vienna when Kurt Schuschnigg became chancellor. Horovitz also made arrangements for the Goldscheiders, who tended to be less well able to deal with practicalities.

In what is essentially a story of escape and success, it is important to remember that nearly all the refugees experienced the Holocaust through family and friends left behind. Close family members of both the Horovitzes and Goldscheiders were killed in concentration camps. Horovitz's sister had emigrated to Holland, but was arrested and ended up in Belsen. She survived the experience and lived to be 98, outliving her son, who was so weakened by his treatment in the camp that he did not live long thereafter. Erich Geiringer, the brother of Ludwig Goldscheider's first wife, Blanka Geiringer, and his young son Heinz were killed in Auschwitz. His wife Fritzi remarried; her second husband was Otto Frank, father of Anne Frank, whose diary records the family's life in hiding from the Nazis in Amsterdam.

The Horovitz and Goldscheider families were able to escape to England because of a mutually beneficial arrangement with Sir Stanley Unwin, Chairman of the publishers George Allen and Unwin and of the Publishers Association. Like other patrons of the refugees, Unwin was a connoisseur of German culture and spoke the language fluently. He had learned much of his trade in Germany on behalf of his publisher uncle, T. Fisher Unwin, at a time when connections with the German book market were much sought after. At his uncle's insistence, Stanley had travelled to Leipzig, then the centre of the German book market, where he sold Unwin books and generally got to know German publishing.[38] In 1927 Unwin wrote to Hermon Ould of the British PEN Club, advising him on how to approach publishers in Germany and suggesting that he would have given him letters of introduction to other publishers had he been allowed a little more time. Unwin was clearly well acquainted with all the major publishers of the time.

Correspondence between Sir Stanley and Phaidon appears to have started as early as 1927. In a letter dated 24 February 1927 from the Phaidon Verlag (then situated at Vienna 1, Himmelpfortgasse 25) to Unwin at his Museum Street offices, Horovitz enquires (in faultless English) about acquiring the German rights to some of Unwin's publications, including a book about Napoleon, a child's history of the world and two English books on contemporary psychology.[39] There is no reference at this stage, however, to any personal contact. Over the next few years, the correspondence between the two publishers was restricted to trade matters.

By 1937 Unwin had moved on from acquiring rights to buying Phaidon books to sell in Britain. A letter of 30 March 1937 from the world-famous bookseller W. A. Foyle underlines the early success of the Phaidon books, as it congratulates Unwin on three titles: *The Paintings of Rembrandt, Vincent van Gogh,* and *The Art of Ancient Egypt.* Together with the rest of the trade, Foyle said, he had never seen a greater bargain offered to booksellers. He was quite sure they would manage to sell thousands of them and was beginning a 'special selling campaign'. His assistants would be in touch with Phaidon for supplies for window decoration.[40]

By November 1936, a personal letter from Béla Horovitz to Stanley Unwin shows that, by then aware of the imminent danger, the two men had worked out a plan of action that would benefit both sides. Essentially, Unwin would buy the Phaidon rights and stock, using money given to him by Horovitz's brother-in-law, Jacques Schupf, who was based in New York. An unspecified 'gift' of money would also be paid to Unwin. Unwin set out some of the details of the takeover of Phaidon in a letter to Horovitz of 14 March 1938, in which he promised to buy specified Phaidon books and materials for the sum of either £6,000 or £7,000, depending on whether copies of *Van Gogh* were delivered in an unfinished or completed state. Phaidon would continue to publish independently in England, using George Allen and Unwin as its distributors. This 'Aryanization' of Phaidon enabled it to continue selling undisturbed in Germany and Austria without revealing its Jewish identity.

Horovitz wrote to Unwin stressing that the technical form of their relationship should be simple, needing a quick and uncomplicated solution.[41] When *El Greco* appeared in 1938, the preliminary work already having been done in Vienna, the advertisements for the book lacked any reference to author or editor (Goldscheider), and as small a reference to Phaidon as possible. The same was true of the title page. Later, any reference to Phaidon was omitted altogether. Other such advertisements in the trade journal *Börsenblatt* advertise what are recognizably Phaidon books with no mention of Phaidon, referring only to the distributors, George Allen and Unwin.

In his autobiography, published in 1960, Sir Stanley Unwin claimed the credit for warning the Horovitzes of the danger from the Nazis: 'I kept urging Dr Horovitz to leave Vienna. I pointed out that when Hitler marched in, which he would do without warning, it would be too late.'[42] It is clear from Horovitz's earlier application for passports, however, that he was well aware of the danger. In 1936 he had petitioned the German ambassador, Franz von Papen, successfully persuading him to exempt Phaidon from the Nazis' ban on Jewish publications being sold in Germany. Clearly, Horovitz had been preparing himself for flight ever since that interview: 'He was convinced that the *Anschluss* was going to happen. Horovitz immediately set about preparing for the worst.'[43]

Horovitz had set up a distribution agreement with Oxford University Press in New York in 1936, so that Phaidon books would be sold in the United States, too. North America, an obvious choice of refuge for Austrian Jews, would have been particularly suitable for Horovitz and Goldscheider because of their business and personal links there. Ungar, one of Phaidon's three original founders, emigrated to the United States in 1938, and the family of Béla Horovitz's wife, Lotte Beller, settled there after World War I. Goldscheider was issued a four-month visa to emigrate to the United States but allowed it to expire; he became a British citizen on 17 August 1946.

Horovitz was in London dealing with the legal details of arrangements with George Allen and Unwin when the Nazis marched into Vienna. Nazi officers arrived almost immediately in the Phaidon Parkring offices, only to be shown that the company was now in the 'Aryan' hands of Sir Stanley Unwin. They still, however, seized archives and the irreplaceable photographic library, which was a major blow.

Later, Sir Stanley Unwin arranged for Ludwig Goldscheider's personal library and papers to be sent on to England. According to Goldscheider's daughter, her father would have found it difficult to work without these books and appreciated the considerable trouble to which his benefactor went. Unwin was also responsible for the safety and well-being of the émigrés; he acted as a guarantor so that they could avoid the mass alien internment in 1940. Typical of his support is a letter dated simply 1938 to the Under-Secretary of State, Aliens Department (Home Office), in which Unwin requests the extension of permits to remain in the United Kingdom on behalf of Dr Horovitz and Mr Goldscheider and their respective families, and in which he confirms the two Austrians' active engagement in the company.[44]

Escape

When the *Anschluss* came, the worst fears of Austrian Jewry were realized. Joseph Horovitz, in a film made to mark its fiftieth anniversary, remembered that 99 per cent of people wore swastikas in their buttonholes in the streets of Vienna hours before the arrival of the Germans.[45] He was struck by the silent, threatening atmosphere. A letter from Béla Horovitz to Unwin written just after the *Anschluss*, on 27 March 1938, conveys the anxiety and uncertainty of the time. He was, he said, just about to leave for Antwerp and hoped to be in London by Tuesday, Wednesday at the latest, with Mr Schupf. He would be grateful if he could be met straight away. He finished on a poignant note, saying that his brother had gone to Vienna and he was still awaiting news from him. His child [Hannah, still a baby] had not yet arrived, but he lived in hope.[46]

Elly Horovitz recalls the children being told they were leaving for a short holiday (school had been closed anyway to mark the *Anschluss*). They packed only sufficient clothes for a few days and left via Italy and Switzerland for Antwerp, where Béla Horovitz joined them. There they stayed with family and were eventually joined by the Goldscheider party, including not only Mr and Mrs Goldscheider, but also Goldscheider's mistress and her husband. In a letter to the Ministry of Justice, Belgium, dated 31 March 1938, Goldscheider wrote that he needed permission to stay in Belgium temporarily and that he had never been politically active: 'The reason for my emigration is purely and simply the National Socialist anti-Semitic laws, which affect me in the harshest possible way.'[47]

Goldscheider's own departure from Vienna had been dramatic. On 12 March 1938, he had received a telephone call from someone in the Chancellor's office, warning him that all Jewish authors should leave Austria immediately. The family packed only their nightclothes, so as not to give away their planned flight. Blanka Goldscheider's friend, the son of a known Nazi, got the necessary papers for them to leave, and they caught the train the same day. It took them two days to get to Paris, where they arrived with minimal cash. They went straight to the house of the Paris Phaidon distributor, Albert Lévy, who provided them with money, some of which the Goldscheiders passed on to destitute refugee friends living in the city. From there the extended Goldscheider party travelled on to Antwerp. They remained there for some three months, and all the children had English lessons. Gaby Goldscheider's English was already quite fluent, as she had had an English nanny in Vienna for some time.

The next step was Britain, but arrival there was not the end of the terror. When war came, there was no guarantee that Britain would not be invaded by the German army, and had that happened the refugees seeking haven there would have been high on the Nazis' list of those to be exterminated.

Libraries at War

The more you destroy them, the louder we call for books.
The war-weary read and read, fed by a Library
Service for Air-raid Shelters and Emergency Teams.

We can still come across them, the pinched economy
Utility war-time things, their coarse paper, their frail covers.
Such brightness in the dark: Finnegan's Wake,

The Grapes of Wrath, The Last Tycoon, Four Quartets,
Put Out More Flags. On benches, underground,
In Plymouth, Southampton, Gateshead, Glasgow,
        in the Moscow Metro
They sit, wearing a scatter of clothing, caught off-guard,

The readers reading, needing it, while terror
Mobilises in sound-waves overhead,
Lost in the latest. Something long. Or funny.

Fire, fear, dictators all have it in for books.
The more you destroy them, the louder we call.

When the last book's returned, there is nothing but the dark.

U. A. Fanthorpe[1]

Until the *Anschluss*, immigration to Britain happened on a small scale. On the whole, refugees arrived at Liverpool Street Station on the boat train, although some who could afford the fare flew to Croydon airport. Generally, those Jewish refugees who were not met by sponsors, hosts or employers were taken to Bloomsbury House in central London, where they were helped to find accommodation and given minimum funds. Many German-speaking refugees went on to settle together, mainly in north London, resulting in the creation of an identifiable community with cultural and political organizations,[2] cafés and other meeting places. 'Finchleystrasse!' was how some bus conductors would announce a certain London stop.

The relief at being out of Nazi hands was enormous, but was tempered with anxiety. For one thing, Britain was no stranger to anti-Semitism; Jews were tolerated rather than accepted, and this attitude continued towards the new immigrants. At the beginning of the nineteenth century there had been a significant wave of Jewish immigrants from Europe, which grew in the second half of the century as a direct consequence of pogroms in Russia.[3] Between 1881 and 1914, some 150,000 European Jews arrived in England, settling largely in London's East End.[4] British Jewish institutions such as the newspaper *The Jewish Chronicle* urged the new immigrants to adapt to British life and not to call too much attention to themselves in public. The 1930s saw open anti-Semitism from Oswald Mosley and his British Fascist Party. There were ugly scenes in London's East End when Mosley's black-shirted supporters clashed with Jewish and non-Jewish protesters.[5] Although this expression of anti-Jewish feeling was short-lived, it revealed a permanent, low-key element of anti-Semitism in Britain, albeit a far cry from the rabid hatred and persecution taking place in German-speaking Europe. British anti-Semitism persisted throughout and after World War II, despite the revelation of the atrocities against Jews during the Holocaust:[6] many German-speaking refugees faced both anti-Semitism and hostility toward them as Germans, the enemy.

One of Mosley's claims was that the Jews were taking British jobs. The Great Depression that followed the American stock market crash of 1929 affected all countries trading with the United States – in effect, the whole industrialized world. Unemployment in Britain rose drastically as a result, although less dramatically than in Germany or the United States.[7] In July 1930, there were over two million unemployed in Britain, and by December the same year two and a half million, in a population of just under 40 million. Oswald Mosley founded the British Union of Fascists, inspired by Mussolini's party in Italy, and skirmishes between the Fascists and their opponents continued until Prime Minister Stanley Baldwin introduced the Public Order Act in 1936 (he did not actually ban the Fascist party).

Refugees and the British alike had to live with Britain's non-intervention against Hitler's increasing annexation of European territory after Prime Minister Neville Chamberlain returned from Munich on 30 September 1938, bearing newly signed vows of Anglo–German friendship and promising peace 'in our time'. Although appeasement must be seen in the context of a population still scarred by the experience of the World War I, nevertheless the refugees often found this attitude hard to bear, thanks to their first-hand experience of Nazi deception and ruthlessness. Generally, however, after the invasion of rump Czechoslovakia the British started to realize that war was inevitable.

The Émigrés in Britain during the War Years

Some people the émigrés encountered displayed their famous British insularity: they seemed to know little or nothing about life on the other side of the Channel, and the refugees told stories that would have been amusing in a less anxious time. Born into the privileged Schüller family of Vienna, where her father, unusually for Jew, was a diplomat, Hilde Kurz was beautiful and blonde (fig. 8).[8] She studied art history at Vienna University with her friend Ernst Gombrich and her future husband, Otto Kurz, both of whom would later work for the Warburg in London. She came to Britain in 1937, when her husband was working at the Institute,[9] but what chance was there for a female art historian to find paid work in Britain, with all its unemployed men? Before becoming a picture researcher, Hilde took on various small jobs to generate some income, including compiling the index for Kenneth Clark's book on Leonardo da Vinci. Through her detailed letters to her sister Ilse in America, she gives an Austrian refugee's impression of attitudes in Britain to the prevailing European situation. On 27 September 1938 she comments on both the politics of appeasement and the reaction of her English neighbours. Having noted that 'ordinary people' had not known until recently where Czechoslovakia was, even at the time of Chamberlain's visit to Berchtesgaden on 15 September, she noticed a change: 'They are completely resigned to the idea of war, know everything about Hitler and say with the greatest calm: isn't it dreadful!' In the same letter she writes that two of her neighbours, having just heard the report of Hitler's speech on the radio, remarked to her mildly: 'We hope you're not a Nazi.'[10]

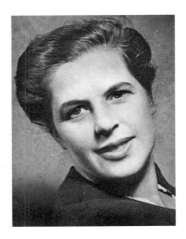

The Horovitz and Goldscheider families eventually arrived from Antwerp at the end of June 1938 and settled in Hampstead, north London. The Horovitzes moved into 23 Lyndhurst Road, which they rented from a German émigré and filled with furniture brought from Germany by earlier arrivals. Many other German and Austrian refugees settled in the area, including their neighbour at number 24, the photographer Bill Brandt. Phaidon was run initially from George Allen and Unwin's premises in Museum Street, Bloomsbury, under the name 'Musarion Press'. Horovitz and Goldscheider were joined in the office by Alice Hammond, a German refugee who stayed with them as secretary and assistant for several decades.

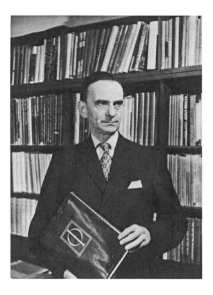

Another émigré who became a key figure at Phaidon, though less well known, was Innozenz Grafe (fig. 9).[11] Born in Vienna in 1916, he studied philosophy for eight semesters at Vienna University between 1934 and 1938, and was awarded a doctorate on 21 July 1938 for a thesis entitled *Qua ratione imperatores romani culti sint a poetis* ('*Why the Roman Emperors were Cultivated by Poets*'). Grafe had known Horovitz before the war and had done some proofreading for Phaidon; he now became an editor, a position he held for many years. He was known within Phaidon as 'Dr G' and, like Horovitz and Goldscheider, could demonstrate his erudition by quoting at length from the Classics. Grafe's father had converted from Judaism to Roman Catholicism, but this would not have been enough to protect Grafe against the impact of the Nuremberg racial laws, and he was forced to leave Vienna in 1938, travelling via Switzerland to England. He was a gentle, scholarly man who loved music, literature and the arts. He was as proficient in mathematics as in philology, but wore his knowledge lightly. He was quietly witty, creating limericks in an instant ('There were two greedy sisters of Edam / Who told Santa Claus how to feed 'em / The elder craved cheese / But the younger cried, 'Please / Bring me lots of smoked salmon from Needham!'), and always exceedingly generous to family and friends. His mother also escaped from Austria and became the housekeeper of Wadham College, Oxford.[12] Her granddaughter Denise remembers spending many a happy occasion in the kitchen at Wadham watching her make *Apfelstrudel* in the proper manner: the table was almost as long as the enormous room, and the pastry covered the whole length.

A good command of English was vital to the rapid integration of the Viennese refugees into British society. It was no mean feat to start life and work anew in a strange language, albeit one that they spoke fairly well. Goldscheider's linguistic skills were in a way more tested than Horovitz's, since he had already written books for the English market. Horovitz was teased about the somewhat Shakespearean turn of phrase with which he would mystify London cabbies. 'Wilt thou convey me to the Square of Leicester?'[13] Kenneth Clark wrote to him from the National Gallery on 17 March 1943, referring to Goldscheider's book on Leonardo and pointing out that English was a such 'peculiar language' that one could live in England all one's life and still write what he diplomatically referred to as not 'ordinary English usage'.[14] Business English was yet another challenge: according to Joseph Horovitz, Béla's son, the company secretary, who was named Stenning, assisted his father with his business correspondence. (Phaidon had taken on Stenning because the firm needed one director who was British.) Horovitz senior once admitted to his son that 'Stenning has pulled another business letter out of me – the hard way: through my nose.'

The correspondence between Horovitz and Goldscheider is mostly in German, though some letters between Ungar and Goldscheider after the war are in English. Alice Hammond, principal secretary at Phaidon, remembers that the working language in the Phaidon offices was English, despite all of the early colleagues being Austrian. Perhaps this was a conscious effort to follow the advice given to aliens not to speak German in public.[15] It may also have been symbolic of the staff's adoption of a new life and language. Grafe and Hammond were both refugees – one from Germany, the other from Austria – and others were taken on not only because they needed work, but also because they were known personally to the directors. For example, Margarethe Boehm, who later worked for the company as a secretary, was the sister of a friend with whom Béla Horovitz had been at the Sophien-Gymnasium in Vienna. Another employee was the daughter of Horovitz's dentist in Austria.

Hardly had the refugees arrived in Britain than war was finally declared on 3 September 1939. This brought new horrors: their host country would be attacked by their own countrymen. Their homeland would in turn be attacked by the Allies, threatening not just family members left behind but German and Austrian culture. Would German churches or Austrian palaces survive a war? What would happen to paintings, furniture, books and manuscripts? This paradox gave rise to complex feelings. Eva Feuchtwang felt that Germany itself and its cultural traditions were being attacked. She felt unable to reconcile her hatred of the Nazis with her love of her country, and turned to psychoanalysis to help her understand her inner conflict.

To add to the refugees' confusion, overnight their status changed to that of 'enemy aliens' after the creation of aliens' tribunals to assess how much of a risk German and Austrian arrivals represented to Britain. The tribunals designated aliens as Category C if they were considered to be loyal to the Allied cause, Category A if they were thought to be loyal to Nazi Germany and Category B if their status was unclear. Category A aliens were interned immediately. In all, 64,244 refugees were registered C and initially exempted from either internment or special restrictions.[16] However, in 1940 there were rumours that the German invasions of Norway and Holland owed their success in part to the existence of fifth columnists (German sympathisers in those countries who facilitated the invasions). As a result, in May 1940 the British government took the step of interning Category B male refugees; the following month, Category C men were interned, too, although Category C women were exempted.[17] All refugees who were not interned were in any case moved from coastal areas, which were deemed sensitive because of the risk of invasion.

Goldscheider and Horovitz appeared before a tribunal, were classified C and exempted from internment on 14 and 20 December 1939 respectively. By contrast, Grafe's story is more typical: without the protection of an influential man like Unwin, he was interned, like most category C male refugees, in June 1940. There are no details of when he was released. Personal accounts of internment show a range of experiences: a terrible fear of being an easy target for invading German forces (the suicide rate was high); boredom and loneliness; but on the other hand, the real pleasure of new friendships and important contacts. The predominantly Jewish population of the camps included a high number of professionals, academics and artists. In order to pass the time usefully, and to improve their employment prospects on release, the internees in some camps set up informal universities; they organized concerts, plays and classes on languages and other subjects.[18] Some artists, including Hellmuth Weissenborn, Kurt Schwitters and Hugo Dachinger, made internment an intensely creative episode despite the unavailability of traditional materials, turning instead, in Weissenborn's case, to linoleum, margarine and a household laundry mangle.[19]

Wilhelm and Eva Feuchtwang were both classified c at an aliens tribunal. Although Eva remarked that the internment policy seemed rather arbitrary, she was touched by the gentleness of the magistrates' questions, which were a stark contrast to her treatment in Holland and Germany. Nevertheless, in 1940 Wilhelm was interned. It was a bleak time, since he had no Establishment contacts who might have been able to plead for his release.[20] Although it is known that he made sets for theatrical productions in Hutchinson Camp and ran the camp journal, he was cut off from his family. Eva visited him once, managing to make her way to Liverpool despite her virtually non-existent English. During her husband's internment, she worked at Adprint with Walter Neurath.

After a public and parliamentary outcry against the internment of known opponents to the Nazi regime, three White Papers identified categories under which internees could apply for release.[21] They specified occupations that would be useful to the British economy or war effort, for example in science and technology. Special personal circumstances that could lead to release were also outlined: bad health, illness or death in the refugee's family.

Those who would be useful to the war effort were released first. The Pioneer Corps (AMPC) had been open to enemy aliens from the outbreak of the war, and joining up guaranteed release. It was a non-combatant corps (combatant corps were open to refugees from 1943) composed of unskilled personnel and largely deployed in manual labour. For this reason the corps was an unpopular choice for the German-speaking refugees who were eager to fight directly against the Nazis and were, for the most part, unsuited to manual work. Harry Fischer, who had pioneered book packaging with

Walter Neurath in Vienna, volunteered however, lacking the contacts to help him find another way to be released; he remained in the unit in Scotland from 1940 to 1943, when he became seriously ill and was discharged.[22] Although he found internment an unpleasant experience, it was in the camp that he met Kurt Levai (later Frank Lloyd[23]), with whom he set up the Marlborough Fine Art Gallery in 1948, an example of the fruitful networking not uncommon in internment.

On the outbreak of war the Horovitzes moved to Bath, where the established refugee community included the writer Stefan Zweig, who was married to Lotte Altmann, a friend of the Horovitzes. The exiles depended on each other for moral and emotional support. Elly Horovitz recalls her father receiving a white feather in the breakfast post, but with hindsight she thinks this suggestion of cowardice was largely a result of widespread ignorance about the refugees and their position, rather than real prejudice.

When it came to avoiding internment, Horovitz and Goldscheider were more fortunate than most other refugees. Sir Stanley Unwin, with his prestige and influence, wrote letters of support on their behalf, underlining the importance of their contribution to the economy, given the profitability of Phaidon Books. One of his letters stresses the irreplaceable nature of Goldscheider's experience and skills, and his 'unique knowledge of the reproduction of pictures of sculpture' as well as the associated technical processes. Unwin noted that Goldscheider's arrival in London was a 'definite asset' to the printing trade,[24] and added that the German authorities would not allow any books bearing Mr Goldscheider's name to be circulated in Germany, indicating how lucky he had been to escape the Nazis. There need be no hesitation in classifying him as a friendly alien. Similarly, a letter of support of 9 August 1940 from the Musarion Press to Goldscheider, signed by H. J. Stenning, Director, shows Goldscheider's importance in financial terms. Some £57,000 worth of art books had been sent to the United States since October 1937, wrote Stenning, with orders in hand for another four volumes, representing a further £10,000. Without Goldscheider, it would be impossible to produce these books.[25] When one considers that £57,000 is the approximate equivalent of £1,140,000 today, it is clear that such work represented a serious contribution to income. This was in stark contrast to the experience of many refugees in Britain who found it difficult to find any, let alone suitable and satisfying, employment.

The Horovitzes soon returned to London, but once the bombing started they and the Goldscheiders moved to Oxford, with Phaidon's new office situated at 14 St Giles. Oxford was an excellent place to net-work for the art publishers: they made contacts with the director of the Ashmolean Museum and with academics who would write books for them. Elly Horovitz recalls that her father organized the move not only for his own family but also for the Goldscheiders, who were distinctly impractical. For a time the two families lived in apartments in the same building in the St Giles area. Ludwig Goldscheider also kept his flat in London, 33 Belsize Court, where he used to go to research his books, paint his pictures and meet friends. Elly remembers her father commuting from Oxford to London, no doubt for meetings with Unwin. As an enemy alien, even a 'friendly' one, he had to report to the police when he left Oxford, when he got to London, when he left London and again when he returned to Oxford.

Publishing during the War Years

Art publishing is a challenging enterprise at the best of times, and the disruption caused by the war made it more difficult on many levels. In a letter to Ludwig Goldscheider from Sir Kenneth Clark, for example, Clark asks forgiveness for not having answered a letter sooner, as it was addressed to a house he had left before the war, then sent on to another house that had been destroyed before the letter reached him.[26] Back in London, the Blitz started in earnest after the strangely calm months of the Phoney War. Books had been burned in May 1933 by triumphant Nazis – now they burned again. Paternoster Row in the City of London was bombed, resulting in the destruction of thousands of books and the ultimate demise of the book wholesalers Simkin's. Before the air raids started, several publishers had moved their premises out of London to safety.

There were enormous difficulties to be overcome at every stage of book production. They included staff shortages, as men were either called up for military service or injured or killed as civilians. Publishing was not considered of national importance, so employees were not exempt from military service. Heroic quantities of books were produced by staff who were 'malnourished, overworked and often elderly'.[27] Bomb damage to plant or stocks and all the inconveniences of evacuation added to the challenge.[28] Even before war broke out, publishers had met to discuss ways of dealing with new legislation, such as the Book Production War Economy Agreement, which was drawn up by publishers but enforceable by law to reduce paper consumption by stipulating the number of words per page, the weight of the paper to be used and so on (fig. 10).[29]

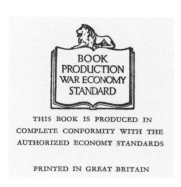

At the same time, the enormous demand for books during the war outstripped supply. Thousands of people had new jobs that required them to learn technical skills; millions had to spend time indoors because of the blackout; relocation to the countryside for war work meant that some were socially isolated; and British and overseas servicemen travelling or waiting for action needed to pass the time. (Penguin's huge sales during wartime may have been due in part to the fact that their small paperbacks fitted neatly into a uniform pocket.) Some people took their thirst for books too far: 'The basement of the publishers Allen and Unwin, where they kept their stock, was requisitioned as a shelter. People flocked in whenever an alert sounded and helped themselves to books. One well-dressed lady took four copies of an expensive art book and tried to sell them to Bumpus, the celebrated bookshop just down the road.'[30]

The Red Cross registered requests from Allied prisoners in Germany for books on art 'comprising the lives of artists, histories of the arts, descriptions of the famous galleries and collections, and volumes on technique'. However, the Nazi authorities stipulated that no books by 'Jews or emigrants' were to be allowed into the camps, a challenge to those supplying art books, given the market's domination by Phaidon.[31] Libraries reported more borrowing than ever. The Publishers' Association, chaired first by Geoffrey Faber and then by Walter Harrap during the war years, supported their members in a practical way, re-creating a wholesale system when Simpkin Marshall was bombed, and successfully fighting off the threat of a purchase tax on books; this was condemned as 'a tax on culture' by J. B. Priestley, who wrote: 'Without books, our civilization would not exist and could not continue in the future, for it is through books that we understand ourselves and each other more fully.'[32] It is little wonder that art books, like those produced by Phaidon, sustained

10 War publishing logo; paper rationing was enforced from 1942 to 1949.

readers and reminded them of the life-affirming qualities of art. A moving letter to Ludwig Goldscheider from Tancred Borenius, editor of *The Burlington Magazine*, dated 27 April 1943, summarizes the prevailing fear for works of art, alluding to 'destruction and dispersion' and noting that Borenius was trying to salvage the 'memory of such things as are in peril of being altogether lost'.[33]

One of the greatest challenges publishers were facing was paper rationing to cut imports. Initially, the paper allocation was based on a formula of 60 per cent of the publisher's paper consumption during the 12 months to August 1939, with four-monthly reassessments of the ration, which fell steadily during the war. Penguin Books was fortunate enough to have used very large quantities of paper during the crucial 12-month period (which for most publishers had been a poor one, reflecting public anxiety and low consumer spending between the Munich crisis and the outbreak of the war) and so were well supplied during the war years. The so-called Moberley Pool was a later version of the paper rationing system in which the government could give priority to certain titles, thereby introducing covert censorship in addition to the more open efforts to support British propaganda;[34] one example of government intervention was their support for the Collins 'Britain in Pictures' series, produced by Adprint. Much dealing was done to obtain the necessary supplies, and not a few publishers took advantage of the Moberley Pool's ruling that new publishers could buy paper on the open market by creating 'new' imprints within their own companies. Frederic Warburg recorded his reaction to hearing that his company's supplies in Plymouth had taken a direct hit, saying that it represented the loss of 150,000 books and half as many again unbound volumes, stereo plates of their most important titles and manuscripts and, worst of all, 20 tons of paper.[35] Only a chance encounter with someone who had bought up large stocks of paper before the war enabled Warburg to continue publishing.

Printers worked unceasingly during the war, with those male and female employees who had not been called up working long hours (not including their additional time on fire-watching). Printing firms also suffered bomb damage to the photographic plates and blocks used to illustrate books, and from the fact that some of these were used as scrap for munitions – a threat to illustrated publishing in particular. With only half the pre-war workforce, an enormous quantity of leaflets, propaganda and books was printed in very difficult circumstances. Indeed, for many printers the war provided a great opportunity, such was the need for information.[36]

In 1937, 11,410 titles of all types of books had been published in Britain; by 1943 the number had fallen to 5,504, a record low. Records kept by *The Bookseller* show that the number of new art books published in 1943 was only around a quarter of the pre-war output, although by 1955 it had more than doubled the pre-war total. However, the war brought an increase of titles in fiction, politics and religion, although this reflects the publishers' interpretation of the market more than the reality of sales. A more concrete indication of the high sales was the figure of £10 million, representing the value of the turnover of Britain's 150 publishers, a figure that remained consistent from at least 1937 until 1941. Equally impressive is the almost unvarying 30 per cent export share of book sales. Exporting was no easy feat in wartime, but it was identified as a lasting and effective form of propaganda. Exports were directed first to the United States, initially with the motive of persuading the Americans to join the war, and then to the dominions: Canada, Australia, New Zealand and South Africa.

Many of the German-speaking refugees were more than willing to join in the war effort to defeat the hated Nazi regime and to show their gratitude to their host country. Even before the war broke out, Ernst Gombrich pointed out in a letter to Esther Simpson of the Academic Assistance Council (later the SPSL) that the émigrés could not simply stand aside while the English had to fight.[37] Many refugees volunteered for activities such as fire-watching. The Warburg scholars Rudi Wittkower and Otto Kurz occasionally fire-watched together; as Wittkower was generously proportioned, he could simply stamp on incendiaries with his huge shoes.[38] Very few refugees, however, succeeded in signing up for active service. One of the first was Michael Kerr, later Sir Michael Kerr QC (son of the eminent German theatre critic Alfred Kerr, and brother of the writer and illustrator Judith Kerr), who was allowed to join the RAF and eventually in 1944 to fly bombers over Belgium, although he first needed to use family connections to speed up his commission.[39] Others managed to play their part using special skills such as their knowledge of the German language; for example, both Ernst Gombrich and George Weidenfeld monitored German wartime broadcasts. In April 1945 Gombrich overheard part of Brückner's Symphony No. 7, which had been composed to mark the death of Wagner, followed by the announcement of Hitler's death. He was the first in Britain to be aware of the event.[40]

Another area in which the refugees could make a contribution was in anti-Nazi propaganda, of which there were two types: first, accurate accounts delivered by the German and Austrian services of the BBC intended to encourage anti-Nazis in Germany; and second, misinformation, or 'black' propaganda, aimed against the Nazi regime and broadcast by the Ministry of Information. Numerous refugees worked in this latter sector, producing German-language programmes intended both to mislead the enemy for military purposes and to undermine the morale of German civilians.[41] As committed anti-Nazis, the refugees were ideally suited to help the propaganda effort, both in broadcasting and in print, as were specially selected anti-Fascist prisoners of war and deserters from the German Army. Ellic Howe's account of black propaganda activities describes forged newspapers, ration cards, handbooks on malingering and leaflets from a German deserters' organization. Millions of documents were dropped on Germany by balloon or distributed by secret agents.

Berthold Wolpe and Elisabeth Friedlander both produced graphic propaganda material.[42] Friedlander had been contacted through Francis Meynell, who had recommended her as a first-class graphic artist. Impressed that she had studied under the great typographer E. R. Weiss, Meynell took her on to complete tasks for the graphic section. Her 'Gothic' lettering was superb, and she reproduced many rubber stamps that were excellent imitations of those used by the *Wehrmacht* and the Nazi party. Her expertise was quickly recognized at the Ministry: few British artists would have been in a position to provide such accurate reproductions of German documents. While it is difficult to quantify the part that forged German documents played in the Allied victory, evidence suggests they deceived the Gestapo and caused disruption to supplies, for example by causing a run on clothing.[43]

There was a comic side to having 'friendly enemy aliens' helping the war effort. Hellmuth Weissenborn told the story of being on fire-watching duty with another refugee. An infantry patrol came round and shouted up a greeting to the two. Picking up the accent in their response, the soldier asked, 'Oh, by the way you're not British?' Weissenborn explained that in fact he was German and his fellow fire-watcher Italian. Far from arousing suspicion, this got the response 'Oh good, reliable enemies'![44]

Although there were no publishers in Britain selling cheap art books, the new arrivals did face some competition. The importance of Zwemmer's art bookshop in Charing Cross Road, London, is acknowledged by many of the refugee publishers and their associates. Zwemmer's was a microcosm of the British contemporary art scene, simultaneously a substitute library for its key figures, a publisher of contemporary art books at a time when they were underrepresented in Britain, and a gallery for contemporary art from 1929.[1] Indeed, Zwemmer's co-editions may have been a model for the refugees' own co-editions. The shop was a source of education and a focal point of networking both in Britain and in Europe. Zwemmer's also had a wider sphere of influence through its role as a supplier to libraries and its part in a new project involving children's art education.

The shop had been founded by the German Richard Jäschke before World War I but was run by the Dutchman Anton Zwemmer after Jäschke was interned as an enemy alien in 1916; Zwemmer bought him out in 1923. It was Zwemmer who turned what had been a foreign language bookshop into a specialist art bookshop. He realized that there were no other retailers supplying art books at that time, a discovery that paid dividends. Fluent in German, French, Dutch and English, he travelled round continental Europe, regularly visiting Leipzig, the centre of the German book trade. Art historians such as Kenneth Clark claimed to have received much of their education at the shop,[2] and Anthony Blunt named Zwemmer's as the best source of art books. Anthony and his brother Wilfred took early pleasure in the beauty of paintings, borrowing prints from Zwemmer's to display at school.[3] The first art history course in Britain did not start until October 1932, and 'Zwemmer provided not only the commercial forum for buying art books, but also ... the leisured and serendipitous aspects of a library'. Henry Moore and other art college students recognized the debt they owed to Zwemmer's generosity.[4] The publishers Oliver Simon and Robert Harling, later to provide support to refugees, were also regular clients.

A list of Zwemmer's publications and authors gives an impression of the art books on the market in Britain between the wars.[5] The emphasis was necessarily on European publications, including the German 'Orbis Pictus' series on ancient world art published by Wasmuth in the 1920s, retailing at only 2s. 6d. per volume. A more expensive German series of monographs was 'Die Kunst des Ostens' ('The Art of the East'), with more than 160 plates each but retailing at

10s 6d., and the 'Junge Kunst' ('Young Art') series, featuring twentieth-century German artists who were little known in Britain, as well as many theoretical books on art history and modern art. Of these, books by Clive Bell and Roger Fry featured in Vaux Halliday's account of the inter-war period, as did *Contemporary British Artists*, edited by Albert Rutherston. The significance of this provision of avant-garde publications can be seen in the example of the modernist designer Ashley Havinder, who came across some Bauhaus books on Moholy-Nagy's typography designs at Zwemmer's that 'had a major impact on his design', for example, for Chrysler cars in 1925. Importantly, Zwemmers carried such seminal contemporary art journals as *Les Cahiers d'Art*, rarely seen in England.[6]

With the demand for more art books in Britain, Zwemmer embarked on a series of co-editions, notably with the Swiss publisher Albert Skira.[7] German publications were well represented, with favourable criticism from reviewers, who remarked on more than one occasion that the Germans seemed so good at producing 'these monuments of combined patience and originality'.[8] Zwemmer's co-editions were by no means cheap: the cover price of a volume on Giotto was £1. 5s., which was the equivalent of half the weekly allowance of a relatively well-off scholarship student such as Henry Moore. The question of how Zwemmer financed his own co-editions and other publications despite the shop's clientele being dominated by impoverished art students can be understood better when it is acknowledged that not only was Anton Zwemmer a consummate businessman, both knowledgeable and cosmopolitan, but that this was a period when Britain was not on the gold standard. That made exports more expensive for the British, but Zwemmer had funds in Holland, which rose in value. This, combined with his innovative approach and virtual monopoly of art book selling for many years, assured his viability.

Zwemmer opened a gallery in 1929, exhibiting contemporary British art but also hosting an exhibition on books and interior design in 1932, called 'Room and Book'.[9] His standing in the art world can be inferred from the calibre of the gallery's advisory board: Herbert Read, Walter Gropius, Moholy-Nagy, [Herbert] Bayer and Havinden. The history of Zwemmer's Gallery provides an example of the role played by chance, then exploited adroitly by networking, in the world of art publications: the first floor of the gallery building was occupied by the London offices of the film magazine *Close-Up*. The editor, Kenneth Macpherson, and his wife, Bryher, apparently exchanged ideas with Zwemmer, because the bookshop started to stock the journal. Later, Zwemmer's was to hold an original exhibition of film stills curated by Paul Rotha, the filmmaker and critic. Two exhibitions were dedicated to refugee art: Fred Uhlman's work in 1938 and the eccentric art collector Jack Bilbo's exhibition in 1940.[10]

Zwemmer's influence, already considerable on art students, critics and professionals, extended yet further: the firm supplied contemporary art books to the major libraries in Britain, such as the art library at the Victoria and Albert Museum in London, which bought their books in 'taxi loads'.[11] In addition, the gallery participated in a scheme that echoed the earlier Viennese project: the provision of art for schools. Zwemmer supplied portfolios of reproductions to local education authorities to be displayed in schools, the London County Council being a major customer. In 1938, the same year that the Society of Art Teachers was formed, Zwemmer's held an unusual exhibition of children's art that gave rise to much discussion on the need for young children to find an outlet for their creativity – some two decades after Cižek's initiative in Vienna (see p. 30 above).[12]

During the war, Zwemmer's profited from the general shortage of books (and perhaps from a hunger for beauty and escapism), publishing art books until around 1950, despite the disruption to supplies. In the post-war period, the bookshop was doubtlessly important to the refugee art publishers Phaidon and Thames & Hudson, and photographs survive of representatives from both companies at Zwemmer receptions in the 1960s. In the pre-war period, however, Zwemmer's must have seemed like a lighthouse, sending out a bright beam into a Britain supplied with a minimum of art books, offering books on Picasso, Cézanne, the Bauhaus and seminal artists and designers, as well as publishing art books in its own right.

Oxford University Press and Teddy Schüller

Some customers remarked on the prices of art books and on the insufficient coverage of art history in English. In 1938, Wilfred Blunt, then drawing master at Eton College, had written to the Oxford University Press lamenting the lack of just the kind of publication the Austrian refugee publishers would later be well equipped to provide:

> A 'companion to art' (the visual arts or even just paintings).
> Such a book is badly needed. There is little at present except
> Bryan (at seven guineas, corresponding to Grove) and the prohibitive Thieme-Becker at £65.[13] A book at a guinea giving
> biographical dates, and explanations of art terms and a fair

number of reproductions, would be invaluable as a reference work, and would I am sure have a very wide sale.[14]

Blunt's request was answered promptly by G. F. J. Cumberlege, Publisher to the University: 'Many thanks for your letter. *The Oxford Companion to Art* is about to be produced, and you will be interested to know that most of it is written and a good deal in type. We hope to publish a year from now.'[15] This proved to be an overly optimistic assessment of the timing of the project, since the first edition did not actually appear until some 30 years later. In a letter to Wilfred Blunt 'to enlist your help', OUP noted: '… the project almost went underground during the war, and since the war it has run into all sorts of unforeseen difficulties, but now it is very much alive.'[16] Indeed, the project seemed almost fated not to happen, so major were the 'difficulties' alluded to; the *Oxford Companion to Art* was not published until 1970.

The idea for the *Companion* was developed by Theodore ('Teddy') Schüller and by those he enlisted to create the book, notably refugee art historians. Teddy, like his cousin Hilde, had had a privileged upbringing in Vienna, where his diplomat grandfather, Richard Schüller, was the centre of family life. After university Teddy worked at the Ullstein publishing giant as the private secretary of Louis Ullstein himself. In 1932, with the rise of Nazism, he saw that the time was right to move to London. A lifelong Anglophile, he already spoke excellent English and was naturalized in 1939.

By the beginning of the war, Schüller was working for Oxford University Press, then based in London (fig. 11). He had the drive, will and imagination to do well in his chosen field,[17] but he was not an organization person and resisted the rules of the institutions that employed him. He worked best by finding senior figures to protect him against the organization, patrons who appreciated his flair and his capacity for making things happen. He was highly strung and volatile, with a fearful temper. Like Walther Neurath and Wolfgang Foges, he came from a culture in which shouting and immoderate criticism were the norm, and he frequently clashed with Anglo-Saxon colleagues who were less familiar with this way of working. It is not known in what capacity he joined OUP, but when the Press moved to Oxford to avoid the Blitz, Schüller moved, too. As a British citizen he was not interned, unlike his brother Erwin, who had come to England around 1939.

In a memo entitled 'Statement of Purpose of "Companion"', Schüller underlined that the planned publication was not meant for art historians or museum officials but rather for the general public,

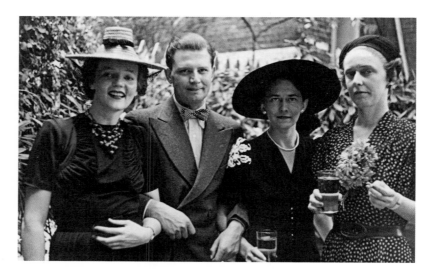

that is 'for people who visit art exhibitions or "see the sights" on holiday; who collect or inherit works of art or frequent antiques shops and auction sales; for students (but not necessarily students of art); for public libraries, and school libraries.... It will stand or fall by two qualities: accuracy and interest.'[18] Schüller's former classmate and friend, Ernst Gombrich, was already involved as a consultant. In a letter to Gombrich, Schüller defined the purpose as 'a book that will give a great many facts shortly, i.e. will contain rather a large number of separate entries, but most of them rather short.'[19]

Despite the planned general appeal of the *Companion*, the standard of scholarship was to be of the highest, and it is here that the project ran aground in its early stages. For various reasons, Olive Cook, its editor in the late 1940s, was not scrupulous enough in her research and could not keep the deadlines set. She was released from her contract in October 1950, having consumed much of the time and money meant for the project. The contributors who could provide the necessary scholarly quality were largely German-speaking refugee art historians, so Schüller's Vienna connections and his networking skills would prove very useful. Schüller drew up a list of people who could author entries to the *Companion*, no doubt after consulting Gombrich. The list included Otto Kurz, who was married to Schüller's cousin Hilde. Kurz was invited to write the entries on Russian art and on 'Fakes', a subject on which he had had a book published by Faber. Other possible contributors included Leopold Ettlinger, Otto Pächt, Nikolaus Pevsner, Rudolf Wittkower and

11 Theodore ('Teddy') Schüller with Oxford University Press colleagues in New York, 1938.

Hugo Buchtal, all of the Warburg Institute. In fact, the involvement of Otto Kurz was by no means a foregone conclusion; on this subject Ben Nicolson wrote to Schüller: 'Of course Dr Kurz of the Warburg Institute ... is far too busy to take on any further work at present. The paucity of scholars in this field is a serious handicap.'[20]

The task of offering employment on a prestigious project was not without pitfalls. Schüller was aware of professional rivalries, such as that between the Warburg and the Courtauld. In a memo regarding Anthony Blunt of the latter institute, Schüller referred to 'the importance of the care required in the choice of the contributors' but pointed out that they wanted Blunt to be a friend rather than a foe, as he had a great deal of influence. To this end, he proposed including some contributors from the Courtauld.[21]

As well as being an essential aid in the choice of writers, Gombrich was an invaluable, if uncompromising critic. His eagle eye noted every mistake in the entries, and his letters hint at the pain he felt at witnessing so many errors:

> Many thanks for letting me see the Botticelli slips – or should I not thank you? Frankly I hate myself in the role of the professional fault finder and I must so often play the discouraging expert ... So I hope you will believe me that it is not for any pleasure that I have to tell you that the entries as they stand are really worse than inadequate ... After all, it is pretty bad, is it not, if an entry starts with the name misprinted and the date of birth wrong?[22]

There follows a whole page of errors, the product of Gombrich's rigorous training under Julius von Schlosser at Vienna University.

Like the *Companion*, *The Oxford History of English Art* was conceived long before the first volume's eventual appearance in 1949. The ninth and final volume appeared in 1978, the whole series representing a mammoth undertaking. Again, the problems of editorship, contributors and checking for accuracy fell to Schüller during his period at OUP. In March 1954, no less a scholar than the Warburg's Hugo Buchthal assessed the latest volume in glowing terms: 'The third volume of the *Oxford History of English Art* is a masterpiece of its kind. The President of Magdalen has produced a book that is both informative and eminently readable.[23]

Another project, *The History of World Art*, was published by OUP in 1950, coinciding unfortunately with the publication of the hugely successful *The Story of Art* from Phaidon. Much had happened between the end of the war and the publication of this great title. The relationship between Sir Stanley Unwin and the Phaidon directors had become a difficult one. Initially, it was extremely cordial, with Horovitz's admiration for the older publisher clear even before he also had reason to be grateful to him.[24] Horovitz's daughter, Elly, remembers Unwin's kindness and support for her family. Unwin, for his part, was a great admirer of Phaidon Press, as is clear from a letter he wrote in 1938 to Horovitz's brother-in-law, Jacques Schupf, in which he expressed his pleasure at having helped such a distinguished fellow publisher and hoped that he could continue to produce fine books in the future.[25] Nevertheless, after a time the working relationship became strained. Both Horovitz and Unwin were strong personalities, and each was used to running his own company. One source of dispute was that Phaidon books were larger format than Allen & Unwin books, and so took up more room in the warehouse. A letter from Unwin as early as 1937 refers to this problem of locating storage space for art books in London.[26] There was also evidently an element of jealousy on Unwin's part towards the popularity of Phaidon books. After all, it was he who had turned around the fortunes of first T. Fisher Unwin and then of the George Allen publishing house, which he had purchased after it had ceased to trade; he was used to being seen as a successful publisher.

Unwin's nephew, Philip, recalled the difficult relationship between Sir Stanley and his uncle, T. Fisher Unwin, and Fisher's 'inordinate jealousy' of his nephew. This pattern was to be repeated: the older, more experienced publisher had to bow to the success of the younger, more innovative publisher. Tensions became obvious fairly early on in London. In a letter of 10 October 1940, Unwin disagreed with Horovitz as to a publishing proposal.[27] Other correspondence contains complaints from both parties about, for example, the responsibility for risk, in terms of both debts to suppliers in Austria and the dangers if London were to be bombed. Such problems exercised the two publishers during much of their business relationship. Finally, on 29 June 1949, Horovitz signalled the end of the working relationship: it was with the greatest regret that he had to inform Unwin of the decision to change the present system of distributing Phaidon art books. Horovitz explained that, to meet all kinds of competition, he considered it vital for Phaidon to take the distribution of its publications into its own hands, and he wished to terminate their agreement by the end of December 1949. He closed the letter asking for Unwin's understanding and expressing his sincerest thanks 'for so many years of co-operation'.[28]

Such understanding was not, however, forthcoming.[29] George Allen & Unwin's reply on behalf of Sir Stanley referred to over 12 years of highly successful collaboration. The writer found it 'hard to believe' that Phaidon wished to terminate the agreement. Listing his objections, Unwin's representative included Unwin's efforts to rescue the Phaidon Press from the Nazis in 1938, pointing out that perhaps no other Englishman could have achieved his success. He also mentioned the support given to Goldscheider and Horovitz when they were threatened with internment in 1940. Nevertheless, Phaidon became independent and moved into its own premises next to the Victoria and Albert Museum, at 1 Cromwell Place; later, with expansion in mind, it moved into number 5 on the same road.

The Allen & Unwin archives hold no correspondence between Horovitz and Unwin after 1949; they had effectively ceased to be on speaking terms. Several years later, after Horovitz's death, the strength of Unwin's continuing resentment towards him became clear. On 22 April 1960, in a letter to Goldscheider, whom Sir Stanley clearly saw as more of an ally than Horovitz, Unwin asked for reactions to the autobiography he was then preparing, *The Truth about a Publisher*. Pointing out that he had tried to be 'scrupulously fair' to Horovitz, despite 'his treatment of me after Hitler's death', he wondered if Goldscheider thought his account fair? Unwin reminded Goldscheider that he and Horovitz had not spoken since their parting.[30]

Goldscheider's reply must have been somewhat challenging. In the next letter, dated 2 May 1960, Unwin explains that he can never forgive Horovitz for introducing into his system the 'horrible virus of anti-Semitism', which had not been there before.[31] Such a confession could be seen as revealing another side to the saviour of the Phaidon directors, and may explain the rather patronizing attitude that he is reputed to have adopted towards them and other refugees that he helped.

Goldscheider himself continued to produce very high quality books, averaging at least one a year. Despite the war, Phaidon brought out books on Classical and Renaissance art, as well as more recent European art. Producing *catalogues raisonnés* of the art at Windsor Castle proved a valuable source of commissions, and 1942 and 1943 saw the publication of catalogues of the Dutch and Flemish drawings compiled by Leo van Puyfelde, surveyor of the Royal Collection in Belgium, whom Horovitz had known before their emigration. Goldscheider went on to work on the later catalogues in the project, which were produced in special leather-bound volumes for Queen Mary. In 1945 it was the eminent art historian Anthony Blunt who wrote the catalogue for the French drawings. A. P. Oppé authored the Sandby drawings in 1947 and the English drawings in 1950, and K. T. Parker the Canaletto drawings. John Pope-Henessy was responsible for the work on Domenichino drawings. These were prestigious authors, and there is no doubt that the Windsor contact represented an acknowledgement of Phaidon's own expertise and reputation. It is remarkable that an enemy alien such as Horovitz was able to gain entry to such exclusive parts of British society as the connection between Phaidon and Windsor Castle indicates. Horovitz's links with Sir Stanley Unwin helped, as did the fact that he had been trading with the United States since 1936, well before his arrival in Britain. Goldscheider, too, had been in contact with museums and galleries all over Europe and was already established as an expert before he came to Britain. In addition, both men were fluent in English, unusual among Austrian refugees.

Ernst Gombrich, The Story of Art and Phaidon

In his programme notes for a concert to celebrate Ernst Gombrich's sixtieth birthday in 1969, for which occasion he had composed *String Quartet No. 5*, Joseph Horovitz, Béla's son, noted the Viennese origins of the 'composer, dedicatee, and three of the performers', the last referring to the Amadeus Quartet. Horovitz explained that the vision of the refugee musicians playing the piece had made him 'realize how much of what was good in Vienna has survived to flourish here and to benefit the whole world of art and culture'.

The Story of Art has its roots in Vienna, but it was conceived and produced in Britain. Gombrich recounted the genesis of the project in an interview in 1994,[32] in which he recalled that during the war he was heavily involved with monitoring German radio broadcasts but kept up some of his scholarly work. The correspondence held personally by Gombrich's granddaughter and executor Leonie Gombrich (kept at the Warburg Institute) contains the details of the project's development.[33] On 19 February 1942, Gombrich received a letter in German from Béla Horovitz, who had got Gombrich's address from Teddy Schüller. According to Horovitz's daughter, Elly Miller, he originally wanted to publish a German version of Dickens' *A Child's History of England*; knowing Gombrich's *Kleine Weltgeschichte* ('*A Little History of the World*'), which Gombrich had written for children, he thought him a suitable author. Horovitz referred in the letter to an article on the educational value of art in England, adding that it seemed to him that Gombrich would be ideally qualified to write such an article and inviting Gombrich to visit him when they were both in London.[34]

By 1943 it becomes clear from the correspondence (in their native German) that Horovitz has invited Gombrich to show him a few chapters of his history of art for young people, which have been duly read and approved by his then sixteen-year-old daughter, Elly. (She relates that the art critic Herbert Read had also been given the manuscript to read, but had rejected it.) On 24 December 1943 Horovitz wrote to Gombrich thanking him for what he had sent, adding: 'I am willing to publish this book.'

This promising start was beset with difficulties, as Gombrich detailed in a revealing letter on 10 April 1945:

> *The Story of Art* is never absent from my mind, and during recent weeks its progress on paper has not been too discouraging. I am glad to say that my health is not too bad, though nearly six years of night work or half-night work have begun to tell a little. I am sure you can imagine that there have been times during the winter when all the energy and strength I had left were absorbed – and had to be absorbed – by my work. However, the coming spring and the coming prospect of 'peace' [*sic*] seem to have raised my spirits or energies and, as I have said, at present *The Story of Art* is not altogether treated as a stepchild.[35]

By May 1945, as Gombrich wrote to a contact, he was 'somewhat less involved and busy at the BBC than previously', but he also admitted that he had perhaps made a hasty decision: 'I have rather rashly signed a contract for a book whose deadline has long since passed.' Apparently, when visiting his parents in Oxford during this period, Gombrich occasionally crossed the road to avoid Horovitz, so embarrassed was he by his own lack of progress.

On 12 August 1945, Gombrich wrote to his would-be publisher offering to repay the advance on the book, but the offer was evidently refused. Horovitz continued to write encouragingly, and he was eventually rewarded with a more promising tone, as in a letter written in 1946: 'As you see from my new address I have now really taken the plunge and have even found a place to live in, but', Gombrich

91

added regretfully, 'the changeover has forcefully brought it home to me what it means to have lost six years.' In the same letter Gombrich indicated that he was reviewing his work, commenting that he now thought there was more 'art' and less 'story' than seemed good for children. By 1948 the project was still taxing enough to be referred to as a 'problem child'. That same year a new contract was drawn up as an acknowledgement of how much circumstances had changed since the original one in 1944. The royalty to be paid to Gombrich was 4 per cent on the cover price of each copy, plus an advance of £100.[36]

Ludwig Goldscheider dealt with one aspect of the project in 1948 – the search for a subtitle:

> I am still trying to think of a formula which would include the fact that the book was really intended for young people (of 14–16 years) without excluding or repelling any adults who might otherwise read it. In the 19th century there was a convenient phrase, 'für jung und alt'. ... There is no equivalent for the German word 'Jugend' in English. Benjamin Britten called one of his pieces 'The Young Person's Guide to the Orchestra', but even that sounds a bit artificial and condescending.[37]

Goldscheider's next letter takes up the same theme:

> It is very difficult to find a sub-title that does not say that this book is intended for the young but which describes this introduction to Art History as a book recommended to:
>
> 1 Everybody
> 2 The Young
> 3 What I always call 'The Innocent Readers'
> 4 The Children
> 5 The Americans
> 6 The Grown-ups as well.[38]

One can assume that there is more than a hint of intended irony in this list, not to mention a touch of intellectual snobbery as regards the Americans, but the readership for the book was a crucial issue.

The Story of Art was finally published in January 1950 to immediate critical acclaim (pl. 3). The publication seems to embody the essence of the refugee publishing experience: the scholarly origins of the work prepared in Vienna; the contact between author and publisher made through another Viennese publisher, if not in pre-war Vienna; the dedication of the book to young people or the 'innocent reader'; and, finally, the project's survival of the long, hard war years to be published in a new, more peaceful Europe – a real symbol of the survival of Viennese values and a 'world of art and culture' referred to in Horovitz's programme notes.

The children of the Phaidon founders made their own contributions to the book. Not only was Elly Miller (fig. 12) credited with having recommended its publication, but Gaby Goldscheider chose the photo for the back of the cover, when her father asked her advice while designing the book. (In reference to another book, Gaby Goldscheider confessed that she had been approached by Otto Frank, her aunt's second husband, about whether a young person such as herself might be interested in reading Anne Frank's diary. She turned it down, feeling that publication would be in bad taste and opportunistic.)

The Story of Art became a world bestseller, selling over six million copies to date and remaining continuously in print. Its sales ensured Phaidon's success as a newly independent publisher. The book's arrival was marked by a much-quoted review in the *Times Literary Supplement*, which compared Gombrich's book with OUP's *The History of World Art* by the American authors E. Upjohn, P. Weingert and J. Mahler.[39] (It is somewhat ironic that Elly Horovitz, who was then working at OUP in New York, had to present this book at a sales meeting, given her own involvement in the rival *Story of Art.*) The two books retailed at 21s. and 32s. 6d., respectively. The reviewer, although anonymous, was widely believed to be Tom Boase, director of the Courtauld Institute. Starting with the OUP volume, he

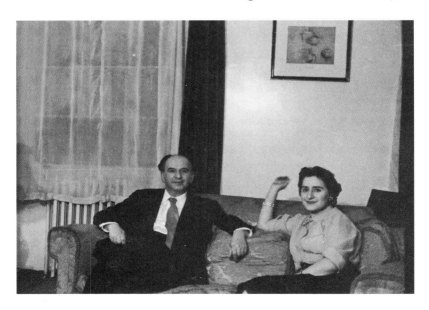

12 Elly (Horovitz) Miller and her father, Béla Horovitz, *c.* early 1950s.

remarked that its claim to be in many ways unique would have been more substantial had its appearance not coincided with the other book. The aims and methods of both, he noted, were strikingly similar: each based the discussion in the text on works represented in the plates, and in many cases the same subjects are selected. The review pointed out that the timing of the publications was in a sense not accidental... 'for they are both reactions to the present state of art historical studies, attempts to pause and take stock. Their outlook belongs to the present moment and is curiously undifferentiated by the continents from which they come.'

The reviewer went on to outline the main differences between the works. He noted the intended readership of the Gombrich title, young people – 'the most exacting class of critics' – remarking that this had led the writer to avoid 'pretentious jargon'. On the style, he was particularly positive: 'He has an easy simplicity which would be admirable in a writer using his native language... a remarkable achievement in one using the language of his adoption.' Finally, the reviewer used the treatment of the same Greek sculpture by both authors as a device for summarizing the differences between them. Gombrich's book, he found, had something new to say on this and almost every subject. He also noted what was to be a trademark of the refugee publishers' work: '[His illustrations] are distributed throughout the book and nearly always on the same page as their textual comments, a most satisfactory arrangement.'

The record sales of *The Story of Art* showed that the British had finally changed their book-buying habits and their attitude to art books. It also confirmed the impact Phaidon books had had on the English book-buying public, although this impact was not down to the Gombrich title alone. Sir Stanley Unwin wrote personally to influential booksellers such as Zwemmer's and had been instrumental in advertising and promoting Phaidon books, for which he clearly had the highest regard, until the rift between him and Horovitz. The influence of art critics such as Anthony Blunt also made a real difference to the acceptance of Phaidon books and recognition of their quality. Philip Hendy, Director of the National Gallery, was another high-profile admirer of Phaidon publications, his approval no doubt also contributing to their success.

The Horovitzes and Goldscheiders were fairly unusual in the refugee community in that their source of income was already in place in Britain on their arrival, providing that the publishing company continued to flourish. Although they had lost many of their possessions

– including treasured books and pictures – they soon began to rebuild their lives. Many years after the end of the war, the families received restitution payments from the Austrian government. The Horovitz family continued to live a comfortable, middle-class life, and Goldscheider also enjoyed a good income, but he must have been less good at organizing his finances, if a letter to a Canadian client for whom he was authenticating some Michelangelo sculptures is anything to go by: 'I am not a rich man – I only live like a rich man, and alas, it has always been my habit, whatever I earn I spend quickly on art expeditions. And most of the time I am a poor man.'[40] In fact, Goldscheider's accounts show that he had a very substantial income at the time. His royalty statement for the year ended 31 March 1945 shows that his commission for that year (4 per cent of £32,098 3s 9d) amounted to £1,283. By way of comparison, in the 1940s it was generally accepted by refugees that it cost a minimum of £3 a week to pay for basic accommodation and food. Still, much of Goldscheider's correspondence bears out his claim that, despite his large income, he often found himself short of funds. Many of his letters are on the subject of royalties or negotiating for income from books. This financial insecurity may have helped him keep in touch with the ordinary readers and buyers of Phaidon books. The Phaidon policy of setting low prices for their books evidently concerned both Goldscheider and Horovitz, whose practice was to print and sell 50,000 copies of books at a relatively small profit margin. On 1 June 1959 Goldscheider wrote:

> I do not think it is the right time for 'cheap books': even these are too expensive for the poor customer and anyone who has a little money would rather buy a bigger book than two small ones. (At least, that's how I feel, and whenever I have been producing [books] I have always asked myself: Would I buy this book at this price? And not regret my purchase?)[41]

Neither Horovitz nor Goldscheider appears to have been a member of any of the many refugee organizations set up in Britain during 1933 to 1945, such as the Austrian Centre or the Friends' Committee for Refugees and Aliens. While the Horovitzes had a regular family life to sustain them, together with the support of their religious community, Ludwig Goldscheider fared less well in this regard. However, it seems that he was greatly appreciated by many who worked with him. This much can be inferred from letters such as one dated 1962 from Irving Stone, author of *The Agony and the Ecstasy*, a book about Michelangelo. Stone corresponded a great deal with Goldscheider about the artist and acknowledged his help in the book, and in a letter to someone at the New York Graphic Society he said that Goldscheider the scholar was full of deep love and sympathy for all kindred souls.[42] On the other hand, Goldscheider was evidently a bitter and often lonely person. Resentment frequently made its way into his correspondence. Fritz Ungar, with whom he had a close if stormy friendship, despite their shared histories, remained in contact with Goldscheider and consulted him on publishing matters. Many of the disputes between the two men started as discussions about money but quickly deteriorated into more personal displays of resentment. In a letter of 19 August 1966, Ungar wrote (in German) that Goldscheider's attacks showed his need to 'inflict pain and to spray poison' and that this seemed to have become his 'general attitude to the world'.[43]

By now it was clear that the Phaidon founders had thrown in their lot with Britain and would neither emigrate to the United States nor return to Austria. They became British citizens. Horovitz never returned to Austria. Many refugees, especially Jewish ones, would not consider returning to the continent, having been betrayed by colleagues and neighbours who may have survived the war. Generally, it was the political émigrés who went back, hoping to create a new socialist Germany and Austria. Of the Phaidon founders, only Goldscheider's attitude to Austria is known, from a letter he wrote in June 1959:

> In Vienna, whenever I am there, I no longer feel at home. It feels like going home to a mother who looks like her son, but who has changed monstrously, who tried years ago to abort him, to poison him, to throttle him ... without succeeding. Against whom no court can rule, and who has only *one* good quality; the ability to make him homesick. Sometimes, this feeling is so strong that I forget that my Austria does not exist any more ... The only thing that has not changed is the cakes, at least that is welcome.[44]

The recipient of Goldscheider's letter, Dr J. C. Witsch, was a director of Phaidon's partner publisher in Germany, Kiepenheuer und Witsch, which Goldscheider was happy to visit. Witsch, a personal friend of German chancellor Konrad Adenauer, revived the name of Phaidon in Germany after the war.

The continuing success of Phaidon was thus achieved not without some personal suffering by those who ran it: resentment, isolation and competition were part of the refugee experience, alongside relief, gratitude and renewal.

Only a few refugees arriving in Britain had the means to set up in the book business or to run existing publishing companies. Many, however, were engaged as employees or freelancers in what can loosely be called the 'book arts': cover and page design, typography and illustration. Certainly there were more employment opportunities in graphic design than there were in the fine arts. So it was that a man such as Hellmuth Weissenborn, despite his career in Leipzig as an artist and academic, worked in England as an illustrator and teacher.

Today, it is unusual for the same person to publish and design a book, except perhaps in the case of a limited edition from a small press, but before World War II it was not so rare. The skills required are summed up in the German term *Buchkunst*, which is more commonly used than its English equivalent, 'book art'. Around 1900, men who designed books or typefaces were referred to in German as 'book artists' or 'lettering artists'.[1] The book arts in Germany experienced something of a renaissance in the first three decades of the twentieth century, and the German-speaking public responded with a new interest in how books looked. Collectors of attractive new books set up many bibliophile societies, and there was a rising interest in special exhibitions devoted to book design, such as BUGRA (International Exhibition for the Book Trade and Graphic Arts), organized by Hugo Steiner-Prag in Leipzig in 1914, and the IBA (International Book Exhibition), also held in Leipzig in 1927. In 1930 a competition was held to judge the 50 most beautiful books. There was a close link between book design and art publishing, and German publishers of the time were interested in the idea of the book as a *Gesamtkunstwerk* (total work of art), a term also associated with the operas of Richard Wagner, implying an aesthetic whole: sight, sound and drama. The look of a book was intended to reflect its contents, producing a harmonious whole. This creative period had little parallel in Britain, where between the end of the Arts and Crafts movement in around 1910 and the arrival of the refugees in the late 1930s, there were fewer changes to the appearance of books, at least in commercial publishing. Smaller presses certainly produced beautiful books with new design, but they had strong European links, and it was not always easy for the refugees to adapt to British traditions.

The differences in British and German approaches evolved from intertwined histories, beginning in the late nineteenth century with the Arts and Crafts movement in Britain.[2] The best-known and most influential member of the movement was William Morris, the socialist writer and artist who embodied a reaction to the effects of the

Industrial Age in Britain, convinced that the quality of manufactured goods had suffered from mass production and that the craftsmen themselves had been diminished by the industrial process. Indeed, for Morris, the craftsman had had his heyday in the Middle Ages, a period from which the Arts and Crafts movement drew philosophical and aesthetic inspiration. This can be seen in Morris' own essay on book design, 'The Ideal Book'.[3] He insisted on fine, handmade paper, hand-cut metal type and deeply black printing ink, and his edition of Chaucer (1891), printed at his own Kelmscott Press, looks much like a medieval book on the page, densely printed right into the margins.

Although Morris' return to a former age was seen by many as failing to address the challenges of industrialization, he did introduce a new philosophical attitude to the arts and crafts. This fresh approach towards the lives and work of those engaged in craftwork was taken up in both Britain and Germany, as was another of Morris' ideals, that of the book as a harmonious whole. Morris' ideas were the starting point for a radical rethinking of the processes of manufacturing. As far as books were concerned, his harking back to the practices of the Middle Ages found few practical followers, but many were drawn to his theory that in order to excel as a craftsman, one had to be contented in one's life and to live among beautiful things. Others were won over by his ideas about how an artefact should be produced through a single process, and by his insistence on high-quality raw materials.

The German reaction to the coming of the machine age was the birth of an association called the Werkbund, created to examine the relationship between industry, goods and the consumer.[4] Among its founder members – including many architects and industrialists – were the publisher Eugen Diederichs and the book designer and illustrator F. H. Ehmke. Members of the movement were dedicated to the idea of beautiful design for the industrial age. In 1914 there was an important exhibition of the Deutscher Werkbund in Cologne. Later, Werkbund members concentrated on the concept of standardization in design.

The turn of the century in Germany and Austria had been dominated by Jugendstil, the German version of art nouveau.[5] Jugendstil may have taken its name from the magazine *Jugend* ('*Youth*'), founded in 1896; the equivalent magazine in England was *The Studio* (1893). The style was particularly adopted in the flourishing applied arts of the time. Jugendstil design typically features swirling, intricate lines and elaborate decoration, and in Germany had been applied indiscriminately to all types of books, whether they were fiction or cookbooks, reducing their individuality and failing to reflect their contents. Anton Kippenberg, who took over Insel Verlag in 1905, was so determined to keep his books free from the over-the-top Germanic style that he employed English book designers and typographers such as Eric Gill.[6] There was an inevitable reaction against the decorative excesses of Jugendstil, but the crusade of the more modern designers only really applied to the typefaces and page design; the ornamental title pages remained examples of Jugendstil decoration.

The German private presses – the first is generally considered to be the Janus Press, founded by Karl Ernst Poeschel and Walter Tiemann in 1907[7] – had common roots in the Arts and Crafts movement but took many forms. Often free from the constraints of commercial considerations, these presses were important workshops for new ideas in printing. The Cranach Press, founded in Weimar 1913 by English-educated Harry Graf Kessler, was one such. Book artists came from many countries to work at the innovative press, helping with the process of cross-pollination in the book arts. One of Kessler's protégés was the letterer and sculptor Eric Gill; others were Emery Walker and Edward Johnston, later to design the classic typeface of the London Underground. Anna Simons, a Berlin-born pupil of Johnston, also played a role in the transfer of ideas: after studying at the Central School of Arts and Crafts and at the Royal College of Art in London, she returned to Germany, where she lectured on Johnston's work and translated his essays into German.[8] Walker and Johnston designed and drew typefaces for Cranach, which were then cut by other Englishmen. The Cranach Press produced many European books in their original languages and was a model of international cooperation before it was interrupted by the outbreak of World War I.

The influential typographer and calligrapher Rudolf Koch – the most striking example of a German whose working life was inspired by the English Victorians – suggested that the Germans profited more from the works of men such as Morris than did the English themselves. The first and most influential of William Morris' colleagues was Thomas James Cobden-Sanderson, who ran Doves Press. His books – printed in Doves Press type, designed by another of Morris' friends, Emery Walker – were highly elegant, characterized by a balance of the typography and overall page design. Another groundbreaking printer, Stanley Morison of the Monotype Corporation, one of the greatest British typographers of the twentieth century and active until 1967, was an admirer of Karl Ernst Poeschel. Poeschel had spent time in the United States and then in England with Cobden-Sanderson and

Morris before returning to the family printing business, Poeschel and Trepte, in Leipzig. Poeschel later took over Insel Verlag, together with Kippenberg. They were responsible for printing many of the Insel colour-plate books. Ironically, Poeschel had more influence in England than he did in Germany, for example at the Curwen Press.[9]

On a visit to Germany in 1922, Morison visited Koch on 4 November and received a specimen of Koch's lettering.[10] The connections between Eric Gill, the English printer who worked for Kippenberg, the German publisher of Insel, and Morison and Koch, are just two of the links in the book world that proved to be vital for refugee book artists who came to Britain in the 1930s.

The New Typography

German printing was in the doldrums at the end of the nineteenth century, for not much in the way of new typefaces had been created since the Walbaum font.[11] In addition, Germans had the unique problem of having two main scripts: Fraktur (blackletter or Gothic) and Antiqua (Roman). Type designers and calligraphers were much exercised by having to choose between the two, the former sometimes associated with Germanness and tradition, the latter with modernity and legibility.[12] It was not until 1941 that the problem of Fraktur versus Roman typefaces was resolved. Nazi policy was not consistent, and there were both modernizers and traditionalists within the party.[13] Whereas Nazi printed matter had been partly produced in the 'German' blackletter until then, with other documents being in the more modern Roman type, the decision was finally made to stop using Fraktur because it was considered 'Jewish'. More to the point, the typeface is notoriously difficult to read, and must have posed problems for those in the newly occupied areas of the Third Reich.

The first three decades of the twentieth century witnessed a major flowering of what was essentially a new art: creating typefaces for mechanical presses. In 1913 the first type exclusively for machine printing was created: 'Imprint'. The movement was particularly lively in Germany. Ruari McLean, an influential designer and printer who made a major contribution to Penguin books, worked in German printing companies in the 1930s, where he noted that the printers washed their hands *before* work – a small gesture, but one that revealed a pride in their craftsmanship in a centuries-old industry.

Typography quickly became the most important element of book design, and education in printing was essential if standards were to be maintained. The influential Leipzig Academy was created in the nineteenth century in the city that was at the centre of German book production. Schools also sprang up elsewhere, each often representing a particular style of design. Senior typographers on the staff were referred to as 'Professor', a sign of their prestige.[14] Most importantly, new and excellent typography – and overall design – became essential for *all* German books produced at that time, whereas in England type and design remained the concern only of bibliophiles and collectors.

Great German typographers were role models for their British counterparts. One such was Paul Renner (1878–1956), who was associated with the Munich school of design. Although he had started his career using traditional German typefaces, Renner made a radical change in the 1920s, deciding to embrace the new technology rather than react against it, as Morris had done.[15] This was a milestone in German typographical history. It was Renner who created the 'Futura' sans-serif typeface, the first such to be widely used and still admired today.

E. R. Weiss, another German typographer, had begun his career as a painter, a significant fact given that the debate between the German Roman and Fraktur type is often seen in terms of painterly typefaces versus architectural ones, or in terms of the influence of French or Mediterranean art on the one hand and the German tradition of painting on the other. Weiss contributed many designs to Insel over the years. Walter Tiemann, also born at the end of the nineteenth century, is credited with having helped make Leipzig the centre of the book arts in Germany, as director of the academy there.[16] Typical of his own simple and tasteful book designs are the three volumes of *Dekameron* he designed for Insel Verlag in 1904.

The contribution of Rudolf Koch (1876–1934) was that '[he] transformed the typography of his own country and visually affected that of England and America'.[17] Koch was responsible for raising standards in printing worldwide. His importance is due to his influence on the next generation of typographers, some of whom were forced to flee Germany, and also to his successful reconciling of arts and crafts, a subject of much discussion and argument in the field of the book arts, where the boundaries are not clearly defined. Koch's inspiration was William Morris, and he berated the English for not respecting his hero. Koch followed Morris's principles in both his life and his work, seeing each book through all its processes, from design to finished product.

Koch's own career had started in Offenbach, where he worked for the prestigious and progressive Klingspor foundry. He was prolific in his short life, printing and teaching as well as producing many new letter designs and typefaces. One of his best-known typefaces was the 'Kochschrift', and he was a champion of the German blackletter, but he also produced elegant Roman typefaces. He was lifelong friends with the Jewish bibliophile Samuel Guggenheim, for whom Koch designed both a haggadah (the Jewish Passover service book) and some biblical tapestries.

Koch's most famous pupil was Berthold Wolpe, a part-time student from 1925 to 1928 at the Technische Lehranstalten in Offenbach. Following his studies, Wolpe became Koch's assistant. A talented craftsman and designer, he worked on tapestries and designed Hebrew lettering for both the haggadah[18] and the tombstone of Julius Goldstein, professor of philosophy and author. From 1929 to 1933 Wolpe taught at the technical school in Offenbach; he also taught scriptwriting in Frankfurt am Main. During this period, he designed his 'Hyperion' alphabet. He also had contact with English typographers, especially Stanley Morison, who commissioned him to design a new typeface for the Monotype Corporation. This typeface, 'Albertus', remains one of Wolpe's greatest designs.

Yet another of Koch's protégés was Fritz Kredel, who studied at the applied arts school in Offenbach before becoming Koch's assistant in 1921 at the age of 21. He was a talented maker of woodcuts and played a significant role in one of Koch's major projects, *Das Blumenbuch* ('*The Flower Book*'). This eight-year-long project was a book of 250 wildflowers, which Koch drew onto wooden blocks that were then cut out for printing by Kredel. The title page of Koch's personal limited editions of the book were cut by Kredel copying Berthold Wolpe's freehand calligraphy; the prints were then hand-coloured. The main project was finished in 1930 before a smaller version, *Das kleine Blumenbuch*, was published by Insel (pls 5 and 6).

Jan Tschichold, although not a pupil of Koch, was profoundly influenced by him. Tschichold, the most innovative of all the typographers of the twentieth century, saw a copy of Koch's *Katechismus eines deutschen Wehrmanns* ('*Catechism of a German Soldier*') at the Leipzig book exhibition in 1914 when he was 12 years old, and bought one with his pocket money.[19]

Koch's reputation was well known to influential craftsmen such as Morison and to British publishers such as Sir Francis Meynell. Koch's biographer noted that in January 1930, during a visit to Germany, Meynell asked Koch to design a number of small typographic ornaments for the Nonesuch Press editions of the *Iliad* and *Odyssey*, due to be published the following year.[20] That same year Koch was invited to London to address the famous Double Crown Club. This was a society created by Oliver Simon, printer and publisher (and later a patron of refugee book artists, as was Francis Meynell), to bring together the elite of the printing community at special dinners to hear a talk by an eminent speaker on some aspect of printing. Often special editions of privately printed books were brought out for these occasions. Shortly after his visit to London, Koch was made an honorary member of the club.

Koch's working philosophy, in particular his devotion to the craft tradition, made an impression on those who studied and worked with him. He was both a convinced nationalist and a Christian, allegiances that inspired him throughout his life. He died in 1934, and so was never put to the test; he did, nevertheless, carry out one commission for Adolf Hitler, although it may have been difficult to refuse such work at that time. He must have been conscious that his relationships with his Jewish friends – Kredel, Wolpe and Guggenheim – would be under scrutiny.[21] He lived to see the introduction of the Reichskulturkammer, with which everyone engaged in the arts had to register. Wolpe would have lost his livelihood had it not been for Koch, who wrote a strong letter of support to the Frankfurt art school authorities, which was enough to protect Wolpe until 1935. Koch did not live to see Kredel, whose wife was Jewish, flee to New York. There is a pleasing circularity about the fact that the Press of the Woolly Whale, located in New York, which helped Kredel to emigrate and for which he provided some book illustrations, happened to own the original Kelmscott Press printing press, which had belonged to William Morris himself. There is the added coincidence that Koch's own typefaces were used on Morris' press.[22]

The fate of one of Koch's major works illustrates how closely printed works could be linked to a country's history. In 1935 his *Map of Germany*, lettered by Wolpe and drawn by Kredel, should have been a huge success for its publisher, Insel. Instead, the book was issued with a distribution ban only three months after its publication because Mussolini had used the map at the Conference of Stresa as an example of German revanchism. The title of the map was then changed to a more appropriate *Germany and Neighbouring Lands*, a process which took 30 months, only to become completely obsolete three months later when Germany annexed Austria.[23]

Finally, there can be no discussion of German design without a look at the Bauhaus, founded in Dessau in 1919 and devoted to versatility rather than a single style. Its members were expected to excel in all areas of art and design – an idea that gave rise to the modern foundation year at art schools everywhere. So it was that many Bauhaus staff and students were engaged in printing and the book arts, taking typography and letter-press design to the next level.[24] The Austrian Herbert Bayer, who was in charge of the school's printing department from 1925 until 1928, changed it from a traditional workshop for hand printing to a modern mechanical print works. His designs for suitable typefaces for the machine presses were dictated by simplicity and functionality. He did not use serifs or capital letters (which in German are far more widely used than in English). He designed pages using asymmetry, much influenced by the Hungarian László Moholy-Nagy and the De Stijl movement, while his typefaces gave the Bauhaus a strong visual identity and embodied a spirit of modernism.

The Bauhaus' sans-serif typefaces had been designed originally by Paul Renner, with his 'Futura' family of letters. Renner had invited to his Munich school Jan Tschichold, who had now finished his training with Walter Tiemann and turned to Bauhaus designers such as El Lissitsky, the Russian constructivist. In 1925, Tschichold published his groundbreaking *Elementare Typographie*. This manifesto of book design not only turned against the old conventions but also brought some order to the playful but somewhat chaotic experiments taking place in the studios of the Futurists and Dadaists.

Cover Design

Like typography, the dust jacket was evolving as an important part of the book in its own right, even if its role was interpreted in different ways. The jacket's original purpose was simply to protect the binding, and it was usually disposed of once the book was bought. After the turn of the century, jackets began to be used as a background for printed information that might advertise the publishing house or the book itself, perhaps by giving an indication of the contents, much as film posters did. Similarly, the design could make the book stand out to attract the attention of prospective buyers. At different times, the jacket became a canvas for artists of various schools: Jugendstil, Expressionism, Neue Sachlichkeit, Constructivism and so on.

Many artists found employment illustrating dust jackets, and many of these also had a grounding in other arts, be it architecture, graphic design or the stage. John Heartfield, a Berliner (born Helmut Herzfelde before Anglicizing his name in protest at World War I), took over the magazine *Die Neue Jugend* with his brother, Wieland Herzfelde, in 1916, and then set up the Malik Verlag. Between 1920 and 1930, Heartfield worked in the theatre as a set and costume designer with Max Reinhardt. Inspired, no doubt, by the relatively new technique of film editing, Heartfield and the artist Georg Grosz jointly invented the technique of photomontage, using it on the book jackets they produced at Malik. This new visual medium could communicate the ideas of its own time in a striking juxtaposition of photographs with print or graphics.[25] Photomontage was ideally suited to the political nature of these books, using topical photographs mixed with graphics as on *Braunbuch über Reichstagsbrand und Hitlerterror* ('*The Brown Book of the Reichstag Fire and the Hitler Terror*', 1933), with a photograph of a Nazi uniform apparently sprinkled with blood, which the artist has superimposed on the photo. The brothers were also credited with the idea of using the spines of their books to make statements about the contents. In this way, even when the books were on shelves, they would still stand out. When the Nazis came to power, many Malik books were seized by the authorities, since they were openly anti-Hitler. Heartfield sought refuge first in Czechoslovakia and then in Britain, where his working life was often very difficult.[26] The British were not used to such harsh images on their books, although Heartfield received occasional commissions for book covers with a left-wing bias.

Penguin Books had their own approach to cover design.[27] Initially, in the 1930s and 1940s, Penguins were presented just with their famous horizontal bands of colour. Jeremy Lewis relates that Penguin's typographer, Hans Schmoller, and its founder, Allen Lane, both loathed picture covers, especially those that pandered to the American taste for what Lane called 'breastsellers'.[28] On the other hand, Penguin books were beginning to look austere compared with their rivals. In the 1950s, when Penguin decided to try picture jackets, Schmoller contacted Abram Games, a graphic designer who had become famous through his wartime poster designs and who knew and worked with many of the refugee book artists, such as F. H. K. Henrion (born H. F. Kohn). Games had married another refugee, Marianne Salfeld, whose father had had to flee his native Hessen because he was Jewish.[29]

Much later, Games noted that the émigré group in England had an influence out of all proportion to their number and commented on the excellence of their training.[30] He commissioned some cover illustrations from Hans Unger, a German–Jewish refugee who had studied in Berlin before emigrating in 1936 to South Africa, where he joined the army as a volunteer. Taken prisoner by the Germans in 1942, Unger escaped and survived, despite being seriously wounded.

After coming to London in 1948, he produced iconic posters for London Transport, among other graphic projects. After 1954 Unger concentrated on mosaic work, decorating, for example, the Penguin Books canteen in Harmondsworth. Ruari McLean declared in his autobiography that, having worked on various projects with Unger, he grew to love him. Unger spent every Christmas with McLean and his family, until the latter moved to Scotland. Tragically, Unger took his own life in 1975; he was not the only Jewish refugee to survive the Holocaust only to commit suicide later.

In Britain, dust jackets were nearly banned by the Ministry of Supply in an effort to reduce the demand for paper. For the refugees, credited with 'introducing the innovative techniques, styles or systems that would transform the look of British books',[31] the measure would have implications: their names were not to be listed on the wrappers, to avoid any waste of paper. In the event, part of the back-wrapper folder was offered to the BBC for printing information.

Jewish Refugee Book Artists in Britain

The work of several book artists was categorized by the Nazis as both degenerate and Jewish, including that of the painter Ludwig Meidner in 1937, thereby rendering him unemployable in Germany. He was forced to flee to Britain, and he returned to Germany only in 1953. Because of the restrictions imposed by the Nazi authorities, book artists such as Milein Cosman, Hans Feibusch, Elisabeth Friedlander and many others were obliged to find refuge and employment in Britain. A number of British 'patrons' aided the book artist refugees. Francis Meynell, who came from a Catholic literary family, set up the Pelican Press in 1916 and worked closely for many years with Stanley Morison. In the 1920s he created the famous Nonesuch Press and was also active in the founding of the Double Crown Club. Despite being to some extent an Establishment figure (he was knighted in 1946), he was a conscientious objector in World War I and later a fervent anti-Nazi, expressing his disapproval for 'people who persecute democrats, exile intellectuals and bait Jews ... I would not consort willingly with Herr von Ribbentrop [then the German ambassador]'.[32] In his autobiography, Meynell makes several references to his familiarity with German book design, citing, for example, the first use in England of Koch's 'Neuland' typeface by his own press.[33]

Elisabeth Friedlander is one of the few women typographers who made their mark. She studied with E. R. Weiss then went to work on the design for *Die Dame*, Ullstein's women's magazine. Her work attracted the attention of the Bauer Type foundry in Frankfurt am Main, which commissioned a font from her. It should have been called 'Friedländer' after her (she dropped the umlaut from her name after emigrating to Britain), but she was advised to avoid the Jewish-sounding name and opted for 'Elisabeth' instead. Fleeing the Nazi regime in Germany, she went to Italy, where she worked for the publisher Mondadori. When Italy passed its own anti-Semitic laws, she was forced to flee again, this time to London. She found work at the Ministry of Information, having been recommended for the post by Meynell. Later she worked on the 'Britain in Pictures' series[34] and undertook commissions for Thames & Hudson. Werner Guttmann, the production manager at Thames & Hudson for some 40 years and himself a refugee, remembers her 'fierce' contribution to the company.[35] She is especially known for her printers' decorations and her endpapers, as well as her designs for the Penguin Music series. One 'brocade-like' design, 'Prelude', was chosen for Bach's *Brandenburg Concerto*, Score 22 in the Penguin series, and was judged one of the 50 best-designed books of 1954 (pl. 7).

Oliver Simon's support for the refugees stemmed perhaps less from a political stance than from an understanding of their suffering based on his own experience of anti-Semitism, albeit to a much lesser degree, as a Jewish boy in a conventional British public school. Simon, the founder of the influential and much-admired Curwen Press, was born into a comfortably off, cultured, assimilated Jewish family. Like Meynell, whom he met when he was 26, Simon had a cosmopolitan outlook and a good understanding of book production in Germany. Robin Kinross summed up the style of the Curwen Press, which, while definitely English, 'was already inflected by a German leaning. The Curwen Press had acquired sympathies with enlightened German traditionalism, in its use of certain typefaces and its attention to the physical qualities of its materials.'[36] Simon, with Béla Horovitz and Hamish Hamilton, published some volumes of 'The Novel Library' series together; according to Elly Miller, the decorated endpapers show the Curwen influence.

Hans Peter Schmoller was born in Berlin in 1916 to Jewish parents, and so was only allowed to start an apprenticeship as a compositor at a Jewish press, in his case Siegfried Scholem. During his apprenticeship he studied typography part-time at the Staatliche Kunstbibliothek in Berlin. From there, Schmoller went to London to study at the Monotype Technical School. Unable to find a job, he set off to Basutoland,[37] where he worked for a Christian missionary press, applying the standards and style of the famous Curwen Press. When war broke out in 1939, Schmoller was interned as an enemy alien, allegedly the only internee in the whole of Basutoland. In the camp he was allowed to read what he liked. He corresponded with Oliver Simon, pointing out a mistake in the typeface of a Curwen Press publication. After learning at the end of the war that his parents had been murdered in concentration camps, Schmoller returned to England, where Oliver Simon, impressed by his eye for detail, offered him a job as his assistant at the Curwen Press. There he stayed until he began his new and influential career at Penguin on the recommendation of Jan Tschichold. He later became famous at Penguin for his obsessive attention to detail, earning himself the nickname 'Half-point Schmoller', a reference to a tiny measure of adjustment.

The Monotype Corporation, a large international company with its own technical school in Fetter Lane, was created to produce and operate American mechanical presses in the nineteenth century, running both monotype and linotype presses on which books and newspapers were printed. (Monotype was the trade name of an automated typesetting system for metal type, invented in the United States by Tolbert Lanston. This process enabled casting machines to cast each letter and space sequentially in type metal from individual matrices.[38]) Stanley Morison was adviser to the Corporation; his connections with German typographers have already been mentioned. Such contacts meant that those who ran Monotype were aware of the plight of some continental typographers. The company later helped Elisabeth Friedlander with a commission to supply printers' borders. It also offered assistance to Hellmuth Weissenborn, who described in an interview for the Imperial War Museum how he had sought support for his work permit before emigrating to Britain in 1938, mentioning Oliver Simon and ICI, another big company known as a supporter of refugees.[39] It was ICI who proposed to Elspeth Juda that she open a studio to further the links between art and industry, teaching young artists how to create design that was genuinely useful to industry. This she did with some success. Juda, born in 1911, had fled to England from Germany with her husband Hans, a journalist and entrepreneur. She became a successful photographer in her own right, having trained with Lucia Moholy-Nagy.

The refugee artists who flowered in Britain – those who were not in need of support, help or patronage – were those who were already well established in their professions. Hans Schleger had the advantage of having worked previously in the United States. He came to Britain as early as 1932, acting on a speech he heard by Goebbels. In Berlin, he had initially worked in film before going to America to work in advertising, a relatively new field. Schleger became director of the Federal Advertising Agency, returning to Berlin after the Wall Street crash in 1929. He was born into a Jewish family whose surname was Schlesinger, but to simplify his identity, perhaps inspired by the Bauhaus ideas that were so important to him, he shortened it to Schleger. In the United States, however, he adopted yet another name, as explained in the biography written by his wife: 'Zero – allegedly in recognition of his position at that time in his life as a young man on the brink of nothing, alone in a new country, with no money, no commissions, no patronage and very little hope.'[40]

Schleger had a chameleon-like ability to adapt to a new environment. His work has been called 'an exile's art: sharply observant, bitter-sweet'.[41] He was naturalized in 1939, as he had already lived for five years in Britain before the war, and his talent was soon recognized: he was rewarded with major commissions, including some cover designs for Penguin Books, and teaching posts at prestigious British art schools. During the war he produced designs for the Ministry of Food and London Transport. In 1969 he was given the title of Royal Designer. Like Schmoller's success story, Schleger's hid a grimmer truth: his mother was also murdered by the Nazis, in 1941. Critics have drawn attention to details in his work that could be interpreted as symbols of captivity and suffering, such as the pinioned butterfly in his Green Man painting.[42]

F. H. K. Henrion and George Him were two more refugee graphic designers who made a contribution to British publishing and who, like Schleger, were able to capitalize on early successes. Henrion studied graphic design in Paris before emigrating to Britain in 1936 after an invitation was issued to him following an exhibition of his posters at the Levant Exhibition in Tel Aviv that year.[43] In England, Henrion designed many covers for the magazine Future, produced by Adprint, and created other book designs for British publishers. During the war he worked for the Ministry of Information and the U.S. Office of War Information. After the war he was employed by the General Post Office and held teaching posts at major British art schools, such as London's Royal College of Art.

George Him was born Jacob Himmelfarb in Lodz and studied at the prestigious Leipzig Academy from 1925 to 1928.[44] With Jan Le Witt, a fellow student at Leipzig, he set up a design studio in Warsaw to produce book designs, illustration and other graphic work. In 1937 their work was exhibited in London, and they managed to emigrate to Britain on the strength of this. In London they re-formed their studio and ran it until Le Witt (now J. Lewitt) left to become a painter. Him had a successful career, designing for exhibitions, animating, illustrating books and teaching, finally being honoured in 1978 as a royal designer for industry.

Several of the refugee book designers were employed during the war by the Ministry of Information. Referring to his Manx internment, Henrion remarked cheerfully that he had moved from the IoM to the MoI![45] The refugees' work for this and other government bodies is a tribute to their special ability to present information in a visually striking way.

Penguin Books and the Paperback Evolution

The 1930s, the decade that saw the arrival of the refugees, also saw the birth of Penguin Books in Britain. This is rightly recognized as one of the milestones in twentieth-century British cultural history, bringing excellent fiction and later non-fiction books to the public at unprecedentedly low prices. The founders of Phaidon Press were justly proud to be considered to have done for art publishing what Penguin did for general publishing. Not only did the refugees make their own mark on these new paperback books, but the refugee book artists brought to such publications the experience of producing books of striking similarity from the continent of Europe.

The identity of the first paperback book is much contested by book historians. The term 'paperback' implies more than simply a cover made of paper rather than cloth or leather; it also implies a book that is cheap, part of a clearly defined series and widely available. The process of its creation might be called 'evolutionary' rather than 'revolutionary'.[46] There is the example of George Hutchinson, 'who had founded his imprint in 1880 and issued paperbacks, "the Sixpenny Blacks", some fifty-five years before Allen Lane's similarly priced Penguins appeared.'[47] The great surge of popularity of cheap fiction – cloth-bound – coincided with the rise of railway travel.[48]

In Germany, at least two lists well-established before World War I fulfilled some of the criteria for modern paperbacks: Insel Verlag and Reclam, both of which are still publishing today. The debut of these series of small, paper-bound books was the result of a lapsing of copyright, enabling the publisher to reproduce without cost works the authors of which had been dead for at least 30 years. But the main precursor of the modern paperback is generally recognized as the Tauchnitz series. Although the covers of these books were not paper, nevertheless the books had a definite identity. They were small and easy to carry, and they provided cheap fiction for a wide market. The paper-bound Tauchnitz editions dated from 1842 and were extremely popular. By the outbreak of World War II, when their production ceased, between 50 and 60 million copies had been sold. The main reason for the end of the series was the arrival of a major foreign competitor: Albatross.

The Albatross series was not only paper-bound but was also cheap and had colour-coded covers to indicate the subject of the books. Introduced in 1932, it began a series of events that brought together German and British book designers and producers. These English-language books were conceived by the international publisher John Holroyd-Reece, born Hermann Riess to a German–Jewish father and an English mother.[49] Holroyd-Reece was well connected, knowing celebrated printers such as Stanley Morison, Hans Mardersteig and Oliver Simon. The second man involved in the creation of Albatross Books was Kurt Enoch, a publisher from Hamburg. He was responsible for distribution and sales, while the editorial office and production was run in Paris by Christian Wegner, who had formerly worked for both Insel and Tauchnitz.[50]

One of the most striking aspects of the Albatross books was their attractive, modern design, a real contrast to the squat, dark Tauchnitz books. The concept must have looked ultra-modern in the 1930s. Although cheapness was to be a feature of the books, no costs were spared in their design and production. They were printed by the Officina Bodoni, Hans Mardersteig's press in Italy, then one of the most prestigious printers in Europe. The Albatross books were an immediate success and sold very well, but by 1936 Enoch, who was Jewish, had to leave Germany; he went to Paris, where he set up Continenta Books.

There are several versions of the story of how Allen Lane came to create Penguin Books, but all concede his debt to Albatross. One version has it that Lane met Kurt Enoch while the latter was distributing French-language books in England. Lane was enormously impressed by the Albatross books, and felt that such a cheap, elegant series, especially in English, would also do well in Britain. Lane, who was in contact with influential people such as Sir Francis Meynell (Meynell had designed some specimen pages for Lane's edition of James Joyce's *Ulysses*) and who in his first publishing role had run The Bodley Head, remembered his father reading to him from a Tauchnitz edition of

Kipling's *Just So Stories*. Another version of the early story of Penguin is recounted by Lane's biographer Jeremy Lewis, who explains that Lane, while still at The Bodley Head, was put in touch with Holroyd-Reece about the possibility of their two firms sharing printing costs on certain titles. Lane adopted the Penguin format as a result of detailed discussions before forming the company. Yet another claim came from an office junior at The Bodley Head, who insisted that he first suggested that sixpenny books would do well. He was asked a few weeks later to take a Tauchnitz and an Albatross book to the printers to get some costings done, but was never credited with having made the initial proposal.[51]

The first Penguins were published in 1935. The similarities with Albatross were striking: paper covers, elegant modern design, a very low cover price (initially sixpence) and high editorial standards. Even the choice of a marine bird for the name of the series and the colophon was common to both the German and British series. Penguin books sold well right from their introduction. Several factors contributed to this success, one being economic. Wages had risen since the Depression, and people had more leisure time, especially in the more affluent south of England. In addition, the 1930s were marked by a move to the political left on the part of British intellectuals, and this fitted in well with the left-of-centre bias of the Penguins. They are rightly credited with the democratization of good fiction and non-fiction publishing, and with changing the reading habits of the British public.[52]

The outbreak of the war helped to further the books' popularity: they were small and light enough to be highly portable, and helped soldiers through periods of inactivity. Penguin Specials was a topical imprint covering subjects related to the war. They were written and produced quickly: schedules could be a remarkable six weeks from the delivery of the manuscript to the book appearing in shops. One title in the series, *The Internment of Aliens* (pl. 8), made a particular impact on one refugee.[53] German-born Ernie Braun had been interned as an enemy alien in 1940. She could hardly believe her eyes when she saw this Penguin Special title, highly critical of the British government's internment policy, on sale in her camp! It was a striking contrast to Nazi Germany, where nobody had dared to criticize the regime. Then and there, Braun decided that she would like to stay in such a tolerant country after the war was over.

Penguin's reception from other publishers, however, was understandably cooler, particularly as it was fortunate that its allocation of paper was calculated as a percentage of the sales over a specified earlier period that coincided with very high sales for the company. Perhaps the most curious reaction was that of Sir Stanley Unwin, who was generally thought to know more about publishing than any man alive. Unwin was determined to prove that cheap paperbacks were doomed to failure: 'He was convinced that only a limited number of books could justify, in sales terms, the long print runs needed to publish at 6d., and that Penguins would die of inanition in due course.'[54] It is ironic that only three years later, Unwin would be taking on Phaidon, with its similar ethos of large print runs, low prices and subsequently democratizing effect on the book-buying public.

Penguin's high output, with its many titles and thousands of copies, meant that there was little time to consider the design of the books. In 1947 Allen Lane took advice from Oliver Simon as to who would be the best master typographer and book designer for the job. In a letter, Lane thanked Simon 'first of all for your suggestion of Tschichold and secondly for being willing to give up so much of your time and to undertake a fairly arduous journey in order to effect the introduction and to sustain me with your advice'.[55]

Jan Tschichold stayed in England to improve Penguins for two years, from 1945 to 1947. He expressed his disdain for British workmanship, noting that in Britain typesetters still worked according to rules that originated in the nineteenth century,[56] and that the average standard of typesetting there was substantially lower than in Switzerland. Tschichold created the *Penguin Composition Rules*, according to which all Penguin books were thereafter designed. He was responsible not just for new books but also for reprints of existing Penguins, specifying the page layout, the typefaces and the paper to be used. When he finally left Penguin in 1949, having redesigned some 500 books inside and out, he was satisfied that he had proved that the cheapest books could be as beautiful as most other, more expensive ones. Paul Renner commented approvingly that Tschichold's work at Penguin was an eminently modern task.[57]

A letter from Allen Lane to Oliver Simon reveals that Lane's decision to take on Hans Schmoller as Tschichold's replacement was at least partly on Simon's advice.[58] Schmoller carried on designing Penguin books, becoming head of production in 1959 and a director at Penguin from 1960 to 1973. Wolpe also worked for Penguin, providing designs that included a Penguin signet. Other refugee artists contributed to Penguin's cover designs, and there was a particularly strong refugee involvement in King Penguins, a series of non-fiction small-format hardbacks; refugees also left their mark on Puffin Books, Penguin's children's imprint.[59]

Book Illustration and Illustrators

Book illustration provided a source of income for many refugees who might have been fine artists had they not been forced to emigrate. The first three decades of the twentieth century were challenging ones, however, because the ascendancy of photography meant that the role of illustration was being re-examined. Illustration required no great language skills, which some refugees were lacking, but book illustration by definition has a connection to a particular text, so in this field of the book arts refugee artists found a voice. There was much competition for such work, and the refugees' success can be seen as proof of their skill and talent. Thus it was that the British public began to read books that showed, for example, pictures of their own countryside as perceived by foreigners, often a fresh and enthusiastic view. Female book illustrators competed for commissions against men, who would not normally have been interested in such work had they been able to continue producing art of their own inspiration. But when war broke out and some men were called up for military service, more opportunities became available to women, both British and refugees.

Rolf Brandt, brother of the famous photographer Bill, illustrated books of fairy tales and whimsical fiction and developed a personal style of drawing that involved new printing techniques such as frottage. His work has been described as having 'strange, uncanny and macabre effects'.[60] Susan Einzig lived from money she earned by illustrating children's books.[61] Walter Trier, the celebrated illustrator of Kästner's children's classic *Emil and the Detectives*, fled to England in 1936, having worked for Ullstein as an illustrator and cartoonist. Even in Britain, Trier managed to make his living by illustrating German books or publications with a German connection.[62] He continued to work with Kästner until the war broke out, travelling to Austria to meet the author, crossing the Swiss border each time. Once this became impossible, Trier began to work in London for the refugee editor Stefan Lorant, providing drawings for *Lilliput* and, later, *Picture Post*. Trier portrayed British life with the keen eye of the foreigner and brought to his illustrations his knowledge and experience of German life, as in his work for Elinor Mordaunt's *Blitz Kids*.[63] For this children's book, published in 1941, Trier used his familiarity with the appearance of Nazi characters as well as the look of English children in the war, with their long socks and school caps. The bombsites in London's East End, which are the setting of the book, feature the familiar tea stalls. Trier was also a contributor to the early development of the modern picture book, in which the artist is the sole creator of the book – the ultimate merging of words and pictures.[64] For Puffin he created landscape-format picture books, drawing on his experience of producing experimental picture books telling stories through the use of full- and double-page illustrations.

Several refugee artists used the technique of wood engraving and woodcutting to make their illustrations, a tradition they shared with the British.[65] A notable revival of the blockbook (in which text and image were cut into the same block) can be seen in Rudolf Koch's *Soldiers' Boots*,[66] and the technique was much used by Expressionist writers and artists, who exploited the strong black and white contrasts and the stark, simple shapes the medium could provide.[67] The technique, perhaps because of its unrefined quality, fell out of favour in England in the nineteenth century but was enjoying a modest revival by the 1930s. British artists such as John Farleigh and Robin Tanner were enthusiasts of woodcutting as a medium of expression, especially of images of the English countryside.

Wiltshire-born Robin Tanner was not only a contemporary of the émigrés but also actively involved in refugee aid. As a Quaker and conscientious objector, Tanner and his wife adopted a German–Jewish adolescent, Dietrich Hanff, whose family died in the death camps. Dietrich went on to assist Tanner in his etching and publishing work. Tanner took on the task of combating anti-Semitism in the English primary schools he visited as an inspector by talking to the children about tolerance. An outstanding example of the connections and coincidences that punctuate the history of English and German book artists can be seen in Tanner's illustrations for *Flowers of the Meadow*, a King Penguin (pls 9 and 10). This book represents the continuation of a line of development from Koch's *Flower Book*, and it is noteworthy that the English project was led by a German refugee art historian, Nikolaus Pevsner. The series was modelled on a German series, 'Insel Library', for the refugee book producer Adprint, which used refugee designers such as Elisabeth Friedlander.

Hellmuth Weissenborn was a refugee book artist *par excellence* for several reasons: he was a publisher in his own right, a book designer, typographer and prolific illustrator, as well as being a painter and printmaker of international reputation. He was one of the refugees whose successful career might be said to be based on the challenges of exile. Traumatic experiences – service in the trenches of World

War I, internment as an enemy alien and life in London during the bombing – stimulated Weissenborn to produce new art (fig. 13). After returning from the Great War, Weissenborn enrolled at both the Leipziger Akademie für graphische Künste und Buchgewerbe and at Leipzig University, where he studied anthropology, completing his doctorate in 1926. After a show of his watercolours in Leipzig, he was asked to join the staff of the academy that same year, becoming one of the youngest professors in the academy's history.

The Leipzig Academy was a prestigious institution, the staff of which included academics from all over the world. In keeping with the city's position as the European centre for publishing and printing, the academy's director in the first 20 years of the twentieth century, Max Seliger, had developed the institute into a unique centre of excellence in the book arts. After World War I, at the time when Weissenborn studied and worked there, the director was Walter Tiemann, a typographer of international reputation. Also on the staff were Hugo Steiner-Prag, the wood-engraver Hans Alexander Müller, and the painter and illustrator Max Schwimmer. Weissenborn produced a great number of printed works, from bookplates, with which he is particularly associated, to larger scale woodcuts.[68] In 1931 he married Edith Halberstam, who was Jewish. Although he was not Jewish himself, Weissenborn's post at the academy was not renewed, and he was forced to emigrate.

During his first few months in London, Weissenborn went from one publisher to another seeking work. He commented that the prevailing English attitude seemed to be that, although his work was better than what was available, this was insufficient reason to change. Weissenborn was interned in 1940 and released on 26 December of that year. He started making woodcuts for illustrations and threw himself into a rediscovered passion for printmaking, which distracted him from the bombs and fires of the Blitz. He also managed to find a reliable source of income from a teaching post in Beckenham in Kent.

Weissenborn was at ease with both the artistic and technical sides of his creativity. He saw no inherent contradiction between the two, and routinely both drew and produced prints in his prolific artistic output, which included book illustrations. In 1943, he had his first solo show of pastels and graphic art at the Archer Gallery in London, where the publisher and printer Baynard asked him to produce a marine alphabet engraved on wood. Also working at Baynard's at that time was Lesley Macdonald, who became Weissenborn's second wife

Patrick, David? Again on the guns in afternoon. 236 Battery leave tonight: most of the officers are in Havre ignorant. All 244 except Smith dined and wined at the Normandie for 10fr. The view is that it could possibly be better placed. Back to Rest Camp 9.30 - great stark ships black with level flecked snow below and big engines and troops arriving.

4. Cold and bright again. Took the section sliding, then work on guns. At 11 came warning to move at 5.30. Packing, Censoring. New servant - Taylor. Asked if he had done anything of the kind before, said 'I've a wife and family and know what comforts are.' Started at 4.45 for station with guns - held up 1½ hours by train across road - 2 hours at station doing nothing, 1½ hours entraining guns - platform all cotton bales and men singing 'The nightingales are singing in the pale moonlight'. ('There's a long long trail awinding'). Sgt. Major did practically all the work. - The long waiting before train starts - men quite silent after first comic cries of 'All tickets' and imitating cattle (35 men in each cattle truck; we have a compartment to 2 officers). As we start at 11 suddenly the silent men all yell 'Hurray' but are silent before

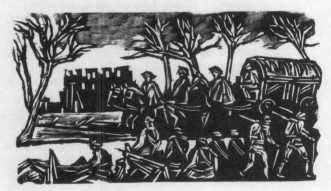

9

13 Page from *The Diary of Edward Thomas*, Whittington Press, 1977, illustrated by Hellmuth Weissenborn.

in 1946. Together they re-established Acorn Press, which published bibliophile editions and illustrated books for children and adults.

From 1943 until the late 1970s Weissenborn illustrated a great number of children's and other books, all beautifully produced and many of which became collectors' items. Most of the books were sold from his London home once a year, at a large party.[69] In 1946, Acorn Press commissioned a book called *The Magic Kite*, illustrated by Wolf Kassemoff-Cohen, Weissenborn's colleague from Beckenham. Kassemoff recalled that he had the impression that Weissenborn had taken on the script to help out the author, Michael Corvin, a fellow refugee and ex-internee from Hutchinson Camp. In 1949 Weissenborn published *A Goethe Chronicle* by Richard Friedenthal, another refugee whom Weissenborn had met in Hutchinson Camp during their internment. Weissenborn also produced many books of his own work, including his prints of bombed-out London. The Whittington Press published many of the most beautiful Weissenborn works, with subject matter ranging from German classics, especially poetry, to English pastoral themes. Common to most of the books Weissenborn illustrated were flora and fauna, whether natural or grotesquely fantastic. He exhibited several times in London and was the subject of two BBC documentary programmes in the 1970s, as part of the 'Arena' series.[70]

After the war, Weissenborn returned to Germany many times, and there were exhibitions of his work in Leipzig in 1957 and 1959, in Berlin in 1969 and at the Gutenberg Museum in Mainz in 1980. In 1979 he was honoured by the German government with the Grand Cross of the Order of Merit for his life's work in art. It can be said that Weissenborn was successful in finding the *juste milieu* between the two cultures. Elements of German Expressionist style can be seen in some of his work, in his heavy use of black and the presence of disturbing monsters and threatening shapes, and he can be counted among the few artists to have successfully sold work of this type in Britain, a country traditionally averse to stark, harsh visual styles of art. The high quality of the craftsmanship and materials meant that the prices of his books excluded them from the mass market, in contrast to the democratizing effect of the refugee publishing houses of Phaidon and Thames & Hudson. The émigré art publishers and book artists made their mark at both ends of the market.

Few book jackets bear the names of those who designed them or of those who designed the type or the layout for the book. Although several book artists eventually found recognition in British society, there were many more who contributed to the look of the British book but remained anonymous, illustrating books with their own peculiar vision of their new host country. These were often artists who had been celebrated in their own field before exile, such as Elisabeth Friedlander and Hellmuth Weissenborn. The process of integration was composed of several stages: the period before the war, with its tradition of interchanges and relationships between book artists; the war years, which created work opportunities for the refugees; and finally their entry into mainstream book art after the war. Initially, at least, these artists had to be content to work behind the scenes. Just as London pedestrians routinely walk past shops in Regent Street the names of which are displayed in Wolpe's 'Albertus' typeface, so British readers take for granted the harmonious appearance of Penguin Books without knowing the names of Tschichold or Schmoller.

There is no doubt that the war itself was responsible for some of the employment opportunities for the refugees. First, many British book artists were away fighting, thereby creating gaps in the work-force. Second, the refugees' very Germanness rendered them suitable for graphic work in propaganda, both 'black' and 'white', which required not only native German speakers but also a deep knowledge and understanding of contemporary German life and culture. The British Ministry of Information was a good early source of employment for the refugees. Later they progressed from such work to more mainstream activities, their portfolios now full of examples of work completed in Britain. However, the war years were also a time when both the British and the refugees were called upon to do unfamiliar work, sometimes potentially beneath the dignity of those asked to carry it out. The enemy aliens, once released from internment, often took on what was to them new types of work: painters becoming book illustrators or established typographers like Elisabeth Friedlander becoming fakers of Nazi German graphics and, later, a designer of logos for, among other things, the shoe shops Dolcis and Saxone.

The freshness and originality of the book artists' work are often remarked upon, in particular where they were commissioned to illustrate life in Britain or the country itself. The line drawings by Weissenborn of the English countryside in books such as *Autumn Fields* are a good example.[71] How strange it must have been for German-born Weissenborn to sketch cricket stumps – but the quality of the image partly reflects the real novelty English life held for the refugees. They noticed and celebrated in their work details that might have been taken for granted by more blasé native artists. The shape of English milk bottles in Weissenborn's bombsite drawings was something that appealed to him. One factor in this wide-eyed, fresh approach was also a lack of cultural background, or knowing why things look as they do in Britain. Ruth Rosenberg, for example, was once asked by the publisher Max Parrish to design a cover for a book on the Coronation.[72] She admitted that she was somewhat at a loss. 'I never had a king or queen,' she said. Parrish answered, 'That is why you are so good at it, because it is so new for you'.[73]

The refugee book artists were grateful for their newfound safety, and for their acceptance and employment in Britain, however hard it was for them to adjust, and they were able to present a more idealized view of their host country than they may have done at a different time in different circumstances. The wartime series 'Britain in Pictures' was a perfect opportunity to show only the more admirable aspects of a country, without any reference to poverty or social injustice. Of course, some refugees – including the photographer Wolf Suschitzky and his sister, Edith Tudor Hart – did portray the other, poorer face of British society in their photographs of industrial hardship published, for example, in *Picture Post*. Committed to social justice, they were attempting in this way to create a more just society, rather than setting out simply to discredit the British government, to whom they owed so much.

The refugee book artists took to Britain their excellent training at colleges such as the Leipzig Academy, where they had received a thorough grounding in skills from typography and printing to illustration. They were part of a long and noble tradition in Germany and Austria, shown in the pride that German printers took in their craft. So it was that the German-speaking refugee book artists could be relied upon for competence and thoroughness, as well as originality. This reliability in turn meant that fellow refugees in publishing could employ them confidently: Elisabeth Friedlander worked for Thames & Hudson after Walter Neurath had come across her work at Adprint, and Hellmuth Weissenborn was employed by Hammond. Networking was beneficial to both parties – and British books looked good.

7 Photography and Printing

The production of art books and other pictorial books has been, inevitably, closely linked with the development of photography. Shortly after the birth of that technology in the mid-nineteenth century, photographs were produced expressly in order to be inserted into books as illustrations. Initially, these reproduced photographs were not printed on the pages of books but pasted in by hand at the top of blank pages – a process known as 'tipping in'.

In the 1920s, photography in Germany and Austria experienced a particularly fruitful phase of development, both stylistically and technically,[1] and photographers joined the professional refugees to Britain. Wolf Suschitzky, born in 1912 and known in Britain mainly as the cameraman on such films such as *Get Carter*, recalled that although he had attended a photography school for three years in Vienna after finishing school, he had found the experience only partly useful to his future career, because the course included technical instruction but little on photography as an art form.[2] Photography was in a pioneering phase, and although many photographers followed a prescribed course of study and apprenticeship, they often took advantage of the form's openness to different approaches to develop their own technique.

Three brothers from the Spender family helped in the process of bringing the new German photography to Britain. The poet Stephen Spender saw photography as sharing the poet's aim to reveal the world more clearly, thereby creating an underlying bond between the two forms; this belief can be seen in the work of Wolfgang Foges' early magazine, *Der Neuen Jugend*. Michael Spender was an optician at the German camera company Leitz, so he knew all about the new lightweight cameras. He was responsible for persuading his photographer brother Humphrey to adopt the relatively small, hand-held Leica camera. Being unencumbered meant photographers could move around more easily and take photos without elaborate preparation, so inspiring the new field of photojournalism.[3] Humphrey later worked on *Picture Post*, the popular British photo journal, which was edited by another refugee, the Hungarian Stefan Lorant.

Trends in photography were also spread through the relatively new field of advertising. One of the very first advertising agencies was Crawford's, which was based in London and also traded as Crawfords Reklame Agentur in Berlin, providing a route by which the new photography was exported successfully to British advertising, particularly in the style called Neue Sachlichkeit ('New Objectivity'). Originating in 1924 and associated with the city of Mannheim, New Objectivity, unlike the Expressionism of early twentieth-century Germany, was defined by its clear, simple images. The focus on the surfaces of material meant that the style was well suited to showing off consumer products and modern, aspirational lifestyles. Photomagazines like *Close-Up* and books showing the new photography were on sale at the admirable Zwemmer's, an island of the avant-garde in a sea of traditional bookshops.

Not only did German and Austrian photographers bring new techniques and styles from German-speaking Europe, they were also able to work whether or not their command of the English language was perfect. Photographs were an ideal medium for the exiles for another reason: as one writer remarked, 'in contrast to the individual schools of painting, photography was largely free of the influence of national idioms.'[4] The rise of photographers was due in part to the huge acceleration in the desire for photographs since World War I, when the image had proved far superior to the word in conveying information about the conflict. Pictorial images were an area in which the German-speaking exiles made a profound mark on British life.

Andor Kraszna-Krausz and Focal Press

It has been claimed that the Hungarian-born photographer and publisher Andor Kraszna-Krausz 'had more influence on the art and science of photography than anyone else in the world'.[5] Long before Marshall McLuhan, he anticipated that the language of pictures would revolutionize printing and publishing. His early life remains something of a mystery, although it is known that he was born in 1904 and by the age of 12 was already a gifted photographer. He never admitted his Jewish heritage, and before 1925 added the 'Kraszna' to his name, apparently to further a myth that his origins lay in the Hungarian aristocracy, although he was said to keep mementos of his Jewish childhood, and his first work as a journalist was for the Jewish cultural magazine *Mùlt-ès-jövó*. A school composition held in the archive at the National Media Museum in Bradford also shows that 'KK' had an early knowledge of English. In the 1920s he studied law in Budapest, where he told a student paper about his career plans: to be a publisher.[6]

After moving from Hungary to Berlin, Kraszna-Krausz began to write as the Berlin correspondent for photographic journals such as *Close-Up*.[7] He worked in Vienna on the journal *Technik* (almost certainly the same publication as *Filmtechnik*).[8] Along with another famous émigré, Erich Kästner, Kraszna-Krausz worked on *Die Weltbühne*

('*The World Stage*'), which was one of the most important left-wing oppo-sition weekly newspapers in Weimar Germany. Initially the paper had been concerned with theatrical reviews, as the name implies, but its outlook had widened to encompass articles of a political nature. Film reviews and film theory were relatively new and exciting topics for a magazine based in 1920s Berlin, the city of Universum Film AG, better known as UFA. UFA was the principal film studio of Weimar Germany and an important influence in world cinema.

One can only imagine the stimulating talks these men had in the hothouse atmosphere of Berlin during the Weimar Republic, a time when creativity seemed to feed on the uncertainty of political life and the resulting social and sexual freedom. Kraszna-Krausz took up a position with the publisher Wilhelm Knapp, editing their new film magazine *Filmtechnik* in 1926 and becoming what one tribute calls 'an experienced editor and author-in-residence of the leading German photography publishing house' at a time when Germany led the world in photography.[9]

When he arrived in England in 1937, Kraszna-Krausz failed to find employment with British publishers, so he set up the Focal Press in London's Fitzroy Square, specializing in books on all aspects of pho-tography. It was at one time the world's largest photography pub-lisher. The first Focal books were translations of works published in Germany by Wilhelm Knapp, who also printed the books for the new British publisher.[10] Kraszna-Krausz's German connections continued with the next books. The 1939 title *Phototips on Children: The Psychology, the Technique and the Art of Child Photography* was written by his Berlin colleague in film criticism, Rudolf Arnheim. The two men were more than colleagues; they were lifelong friends, and many of Arnheim's thoughts on visual culture are evident in Kraszna-Krausz's work.

In common with other refugees who contributed to the visual culture in Britain by using imagery to explain and illustrate in an original way, Kraszna-Krausz championed accessibility in his publi-cations. John Chittock, who worked at Focal for many years, noted the important stylistic character of the Focal books: '[Kraszna-Krausz] extolled the use of plain English, short sentences and simple line illustrations to make photography comprehensible to everyone. And the *All-In-One-Camera* Book went on to sell over one million copies worldwide, the first of hundreds of books later to appear from Focal Press.'[11] Even in 1945, the presence of German influence is acknowl-edged by the English author C. Douglas Miller. In the introduction to *Mountain Photography: Its Art and Technique in Britain and Abroad*, which

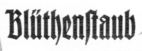

Blüthenstaub

Freunde, der Boden ist arm,
wir müßen reichlichen Samen
Ausstreun, daß uns doch nur
mäßige Erndten gedeihn.

ir suchen überall das Unbedingte, und finden immer nur Dinge.

~

Die Bezeichnung durch Töne und Striche ist eine bewunderns-
würdige Abstrakzion. Vier Buchstaben bezeichnen mir Gott; einige
Striche eine Million Dinge. Wie leicht wird hier die Handhabung
des Universums, wie anschaulich die Konzentrizität der Geister-
welt! Die Sprachlehre ist die Dynamik des Geisterreichs. Ein
Kommandowort bewegt Armeen; das Wort Freyheit Nazionen.

~

Der Weltstaat ist der Körper, den die schöne Welt, die gesellige
Welt, beseelt. Er ist ihr nothwendiges Organ.

~

Lehrjahre sind für den poetischen, akademische Jahre für den
philosophischen Jünger. Akademie sollte ein durchaus philoso-
phisches Institut seyn: nur Eine Facultät; die ganze Einrichtung
zur Erregung und zweckmäßigen Übung der Denkkraft organisirt.

~

Lehrjahre im vorzüglichen Sinn sind die Lehrjahre der Kunst

9

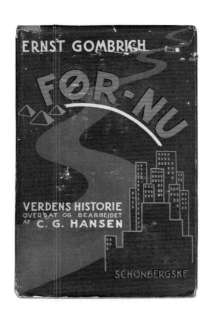

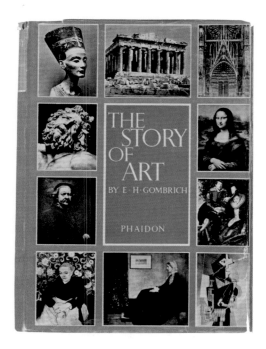

PL.2 Cover of *Weltgeschichte* by E. H. Gombrich, Schønbergske Danish edition, 1937

PL.3 Cover of *The Story of Art* by E. H. Gombrich, Phaidon, 1950

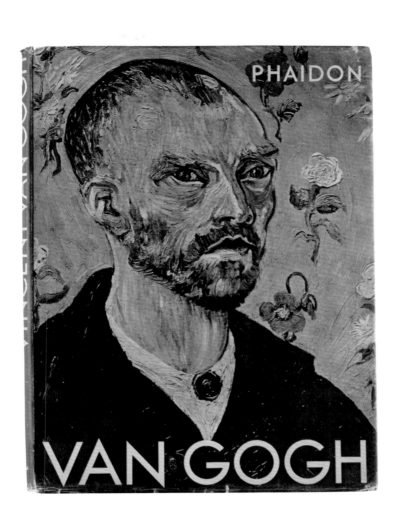

PL.4 Cover of *Van Gogh* by Wilhelm Uhde, Phaidon, 1936

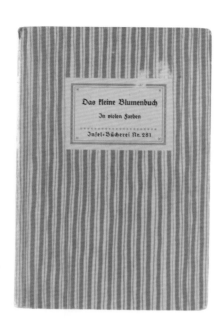

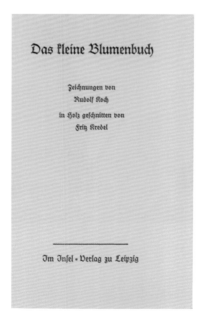

PL.5 Cover of *Das kleine Blumenbuch* by Rudolf Koch, Insel, 1933;
      illustrated by Fritz Kredel

PL.6 Title page of *Das kleine Blumenbuch*, Insel, 1933

still bore the label 'Book Production War Economy Standard', the author thanked his wife for help 'in translation of many passages of polysyllabic German'. Additionally, he expressed his gratitude to 'A. Kraszna-Krausz for bringing to my notice many photographs from continental sources and for making available his own library of mountain books'.[12]

The appeal of the Focal Press books can perhaps be attributed to the fact that the manuscripts were double-checked for accuracy by international authorities on each specific subject. In addition, they were researched thoroughly before publication, and the copious use of line drawings set a style of clarity that became instantly recognizable as that of the Focal style. Kraszna-Krausz also shared an insistence on good page design with other prestigious refugee publishers, such as Ludwig Goldscheider and Walter Neurath.

Kraszna-Krausz was both creative and active in his approach to war work, submitting a wide range of ideas to support the British war effort. Some were rather eccentric, from translating rousing anti-German Hungarian folk songs to encouraging housewives to save food scraps through his use of photographs of pigs.[13] However, he helped most through books: he could provide the Royal Navy with German editions about Germany, no doubt dating from his publishing career at Knapp in Berlin. On 16 August 1943 Lieutenant RNVR Hippisley-Coxe wrote to Kraszna-Krausz, thanking him for his loan of topographical books on Germany.

The reproduction of photographs for use in art books had been a challenge for printers and publishers throughout the nineteenth century, although beautiful colour prints often resulted from challenging processes such as lithography. The advances in photogravure were well established before Phaidon's transition from publishing classics and cultural histories to art books. As Viennese publishers, the Phaidon founders were operating at the centre of developments in reproduction and were able to take up the use of photogravure. This technique, although originally created in the 1830s, had been developed in 1878 by the Czech-Viennese painter Klaus Klietsch (Klič). The process, which is still in use today, is referred to as the Talbot-Klič process. Not only was it used to reproduce works of art to illustrate books, but the deep, subtle, dark tones soon became familiar to the British public in the 1940s from the pages of *Picture Post*.

Béla Horovitz acknowledged his admiration of the Swiss publisher Albert Skira and often had Phaidon books printed in Switzerland (fig. 14), but he wanted to avoid the use of colour reproductions favoured by Skira, which made his books expensive.[14] Horovitz preferred to use black and white in the best possible way, so showing nuances of tone but also keeping prices low. Black-and-white photography was highly sophisticated in the 1920s, and reproduction had made progress in the form of photogravure, all in the publishers' favour (pls 11 and 12). The arrival of good cheap colour reproduction would be the next big step.

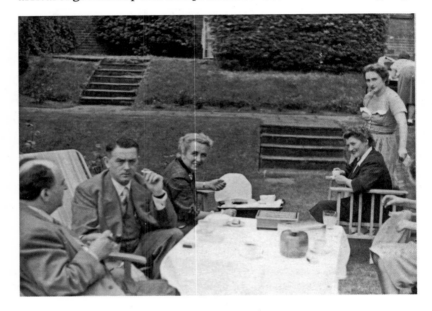

14 The Horovitzes and Millers with their Swiss blockmaker, Schwitter, in Switzerland, 1950.

Both the book production company Adprint and the art publishing house Thames & Hudson had their roots in the Vienna of the 1920s, the First Republic. After World War I, the Social Democratic municipal government of Vienna had introduced an extensive programme intended to improve the lives of the city's large working-class population and to reach children and young people, who formed the focal point of a new area of study in fields such as psychology and education, by setting up schools and childcare centres.[1] Its aim was to open up the world of images as a way of making the real world more comprehensible to all.

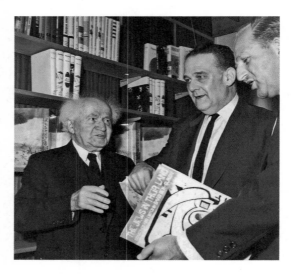

By 1937 the émigré Wolfgang Foges, a Viennese publisher (fig. 15; see also pp. 16–19 above), had founded Adprint – a composite of 'advertising' and 'printing' – in Britain, specializing in colour printing and producing greetings cards and other commercial material. Adprint was financed by the Charles Tennant Group, with the businessman Lord Glenconner at its head. It was incorporated into the group in 1938. Erica Barrett, whose mother Hilde Kurz worked at Adprint as an illustrations editor and picture researcher, and who remembers playing in the premises in Newman Street as a child, recalls that the office was essentially one large space, with the colour-block presses in the centre. Employees worked in small cubicles, and at the side were two photographic studios, set up with models for use as photographic illustrations for Adprint's many children's books. Alice Harrap, Foges' first employee, wrote: 'The planning and production was carried out

15 Wolfgang Foges with David Ben-Gurion, first Prime Minister of Israel, *c.* early 1960s.

in Adprint's offices, mainly by members of staff, e.g. typographers, art historians, editors and photographers (colour).'[2]

Foges employed a number of refugees from Austria and Germany. One critic referred to 'the palpable European accent discernible in Adprint's own style, which surely owes a great deal to befriended émigrés and refugees'.[3] Walter Neurath, who arrived in Britain with considerable experience of publishing fine books in Vienna, provided the essential expertise in book production that Foges lacked.[4] Book packaging, sometimes known as 'out-house publishing', had been thought up by Fischer and Neurath in Vienna. It was especially practical during the 1940s, when paper rationing was in operation. Adprint 'packaged' books for other publishers: the firm dreamed up the ideas, commissioned the authors and designed and produced the books, which publishers then warehoused, marketed and sold. Adprint created books for the English publisher William Collins, who had a large paper quota, thereby bypassing the problem they would have had as a new publisher had they chosen to publish the books themselves.

Foges' working practice is chronicled in a short history of book packaging, which notes that he had been a publisher in Vienna, producing books with illustrations chosen by 'picture researchers' and integrated into the text. 'British publishers of the time had little or no experience in this field ("picture research" as such did not exist), so when Foges arrived in England he found a new and unexploited market for his visually orientated books.'[5] In fact, it seems unlikely that Foges produced books as such before emigration, concentrating instead on quality magazines, but for these he would indeed have used picture research.

Adprint and the Development of Colour Book Illustration

One of Adprint's claims to fame was its use of integrated illustrations. Previously, illustrations had been grouped together at the end or in the middle of a book, printed on special photographic paper. Phaidon books, for example, either featured tipped-in plates or had the illustration pages in their monographs and other works put in where they looked balanced, rather than integrating them with the text in the way that has since become normal practice. Sourcing the illustrations was a big responsibility, and picture research was a major activity at Adprint. Hilde Kurz, the art historian who had studied with Gombrich in her native Vienna, collected her own pictorial library for her work at Adprint, often finding prints by trawling through second-hand shops in London, and even discovering pictures on the back of scrap paper. She knew many émigré artists in England who supplied her with material, including Bettina Ehrlich and Katerina Wilczynski.[6]

Not only was picture research a relatively unknown occupation; picture archives themselves were also unusual. Museums in the 1930s did not generally have photo archives of their collections. Because of this, good colour reproductions represented a source of potential income for art publishers.[7] Picture research and picture archiving owe their origins largely to one of the many refugee Adprint staff, Ruth Rosenberg. Born in 1905 into a non-religious Jewish family in Berlin, Rosenberg matriculated in Italy before studying the history of art at Freiburg, where she was well aware of the Bauhaus and its design ethos.[8] After a short period as an auxiliary worker at a museum, she went to work in the photographic section of the *Berliner Illustrirte* (published by Ullstein), which she maintains was the world's first illustrated newspaper. A history of the newspaper claims that it was one of a new kind, founded in 1891, when 'picture editor was a brand new profession'.[9] There Rosenberg learned how to see pictures from a journalistic point of view and began to recognize a need for a way to organize the visual material. She began a card index of illustrations, much to the satisfaction of her employers.

Through her work Rosenberg got to know several celebrated photographers, which was to prove useful when she emigrated, assisted in this by her Zionist contacts. She then received an introduction to the Warburg Institute, where scholars put her in touch with Adprint; perhaps this introduction came through Otto Kurz, the refugee art historian whose wife, Hilde, already worked there. Rosenberg's unusual experience as a picture researcher and archivist must have made her the ideal employee for Adprint. On her departure from Max Parrish Ltd., where she worked for some ten years after the reorganization of Adprint, she took her large and impressive picture library with her to Thames & Hudson.[10]

Foges' first big project at Adprint was to bring books with excellent colour illustrations to the British public at affordable prices. Colour printing was well established technically by the 1930s – by late in the decade the main challenge was improving and maintaining the quality through long print runs. Adprint books contained many photographs, as well as Isotype graphics (see pp. 57–59). The director of photography, Paul Rotha, made heavy use of refugee photographers, including Wolf Suschitzky[11] and his sister Edith

Tudor Hart, Bill Brandt and Zoltan Wegner. It is possible that John Heartfield also worked on covers, but as much of the work was uncredited this is hard to confirm. The dust jacket for *The Battle for Health* (pl. 17) looks remarkably like a John Heartfield montage but could also be by Suschitzky.[12] For such books, the refugees were the ideal choice of photographers, as their social realism was still unusual in Britain. After the war the successful photographic theme was continued, in particular in children's books. The clarity and appeal of the colour photographs continued to be a selling point of the books until Adprint's demise in the late 1940s. Their impact was striking, if not always aesthetically pleasing. One writer noted their 'continental' sense of design and their 'uncomfortable mixture of roman and sans-serif type-faces'. The arrangement of illustrations was found to be 'eccentric', and the 'bold Isotype charts, emphasized by their use of colour, can seem strangely isolated from their neighbouring pages'.[13]

Having seen how quickly Penguin Books succeeded after its inception in 1935, Foges and Neurath came up with the idea of King Penguins in 1937, taking as their inspiration the Insel Verlag and adopting the small format, hard boards and decorative, small print covers of that publisher. They pitched the project to Allen Lane, with the first two books to be Redouté's *Roses* (pl. 13) and Gould's *Birds of Britain*, whose colour plates were out of print. Lane liked the idea, despite the fact that the cover price would have to be one shilling (double that of the sixpenny Penguin paperbacks). The colour printing proved problematic – the printers' achievement has been called 'superhuman'[14] – and the project was delayed by the need to find a competent British printer, since Austria and Czechoslovakia had been occupied. The first two King Penguins appeared in 1939.

It had been calculated that 20,000 copies would have to be sold for the books to be profitable, but sales were poor. So too was the critical reception. The appearance was pronounced 'humble', and the standard of colour printing found to be low and the binding shabby.[15] John Piper, the eminent British artist, said of the colour reproductions that they looked 'like a mess on the bathroom linoleum'.[16] Allen Lane cannot have blamed Foges or Neurath, however, as Neurath's daughter, Constance, remembers him attending her parents' many parties, where he was very sociable. Nevertheless, the initial results demonstrate the difficulty that the Austrian publishers had in conveying their ideas on colour printing and imposing their exacting standards on British printers.

Adprint produced three further King Penguin titles, including *Caricature* by E. H. Gombrich (pl.14). *Caricature* set the tone for the King Penguins, which from then on were generally considered to be as scholarly as any books produced by their competitor, the authoritative Oxford University Press.[17] Another development in the next three titles concerned the editorship of the series passing in 1941 to the refugee art historian Nikolaus Pevsner, who replaced Elizabeth Senior, who had been killed by a bomb in 1940.[18] The subject areas of some of the books seem also to have been inspired by Insel, such as the inclusion of natural history and Pevsner's own field of art history. Jan Tschichold had previously worked at Insel and would have been familiar with the layout and other design elements of the 'Insel Library' series. Penguin took over the production of the series from Adprint after the first five books. With Allen Lane's support, Pevsner became more adventurous and used his expertise increasingly on the books, with their attractive illustrations in a small space.[19] Ultimately, the series added to Penguin's prestige, though without ever being very profitable.

'Britain in Pictures'

Adprint's biggest success was a series of books packaged for Collins and illustrated with both black-and-white and colour photographs: 'Britain in Pictures'.[20] The series was the brainchild of a charismatic woman named Hilde Matheson, who met German-speaking refugees during the course of her work at the Joint Broadcasting Committee, where she was made director in 1939. Initially the committee was set up to improve international understanding by means of broadcasting, its main task being to diffuse positive propaganda about Britain through the broadcasting systems of other countries. As Matheson's chronicler related, 'With her usual flair and energy she recruited foreign nationals, often émigrés from the Nazi and Fascist dictatorships, and used them to communicate material put together by her team.'[21]

The concept of 'Britain in Pictures' was based on an existing German series of photographic books called 'Die Blauen Bücher' ('The Blue Books'; pl.15), created in 1907 by the publisher K. Langewiesche. Whereas the first German volumes had covered Classical art, the subject matter changed when World War I broke out. The publisher dedicated the 1915 volume to the soldiers in the field, and it was well received. By 1926 he was strengthening his nationalistic approach by publishing a number of books on the German landscape and vernacular architecture, which, with their idyllic pictures of a perfect world, found their buyers mainly among Germans abroad, although Germans who felt that their homeland was threatened bought the books too.[22] 'Britain in Pictures' (pl.16) was, similarly, intended both to inspire those at home and to stimulate the sympathy of those abroad, encouraging people in the Americas, the Empire and the dominions to support the war effort. They were widely sold abroad, with an Adprint office in the Bahamas handling sales to the United States.[23] The conception and success of 'Britain in Pictures', the first volume of which was published in 1941 and the last in 1950, was in some ways the result of the coming together of an exceptional group of people, some British and some German-speaking refugees, and the pooling of their collective abilities.

Adprint's refugee employees designed the books, researched the photographs and managed the printing. Unlike 'The Blue Books', in which there was a minimum of text – a short introduction and captions for the photographs – the text in the 'Britain in Pictures' volumes was as important and informative as the photographs. Typically for Adprint books, the images were integrated into the text. Hilde Kurz was told by Walter Neurath that all the pictures should be orientated the same way as the text because, he said, nobody could be bothered to keep turning the book round to see the pictures.

The authors who wrote the text for these books were often high profile, including Rose Macaulay, Vita Sackville-West and Virginia Woolf. 'Britain in Pictures' eventually included some 126 titles on subjects such as country houses and British children. The series was recognized as having propaganda value: the books all shared 'an uncomplicated love of Britain and things British, and an urge to educate and explain [is] among its most attractive features'.[24] Readers probably had no idea that these quintessentially British books were produced by German-speaking refugees. On the strength of the 'Britain in Pictures' role in boosting morale, Neurath was released after only two weeks internment on the Isle of Man.[25] He was soon back at work on the books, and British naturalization followed.

Although sales were excellent (as they generally were for books produced in book-starved Britain during the war) and the public loved 'Britain in Pictures', adverse comments were made about the experimental colour printing, as had been done in reference to some of the King Penguins. John Betjeman, who wrote the volume *English Cities and Small Towns* (1943) and who was friendly with John Piper, expressed his horror at the quality of the printing. In a letter to Oliver Stonor, who had reviewed his book, Betjeman wrote: 'What a pity that book is reproduced in urine by those filthy Austrian Crooks Adprints Ltd.'[26] (One cannot help wondering whether this reaction may, at least in part, have been influenced by Betjeman's dislike of things German and Austrian in general, and in particular of the work of Nikolaus Pevsner, his arch-enemy and editor of a rival series to Betjeman's own 'Shell Guides', on the buildings of Britain.[27]) Not all volumes of 'Britain in Pictures' were reviewed, but this was partly due to the paper restrictions of the time, which limited the number of reviews periodicals could print.[28] Although the critic Philip Toynbee dismissed the series as 'non-books for non-readers', the excellent sales figures clearly indicate that his view was not widely held.[29]

The Role of Refugee Women

Not only did readers who bought the 'Britain in Pictures' not realize that this quietly patriotic series was produced by Austrians and Germans, but they would also probably have been surprised to learn of the calibre of the scholars responsible for the research and production. Needing to earn a living in their country of refuge, art historians were reduced to designing the page to accommodate text written by other academics.

Much of the production work at Adprint was done by refugee women, including Alice Harrap (née Kun), Elisabeth Friedlander, Hilde Kurz, Elisabeth Ullmann, Ruth Rosenberg, Eva Neurath (then Feuchtwang) and Marie Neurath (married to Otto). They needed to earn money and were often temporarily their family's main breadwinner, at times during the internment of their husbands (only one of the Adprint women, Marie Neurath, was herself interned). Some of these women took on relatively menial tasks while their husbands continued with more satisfying intellectual work.[30] Hilde Kurz organized illustrations for 'Britain in Pictures', an activity of which her daughter thought she was probably ashamed, considering it beneath her ability as an art historian; meanwhile, her husband, Otto, worked at the Warburg, the most respected centre of art history. In truth, the Warburg did not pay him a living wage, but at least he was able to pursue his career as an art historian.

Another trend among refugee women, although not exclusive to them, was that they began to develop careers in exile that would probably not have been an option had they stayed at home, given their middle-class backgrounds. Alice Kun, born in Budapest in 1914, first came to England in 1931 in order to perfect her English. She stayed with the Foyle family, well known in book and bookselling circles.[31]

She visited the family subsequently, first while she followed a short-hand course at Pitmans and then as a commission agent for her father's business in London. In 1937 Alice married William Richard Foyle, known as 'Dick', the son of William A. Foyle, who with his brother Gilbert had founded the prestigious London bookshop.[32] Alice must have returned to Vienna before the 1938 *Anschluss*, because she met Wolfgang Foges there. After emigration, she became Foges' secretary, earning £3.10s. a week.

When Adprint ceased to flourish at the end of the 1940s, Alice Foyle sought an export market in an attempt to rescue the publishing house. Although she had some success, Walter Neurath left, and Lord Glenconnor withdrew his backing. Alice became sales director for the publisher William Harvey at Purnell, which had bought Adprint. In 1959, she left to work for the Golden Press and Western Printing as their overseas licensing agent, eventually also taking on the agency for the Italian publishing giant Mondadori, for whom she eventually worked exclusively. She became a major figure in publishing rights, famously booking two suites in a hotel in Frankfurt during the annual Book Fair and rushing from one to the other to maximize business opportunities. The experience of having run Adprint in its early days when its male refugee staff were interned, of dealing with new and experimental printing techniques and of coping with the difficulty of publishing in wartime all proved useful in shaping Alice Foyle's later career, as did the many useful contacts she had made through both publishing and printing circles. After her first husband died in 1957, Alice married Paull Harrap, whose family company, George G. Harrap, had published many of the Adprint-designed books in the 1940s.

Isotype Graphics

As the war progressed, Adprint began to focus on books that looked towards the probable shape of post-war Britain. A new series of books was launched, 'The New Democracy', illustrated with photographs, diagrams and other graphic information about, for example, public health and education (pl. 17). The refugee couple Otto and Marie Neurath (no relation to Walter) provided Isotype graphics[33] to illustrate statistical data. The two were highly qualified for the task. Marie, née Reidemeister, was born in Brunswick and had met Otto Neurath on a study trip to Vienna, by which time he was already a well-established figure in the Wiener Kreis, the Vienna school of philosophy, as a Social Democrat with a keen interest in public education.

The municipal authorities needed to explain the new social housing programme and other welfare initiatives to the Viennese, and Otto Neurath created a museum for social and economic history for the purpose on 1 January 1925.[34] There he developed his system of pictorial statistics, Isotype (International System of Typographical Picture Education), which presents statistical information in picture form, making it instantly more accessible even to those unused to charts (pl. 18). Neurath's graphic language is still in use today.

Otto Neurath, Marie Reidemeister and Gerd Arntz, their art director, had not worked together for long before they realized they would have to flee Vienna in the face of the approaching Nazi threat. They went first to Holland, which proved to be a poor choice both because there were few commissions forthcoming and because the Germans invaded in May 1940. Neurath and Reidemeister left for England in a small boat with some 20 other refugees; Arntz stayed behind and was conscripted into the German army. Otto and Marie's arrival coincided with the government's mass internment policy, and they were sent eventually to the Isle of Man. They married at the end of their internment, and on their release they settled in Oxford, where they were well received both professionally and socially. Orders came in steadily for graphic work, helped by the film-maker Paul Rotha, who was familiar with Isotypes and saw that they could be used in the documentaries he was making, some of which were on behalf of the Ministry of Information. Also part of the loosely defined circle of journalists, publishers and designers working for the Ministry of Information was Wolfgang Foges, who had known and admired the work done by the Neuraths in Vienna.[35]

Isotypes were an obvious choice for Adprint's 'New Democracy' series, which was intended to educate the British about the new post-war Britain and which dealt with subjects such as healthcare, women and work, and human problems in industry. Otto and Marie Neurath employed the refugee Ernie Braun, who had been interned with Marie, as a general assistant and 'guinea pig' – another instance of networking in the camps that led to fruitful collaboration. Ernie believed that as long as she herself understood the graphics, then the general public probably would, too.

After Otto Neurath died unexpectedly in 1945, Marie continued to run the company, often commuting to London from Oxford to deal with orders. Eventually, Marie (known generally as 'Mary' in England) came to live in Pond Street, Hampstead, near a number of other refugee book artists.[36] She was responsible for many illustrated children's books, and continued to uphold the standards set by the earlier Isotype books, including the beautiful *Railways Under London* (Max Parrish Ltd., 1948).

The role of Max Parrish as one of the British editors at Adprint was particularly significant, in that he was one of several employees who went on to work for Thames & Hudson some decades later, so helping to keep alive the original aims and standards of Adprint. Parrish had worked for the Ministry of Information as deputy director in the Publications Division, a subdivision of the General Production, where his role had been to provide books as a form of popular illustrated documentary, incorporating a straightforward editorial structure that matched the text with pictures, maps and diagrams to provide a visual record of the story. His obituary in *The Times* (3 March 1970) recorded that the books were so successful 'they came to play their own part in supporting the national will and pride.' According to Ruth Rosenberg, Parrish's wife, Mona, had been the head of the *Picture Post* library, so the couple had a common interest in the provision of visual material for publications intended to have a wide public appeal.[37]

The End of Adprint

By 1949 Adprint was struggling financially. After a row with Wolfgang Foges about the directorship, Walter and Eva Neurath left to start their own publishing house, Thames & Hudson. The eventual separation of Neurath and Foges was probably inevitable: all the accounts of their falling out allude to their rivalry and personality clashes. It is easy to see that the two Viennese – both experienced, ambitious and creative – would have clashed over the credit for the 'Britain in Pictures' series, which had represented a milestone in publishing history. Like other instances of bitter rivalry in the story of refugee publishing, normal business competition was given an extra dimension by feelings of betrayal by compatriots.

Years later, an exchange of letters in *The Bookseller* reveals the bitterness behind the scenes. Referring to an article published on the occasion of Thames & Hudson's tenth anniversary, which included the 'Britain in Pictures' series among Neurath's achievements, Foges wrote to the editor:

> As the managing director of Adprint Ltd, I should like to point out that the 'Britain in Pictures' series of books was produced by Adprint Ltd (as is acknowledged in each title). Mr Walter Neurath, as an employee of Adprint from 1938 to 1949, naturally played an important part in planning

the 'Britain in Pictures' series; but I am sure he would be the first to agree that your statement might lead to some misconceptions.[38]

Neurath's response follows:

Mr Wolfgang Foges has sent me a copy of the letter which appears above. The 'Britain in Pictures' was planned and produced during the time when I was firstly production manager and subsequently a director of Messrs Adprint Ltd. The article in last week's *Bookseller* does not tend to mislead on this point as Mr Foges suggests. It did not highlight Adprint, but then I did not read it as an article on 'Britain in Pictures' and I think it was quite right not to stress that series of slim volumes planned 20 years ago.

One wonders if Neurath intended the slight implied in referring to the series as 'slim volumes', suggesting a lightweight quality. In any case, the relationship between Neurath and Foges remained bitter.

After the demise of Adprint, Foges went on to two important new publishing ventures: Future Books, intended for those in leadership positions,[39] and Aldus Books, the list of which might be described as educational, with some specialism in the natural sciences. After his long and varied career in England, Foges, who had a long-standing interest in the emerging African nations, became a consultant on a project creating textbooks for the new post-colonial era in Africa. Once again, with his undiminished ardour for accessible education for all and his sense of social justice, he was at the forefront of publishing. His son remembers future African leaders such as Kwame Nkrumah, the first President of Ghana, coming to their house.

Foges was a tremendous character, with a huge physical presence. One writer who worked with him remembers him sitting in his office puffing out clouds of cigar smoke, shouting, 'What do we think about Indian religion?'[40] Charming and angry by turns, he had friends from the most varied backgrounds, one being the fork-bending Uri Geller. He died in 1986, without having fulfilled his wish to chronicle the story of Adprint. His contribution to the development of British illustrated publishing is generally underestimated, but Adprint's legacy can be better appreciated when it is borne in mind that it was also responsible for the production of 'The New Naturalist', a series still in print today that remains universally respected in the field of natural history. Foges' son, Peter, points out that although his father's business judgement was often lacking, his creativity left behind a superb heritage, leading not only indirectly

to the creation of Thames & Hudson but also to the present generation of educational illustrated books created by publishers such as
Dorling Kindersley and Mitchell Beazley.

9   **The Birth of Thames & Hudson**

British Women Go to War, by J. B. Priestley, was published in 1943. The original impetus behind the book came from Wolfgang Foges and Percy Hennell, who took the photos; like 'Britain in Pictures' it had been packaged by Adprint for Collins, with attractive Isotypes on the endpapers.[1] Walter Neurath, at the time Adprint's production manager, travelled to Scotland to oversee the printing. He had run his own publishing company in Vienna before emigrating, and was clearly capable of doing so again; meticulous, responsible and entrepreneurial, he always wanted to lead from the front.

Walter Neurath had been interned with Wilhelm Feuchtwang on the Isle of Man. When he was released after only two weeks, Feuchtwang, who remained interned, asked Neurath to look up his wife, Eva. Neurath took Eva out to lunch and the two clicked immediately. He offered her work at Adprint, presumably in late 1940. The opportunity was most welcome; Eva was so desperate for an income that she had been on the point of taking up employment as a domestic servant. Although both were married to other people, they were attracted to each other and were united by their passion for good quality books.

On a holiday in France in 1949, Walter Neurath and Eva Feuchtwang decided to found their own publishing house, to be named Thames & Hudson for the major rivers of London and New York. They had close links with museums and other publishers in America, in particular Harry Abrams, with whom they planned to make distribution contracts. The firm's colophon was, and still is, two dolphins, one facing east and one west. Understanding fully the crucial role of the printer in their enterprise, they also invited into the partnership as directors John Jarrold, a Norwich-based printer, and Gilchrist and Co. Ltd. of Leeds, now no longer in existence; Gilchrist and Co. made the blocks used to print photographs.

In general, Neurath commissioned titles for publication. One notable exception was the very first Thames & Hudson publication, the black-and-white *English Cathedrals* (pl. 19), which came out in 1950 with photographs by the Swiss photographer and publisher Martin Hürlimann.[2] Eva Feuchtwang had seen the proofs of the book at Collins, which had decided not to publish it because of cost. Eva asked if she could publish it instead, and Neurath bought 13,000 sets of illustrations, having pre-sold 10,000 copies of the finished book to an American publisher. 'The English book-buying public, still suffering from the "economy" production standards of the post-war years, had not been offered such a handsome volume for more than a decade. ... It remained in print until 1971, when total sales exceeded 20,000.'[3]

Despite this intial success, the problems Thames & Hudson encountered in its early days were legion. As the illustrator Hellmuth Weissenborn ruefully remarked, the British were not keen on innovation; if things were acceptable, they saw little point in changing them to make improvements. Publishers were at first reluctant to take on initiatives connected with the new, international way of selling books. Sometimes Thames & Hudson's own staff were hesitant about adapting to different ways of working, being used to 'less adventurous British publishing houses'.[4]

In 1951 Neurath's second wife, Montessori teacher and trainee child therapist Marianne, died unexpectedly. Walter and Eva waited two years, then married in 1953. He was her third husband and she his third wife. They were a good team: partners in private as well as professional life, left-liberal in their politics, charming, keen on public education and generous in their entertaining, their social circle included the leading lights of contemporary cultural life (fig. 16).

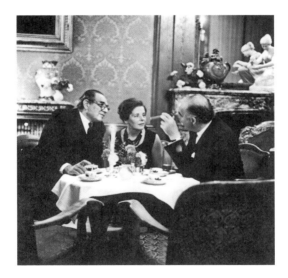

In its first year of trading, 1950, Thames & Hudson published a total of ten titles, including Albert Einstein's *Out of My Later Years* and several French titles, not all of them art books, although they were all illustrated. Thirteen more titles appeared in 1951, including Martin Hürlimann's *French Cathedrals* and Kerenyi's *The Gods of the Greeks*, defining the publisher's two main fields of specialization,

16 Walter and Eva Neurath with George Weidenfeld (right) at the Frankfurt Book Fair, *c.*1960s.

photography and archaeology. Publication of the former title coincided with the launch of a campaign to support parish churches, and the heavy press coverage greatly helped sales of the Thames & Hudson volume: Hürlimann's book outsold all previous publications.

The particular debt that Thames & Hudson owed to Martin Hürlimann is obvious from reviews, particularly in *The Times Literary Supplement*, in which *English Cathedrals* was compared favourably with two other books on a similar subject: *Portrait of Lincoln Cathedral* by G. H. Cook, published by Phoenix House in 1950, and *The English Cathedrals* by John Harvey, with photos by Herbert Felton, published by Batsford. Having complained that Hürlimann's text was a little 'Germanic', the reviewer nevertheless observed: 'When we come to look at the photographs by which these books are primarily to be judged, Mr Hürlimann's seem incomparably the best. He has avoided the 1930-ish Continental trick of taking the worm's-eye views, his pictures are large and well produced in photogravure of a greenish-grey tinge.'[5]

After dismissing Cook's photographs as 'mostly of the dull kind', the reviewer attempts to pinpoint Hürlimann's superior view: 'Mr Hürlimann gets something more than the average professional photographer, whether it be an effect of light on mouldings or of a long-drawn vista. He knows where to stand, where to look, how to print his negative.' The Phoenix publication is criticized for its poor reproduction: 'The fault lies with the printing', the reviewer points out, adding that 'over-heavy sepia' might be acceptable for the 'usual ham volume of agency photographs' but was not adequate for the task of showing cathedrals. In reply to the reviewer's mention of several English cathedrals not covered in the volume, Eva Feuchtwang explained in a letter published in the next issue that the omission was because Thames & Hudson's next volume on the theme, *English Parish Churches*, by Olive Cook, was already in preparation – thereby enabling the publishers to publicize their new book. A *Times Literary Supplement* review of Hürlimann's book on Athens, meanwhile, emphasized an aspect of the book that would no doubt have pleased Eva, referring to some of the plates as being in colour 'of an unparalleled accuracy and delicacy'.[6]

Thames & Hudson initially had a mixed general list, but eventually, like Phaidon, they came to specialize in art. A quotation used in an advertisement for *Rembrandt* by Ludwig Münz underlines one book's prestige: 'Of this book the art critic of *The New York Times* writes: "Dr Münz's remarks on the development of the artist and of the man, as well as his notes on the etchings and drawings, are penetrating, reliable and readable. The many excellent and well-chosen drawings alone make this book a valuable possession.'[7]

1952 saw the publication of *Art Treasures of the Louvre* by R. Huyghe – a major international project that involved photographing paintings in the Louvre and arranging for the book to be designed and manufactured in New York. This sort of venture was to become part of Thames & Hudson's stock in trade. By this time the company merited column space in *The Bookseller*, which reported the reaction to their publication *Boats and Boatmen* by T. C. Lethbridge.[8] In that same year, quotes (known in publishing as 'puffs') appeared in their advertisements. John Betjeman, who had evidently overlooked the fact that the book in question was produced by one of the 'filthy Austrian crooks', called *A Matter of Conscience* by Werner Bergengruen 'an exciting tale of detection' and 'a profound study of temptation'.[9] Neurath told *The Bookseller*: 'When I read Bergengruen's book two years ago I was so impressed with its quality and its significance for the present day that I felt it a matter of conscience to publish it.'[10] Bergengruen had been opposed to Nazism and had therefore been excluded from the Reichsschriftumskammer (the Nazi writers' guild); several of his books had been banned for their implied anti-Nazi message.[11]

Eva Neurath

While Walter brought to the partnership his business acumen and networking skills, Eva, although not trained in layout and design, contributed her experience of working with books and with art, along with her strong sense of composition and the fine sense of colour for which she became known. Her search for excellence in colour reproduction was tested when producing *The National Gallery, London*, which came out in 1955. The photographic blockmakers, Gilchrist, received back the proofs with Eva's colour corrections on them: 'She took each proof to the National Gallery, stood in front of the paintings, and meticulously marked each proof with dozens of notes. "Over in red." "Lacks detail." "Too blue." ...' The more corrections Eva made on the third, fourth and fifth proofs, the further away from the original the reproduction became. In a despairing attempt to get it right, the etcher concerned was put on the train to London with his last revised proof and taken by Eva to the National Gallery. Unfortunately, the etcher could not see that his choice of colour was wrong, causing Walter to lament the lack of craftsmanship and point out that colour is more important in art books than in commercial colour brochures. Ultimately, however, the book was printed

167

satisfactorily, and the catalogue observed: 'Each plate has been made with infinite care for colour value and relationship, reaching a new level of splendour in the art of colour reproduction.'[12]

Shared German origins alone were not enough to create a bond between Eva Neurath and other employees such as fellow Berliner Ruth Rosenberg; her relations were professional rather than personal. Nevertheless, some employees remember her as warm in her dealings with staff, despite her seniority. Michael Hall enjoyed a close and friendly working relationship with Eva as an editor at Thames & Hudson from 1982 to 1989. He remembers that her German culture pervaded the company: it was simply assumed that one knew about Thomas Mann and European opera. Although, like her husband, she had a great respect for English values and a curiosity about British traditions, Hall recalls being asked many times if he spoke German, presumably because Eva assumed that any cultured person had a good command of other languages. When he was assisting with the editing of Thames & Hudson's new book on the Bayeux Tapestry, for which fresh photographs were taken, she called him over. 'Have you seen my Leporello?' she said, pulling out the concertina of folded photographs for the book. He wished afterwards that he had asked innocently if it was her list of lovers, but at the time he merely let her know that he was familiar with Mozart's *Don Giovanni*.

Eva Neurath's method of working was 'hands on'. She and Michael Hall would often sit on the floor with the work spread out in front of them, frequently at the Neurath home in Highgate. She thought in terms of spreads and liked to see the 'rhythm' of a book as a whole. According to Hall, Constance Neurath, later Thames & Hudson's art director, learned much of the craft of book design from Eva, who passed on experience gained through years of working at Adprint. Hall, too, was deeply influenced by Eva. He had never met anyone with such visual intelligence and such an understanding of the way books worked: 'It's not just the text, it's not just the pictures, it's the way they are combined that matters.' In Hall's opinion, few people instinctively grasped this essential philosophy; Eva did.

Eva was an obsessive worker as well as a clever publisher. Stephan Feuchtwang, her son from her second marriage, was sent to boarding school so that his mother could work more easily (he would later become a professor at the London School of Economics). One example of her creativity was her decision to republish four 'Britain in Pictures' volumes in one book, to be called *Aspects of English Literature*; Anthony Burgess wrote the new introduction. She reused the backlist in similarly creative ways, republishing *Panorama of the Middle Ages* chapter by chapter, as separate volumes. One of her particularly successful 'recycling' ideas was to produce a picture book version of the fairly heavyweight history book *The New Sobriety: 1914–33: Art and Politics in the Weimar Years*. She designed the book to look like a 1930s edition, with striking, Bauhaus-inspired red, white and black covers.

When war broke out in 1939 and Eva had felt unable to reconcile her hatred of the Nazis with her love of Germany, she had sought psychoanalysis from a Jungian analyst to help her understand her inner conflict. She became very interested in Jung's ideas, as did Walter Neurath, and they later travelled to hear him speak, inviting some of the conference participants to become Thames & Hudson authors. Eva maintained that Jungian ideas, in particular the concept of the past in the present, formed the basis for some of the books they published. Even a cursory reading of Jung suggests how his writings might have helped her make sense of the contemporary world, in particular his notion of archetypes and the universality of mythology – and so inspire Thames & Hudson's interest in art and archaeology (pl. 22).

Herbert Read

The art historian Herbert Read was a taste-maker, cultural impresario, and public and private supporter of the German-speaking refugees. He held a post at the Victoria and Albert Museum, wrote and broadcast on the arts, including editing for a time from 1933 the prestigious *Burlington Magazine* (for which refugee scholars including Erwin Panofsky and Friedrich Antal also wrote), and was partly responsible for the creation of the Institute for the Contemporary Arts (ICA) in 1946. He had become familiar with contemporary European art while studying in Leeds (see also p. 41 above). Read deeply believed that even modern art was for all, remarking that ultimately art should so dominate life that there would no longer be works of art, just art. Art would then be the way of life.[13] He fell out with Kenneth Clark because of Read's conviction that 'advanced art' was out of touch with reality: Read saw it as a question of elitism versus art for all.

Read's ideas clearly chimed with the ethos of the founders of Thames & Hudson, who were committed to the same ideal: making their art books accessible to those who might not have had a university education (fig. 17). Read also shared with Eva Neurath an interest in the ideas of Carl Jung. He was an enthusiast for modernism, anathema to so many of his contemporaries in Britain. He saw his role as making his fellow countrymen aware of significant developments on

169

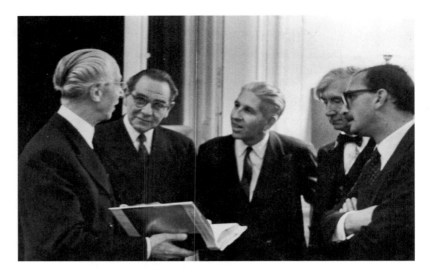

the continent, believing that modernism could inspire people to a new way of life. He used the example of a Paul Nash landscape as a painting revitalized by the painter's contact with Surrealism. 'Ultimately, Read was interested in fusing that which was distinctly English and often parochial to that which was European and cosmopolitan.'[14]

Read's interest in the German-speaking world (in part, perhaps, because his second wife, Ludo, was half-German) meant that even before the war he was aware of the dangers posed by Nazism to Jewish or avant-garde artists. He had met the Bauhaus architect Walter Gropius and the photographer and artist László Moholy-Nagy, and took a keen interest in their work and careers. He was, however, not uncritical: he rather discourteously referred to Ernst Gombrich's art criticism as a 'Viennese pastry approach', claiming that the art historians of the Viennese school were afraid of the senses.[15] And Read was not insensitive. He was more aware than many other Englishmen of what his biographer called the 'grim nightmare of Spain and Germany'. He helped save at least one life by arranging for the German–Jewish refugee Leonie Cohn to enter England in December 1938. She looked after Thomas, the Reads' young son, and did some light housekeeping,[16] later becoming a producer at the BBC as well as editing at least one volume of local history.

Read was an important friend of the Neuraths, a central figure in their widening circle of movers and shakers in the British art world. His special contribution was to heighten their interest in modern art, bringing Thames & Hudson a new and rich theme for publication.

17 Party at Gallimard to launch the Thames & Hudson title *Sumer*, 1960:
   (left to right) Georges Salles, Walter Neurath, Claude Gallimard,
   Herbert Read and Giangiacomo Feltrinelli.

He wrote many seminal books on art, including two on modern art for Faber & Faber, and later produced at least one on the same subject for Thames & Hudson, in addition to being the general editor on another.

Jarrold of Norwich, Printers

'Britain in Pictures' had been celebrated for its integrated pictures and text, and the same approach was continued in the Thames & Hudson 'World of Art' series. But for some larger, more expensive titles, such as *The Dawn of Civilization* and the series that followed it, 'Great Civilizations', Neurath favoured the 'layer cake' format, with text sections on heavy matt paper alternating with pictures on thinner, glossier stock. This facilitated the printing of co-editions in several different languages: the text for each language was printed separately, while the picture sections – both black-and-white and colour – were printed together for all editions. The economies of scale this achieved allowed for the use of very high-quality materials and techniques while keeping prices down.

An art publishing house, it could be argued, is only as good as the printer who reproduces the text and photographs in its books. Neurath chose the printer Jarrold of Norwich, a company established in the eighteenth century that had become known for its use of innovative technology. This must have been due to the influence of H. John Jarrold, who had studied printing and bookbinding in Leipzig before the war and went there again after:[17] 'In 1946 John Jarrold went to Germany to inspect and report on German printing. [He later went] to the East German Leipzig Fair. These visits confirmed the pre-war impression that the German industry had been technically advanced in colour photography and offset printing.'[18] Jarrold had also noticed that working conditions in Britain were inferior to those in Germany, citing the lack of cleaning facilities for printers, who attracted little prestige. Walter Neurath certainly used the reputation of German printers to his advantage. Faced with delays in Britain, Neurath urged his German printer to work night shifts in order to complete the work on time. To counter the printers' protests, he said: 'I know that you and your workforce are *craftsmen*. I know that you take great pride in your achievements.'[19]

Jarrold's early training at the heart of the German book industry in Leipzig and his continuing links with it put him in the company of such important members of the book establishment as Sir Stanley Unwin, Christopher Foyle and Ruari McLean, all of whom also had links with the refugee publishers. The Jarrold house journal,

The Jarrold Magazine, provides a useful insight into the workings of a British printing company in the post-war years. In each issue there was a section entitled 'Departmental Round-up', which, as the name implies, was a summary of the work done in a particular department. Sometimes there was mention of the difficulty that work represented, an important reminder of the tremendous challenge of reproducing photographs accurately, swiftly and cheaply at that time.

It may have been in 1948 that Neurath realized the potential of partnership with Jarrold, because the printers used the occasion of their 125th anniversary to demonstrate the scope of their new machinery. A special issue of the house journal describes how some 200 guests, mostly clients, were invited to Norwich for the day on a specially chartered steam train.[20] They were shown round the printing works and given a festive lunch, but the highlight was to come on their return journey. When they got on the train back to London, they were presented with colour prints of photographs taken of them during their visit to the works just seven hours earlier, an unprecedented feat of timing and skill. Listed among the guests were W. Neurath and Miss Seidmann of Adprint, Dr Béla Horovitz (Jarrold's printed Phaidon's *Rodin* in 1950, although Elly Miller recalls that they were not Horovitz's favourite printer), Sir Stanley Unwin, André Deutsch, and Ian and Walter Harrap, as well as representatives from Penguin Books and many others.[21]

As far as Thames & Hudson was concerned, the most useful advance introduced by Jarrold was the Double Quad Demy. The house journal records the arrival of the four-colour press in 1948, pointing out that it was 'still the largest of its kind in Europe' and giving its nicknames: 'Jarrold's Folly' or 'Frankenstein'. The Harris four-colour sheet-fed litho press, which had a sheet size of 1,752 × 1,270 mm, had been shipped from the United States on the *Queen Mary*. Operated by the brothers Charles and William Kent, it was the first large four-colour litho press to be installed in Britain. Once established, it was in continuous production for over 30 years, serving mainly the growing market for children's annuals.[22] In 1949 the press was on double shift for a considerable time. Its 'teething problems [were] related to the difference in technique required for single-colour and four-colour printing and involved almost everything, including inks, plates, blankets, solutions, retouching and assembling'. The press was referred to in an earlier article as 'the biggest headache in the world'.[23] The reason for the introduction of the new press is explained in the company history: 'It was a decision based on sound market forecasting. Following World War II a rise in the birth rate meant a predictable peak in demand for children's books.'[24]

The four-colour press was also ideal to cope with the demands of Thames & Hudson. Not only was there a large market for attractive, affordable publications in a post-war Britain still starved of books and, it could be said, of beauty and art, but printers were also finding it difficult to meet the demand. As Jarrold comments in 1949: 'The printing industry is at present passing through a time of extreme demand for its products. The number of new apprentices during the war was insufficient to replace those who reached retirement age.'[25]

The new four-colour press in no way solved all the previous problems of accurate reproduction. One 'Departmental Round-up' article deals with the job of the 'retoucher' or 'litho artist', explaining the process as follows:

> The artists get the negatives, one for each of the colours
> in which the job will be printed. Although filters are used
> on the camera when colour separation negatives are made,
> it is not possible to make consistently perfect reproductions
> of colour tones. So the artists treat the negatives with chemi-
> cals to complete the job manually. From these negatives,
> positives are made, then *these* are corrected manually too.[26]

Understanding this technique gives an insight into the importance of the role of Eva Neurath, with her ability to detect discrepancies between original and reproduction by seeing nuances of colour shades that others could not.

The special position of Jarrold was revealed in an article that appeared in the *Financial Times* in 1964.[27] Citing publishers Thames & Hudson, Weidenfeld & Nicolson and Hamlyn (the two last, themselves émigré publishers, being the ones most directly influenced by Thames & Hudson's methods), the author pointed out that their books, which were 'richly illustrated', with 'complicated layout', were largely printed by companies in Czechoslovakia, Italy and Holland. The reasons were listed as follows: first, international co-publishing invited the contribution of foreign printers, as they were better suited to printing foreign languages; second, the quality of colour printing was simply better abroad; third, printers in Britain did not take publishers' demands seriously, considering them 'rather a whim'; and finally, printers in Britain were poor at keeping to delivery dates. This dreary picture of British workmanship corresponds to the received idea of a time when standards of craftsmanship had fallen and unions were often in conflict with management.

However, Jarrold was not part of this negative picture. The author emphasizes that 'The World of Art' series, which started with a volume on Picasso, was printed entirely by Jarrold, including the French edition. The series also went to Finland and Spain in their own languages. Hamlyn, too, was having similar work done by Jarrold. The final point of the article makes it clear that Jarrold was a significant factor in Thames & Hudson's early success: 'It is not that British printers *cannot* print high colour; some can: look at Jarrold's. But the trouble is there aren't enough of them.'

Walter Neurath got on well with John Jarrold but was not beyond criticizing the printer in his relentless pursuit of high standards in all areas of book production.[28] Elly Horovitz notes that the crucial relationship between publisher and printer depends on the best possible communication skills, and that for the German-speaking refugees this cannot always have been easy. John Jarrold, too, attempted to explain the dialogue in an article written in the 1960s: 'The client should discuss printing with both the designer and printer as early as possible. The design has the function of giving information – both the designer and the printer should understand the aim of the literature they were producing.'[29] The sympathy that existed between this master printer and his émigré clients was crucial to the process.

Werner Guttmann and Shalom Schotten

The production and art departments at Thames & Hudson had émigré staff for decades, many with long and successful careers. The refugee publishers would not have been in a position to employ unsuitable refugee staff out of sympathy alone; certainly, the Thames & Hudson founders could not have afforded to do so. However, the employers had confidence in the skills and attitude to work of their fellow refugees. Production and design are fields in which accuracy and discipline are essential, with production also requiring interpersonal skills. The long tradition of pride in the craft of skilled printing corresponds to a stereotypical image of German workmen, but has an element of truth in it.

Eva Neurath was friendly with Berlin-born Werner Guttmann, who was responsible for production at Thames & Hudson for some forty years.[30] Editor Michael Hall found Guttmann quite intimidating in the 1980s, especially when he barked out instructions – no doubt in part reflecting the unusual importance and responsibility of a production manager in the creation of illustrated books. However, Guttmann warmed to Hall on discovering that they shared a love of classical music. Born in 1924, Guttmann came from a Jewish family living in Berlin, where his father was a prominent lawyer, and went to school in Switzerland after 1933. His father's brother, Peter, came to England in 1936 and bought the defunct general publishing house Hammond and Hammond, and Werner and his father followed in November 1938. His mother remained in Berlin and died in the Holocaust. After completing his schooling at Kings College Wimbledon, Guttmann initially embarked on a scientific and technical career, working briefly for a metallurgical company, which qualified as war work; the alternative, he said, would have been the Pioneer Corps. In 1947 he went to work for his uncle at Hammond and Hammond, where, as the company's staff numbered about ten, with few clear delineations of responsibility, it was inevitable that he should learn different publishing skills: packaging, production and publicity. Design for the list was not challenging, as most of the product was general or fiction books. While on holiday in France, Guttmann sought out orders on his own initiative. Encouraged by his success, and no doubt made confident by his fluency in three languages, he took on the representation of other publishers, notably Weidenfeld & Nicolson and Putnams.

During his time at Hammond and Hammond, Guttmann spent six months at the printers Morrison and Gibb in Edinburgh, working closely with compositors, typesetters and printers, and learning the craft of hot-metal printing. It was through his involvement with the production of the journal *Athene*, the magazine for the Society for Education through Art, that he became interested in art books. The society's president was Herbert Read, who worked closely with the Neuraths and whom Guttmann got to know. Guttmann first saw Thames & Hudson books in an exhibition at the Festival Hall and was attracted to the idea of art book production. He was asked to come to an informal interview by Walter Neurath in 1960 and quickly became responsible for the crucial task of Thames & Hudson production. In an interview for the British Library, he mentions his special rapport with his fellow Berliner, Eva Neurath.[31]

On the challenge of overseeing co-editions, Guttmann comments that when foreign publishers had to fit their text to the already fixed illustrations, there was often a discrepancy in the amount of space required; German, for example, needs more pages than English. Part of the expertise of Thames & Hudson lay in the ability to create the right amount of text space. Guttmann had to manage the delicate process of ensuring that all the foreign texts could be set with no loss of scholarship and accuracy, bearing in mind that the greater the number of foreign publishers involved, the higher Thames & Hudson's profit margin would be.

Success and subsequent expansion meant that Thames & Hudson had to look for other printers beyond Jarrold's; according to Guttmann, printers that the firm was using in the UK, Holland and Germany lacked the capacity to produce large series. Thomas Neurath recalls trips to printers in Holland and Germany with his father before Guttmann arrived on the scene – cooperation with foreign printers was not a new concept for the company. But while his British colleagues were sceptical about European printers, Guttmann's combination of printing experience, native German language skills and familiarity with continental culture made him ideally placed to find German and other European printers for Thames & Hudson's big projects, such as *The Dawn of Civilization*. This book was published in more than eight languages after three years of work. The catalogue ran the note, 'The total first printing of this great book will be over 200,000 copies, representing not only a marvel of book production but also the finest example of international co-operation ever known.'[32] The printing blocks were made by five different companies in Europe and sent to one printer in Cologne, an amazing publishing feat.

With some pride, Guttmann relates that other publishers in Britain watched where Thames & Hudson printed, then followed. Various refugee publishers later continued this pioneering work in finding the best printers: for example, the refugee publisher Paul Hamlyn later became the first publisher in Britian to have his books printed in East Asia, a practice that would later become standard among illustrated publishers.

'Jacket designs were – and still are – a source of constant debate. A few outside jacket designers were employed in the early years, but the task of briefing them adequately proved difficult, and for the past twenty years all jackets for T&H books have been initiated by our own designers.'[33] The dust jacket artist is a significant member of the publishing team, a link between the book and the public. According to the refugee book artist Shalom Schotten, it is the role of the dust jacket to stand out in a bookshop while not conflicting with the contents of the book or the image of the publisher. Walter Neurath insisted on a 'monumental' approach to jackets, by which he meant that the design should fill the entire cover, including the spine, and that the lettering should be large.

Shalom Schotten spent 45 years designing covers in house at Thames & Hudson. Following his long and difficult escape from the

Nazis in Austria, via Czechoslovakia, he spent years in France. His subsequent itinerary meant that he was exposed to a multiplicity of influences, which he was able to convert into his own distinctive designs. His family moved to Tel Aviv in 1951, and after military service in the Israeli army in about 1955, he found work as a signwriter, helping to make silkscreen posters. He then moved to the graphic designer Grundmann. This marked a turning point in his life, for Grundmann had worked at the Festival of Britain with such influential graphic artists as Henrion and Abram Games, and so introduced Schotten to European design at one of its most creative periods. He started to read the Swiss journal *Graphis*, and although he was only the studio assistant, he used Grundmann's facilities to create his own designs.

Now eager to earn his living in art and design, Schotten came to England to attend the London College of Printing (LCP). Realizing that the college had only a limited contribution to make to his training, given his already considerable experience, he selected only some parts of the course. At the LCP he met Rolf Brandt, Tom Eckersley and George Adams (born in Austria as Georg Teltscher), formerly of the Bauhaus. (Adams was the artistic consultant to Thames & Hudson for some 20 years, but Thomas Neurath remembers there being difficulties between Adams and his father, because of Walter Neurath's own pretensions to graphic design ability and his unwillingness to accept the advice of Adams, an expert designer.) Adams had designed hundreds of dust jackets, including many for Thames & Hudson (pls 20 and 23), to which company he introduced Schotten. He had been commissioned to design a book entitled *Ancient Near East* but had to go to the United States, so he asked Schotten to complete the work in his absence. Although Schotten had no book design experience, he was a creative and competent designer and was also skilled in fitting maps together, a talent he had acquired during his Israeli army training. Walter Neurath was pleased with Schotten's work and offered him more. Once he was on the staff, the more sought-after dust jackets were given to him rather than to two members of staff who had completed their training at the LCP – another indication of Neurath's recognition of the potential of those who, like himself, had not completed their formal studies. Schotten often found working with the Neuraths difficult and restricting, but he recognized the value of their exacting standards in his recounting of a small incident at work. Inspecting a rough for a cover, Walter Neurath remarked that the design was slightly out of line. Schotten at first disputed the mistake – but he later saw that he was wrong and admitted as much to Neurath, who became much more accommodating and friendly towards him.

In 1975 Schotten's design for a book of archaeological maps won the Silver Eagle award at the Nice International Festival of the Book. Although the Neuraths' direction of the design of covers was firm, the cover artist contributed his or her own knowledge and cultural heritage. When Schotten was asked to design the cover for a book about David Hockney, his knowledge of the painter led him to the notion of reflection, a frequent leitmotif in Hockney's work, for example in his swimming pool paintings. Schotten's chosen image for the cover shows a detail of a Hockney self-portrait with the artist standing in front of a mirror in which he is reflected (pl. 20). When Schotten enlarged the image for the design, he found that the edges of the figure of Hockney and his mirror reflection became slightly blurred, thus creating new suggestions about reflection and identity. Schotten referred to this example of unpredictability or chance as a recognized part of the artistic tradition, for example in Japanese calligraphy, where irregularities are to be embraced rather than rejected. He then chose to emphasize the idea of reflection by creating a book title that had its own reflection in upside-down lettering.

Art Books for All

Walter Neurath died in 1967, aged only 63. He had been a passionate defender of Britain, and when the teenaged Thomas complained to his father about how stuffy British society was, Walter Neurath praised the country as the only one to uphold real tolerance and liberal values. Walter's memory is kept alive not only through Thames & Hudson books, but also through prizes and lectures created to celebrate his life's work. His obituary in *The Bookseller* described the challenge he encountered in his adopted country: "'I found the market for art books in England to be non-existent," he used to say, "so we had to create art books in disguise.'" He certainly succeeded in his aim of creating art books that would appeal to British readers.[34] The tributes paid in the trade and general press were a reflection of his significant role in the publishing world. Although it is true that the post-war period was a propitious one for art publishers generally, nevertheless Neurath's range of talents and experience ensured that he was able to take advantage of the situation.

A comparison can be made between the direction of the two great émigré art houses, Phaidon and Thames & Hudson, in the early 1950s by looking at the thrust of their advertisements in the trade journals. Phaidon's *The Treasures of the Great National Galleries* by Hans Tietze, priced at 35s., was for them perhaps a relatively popular art book at a low price. It is featured in *The Bookseller* under the subtitle 'For the cultured tourist' and includes praise from the *New Yorker* as 'such an excellent idea that one wonders why it had never been done before – at least in a single moderately priced volume'.[35] Two weeks later, a Thames & Hudson advertisement for *How to Understand Modern Art* sets out to appeal more to the non-specialist, including the recommendation 'without employing the confusing and often meaningless jargon beloved of art critics. This is the book the average man has been waiting for!'[36] The latter assessment chimes very much with a quote from Cyril Connolly appreciated still by the present-day Neuraths, that their books were 'for the omnivorous, middlebrow reader'.

However, there were also unfavourable reactions to the publications of the refugees from those who did not see the democratization of the arts as a desirable trend. In an undated letter from the mid-sixties in reaction to a fine art publishing proposal, the author revealed his opinion of the émigré publishers:

> There's a lot of decent publishing that needs to be done, both from the academic aspect, and also from the point of view of this new modish and quasi-popular market which certainly exists now, and didn't a few years ago. It seems to me that the people concerned in this, Phaidon in the former and Thames and Hudson in the latter, are both inadequate in publishing terms: by not producing properly rigorous academic books, or by issuing this stream of badly-written, ill-conceived and poorly-illustrated *World of Art Series*, and all their related junk.'[37]

The Thames & Hudson 'World of Art' series had been conceived in 1958 and designed with a series identity: a black spine and small, pocket-sized format. This affordable and recognizable series, like Penguin Books, was an immediate success. Within seven years there were 49 titles in the 'World of Art' series, and they still sell well today, despite heavy competition.

Thames & Hudson's tenth year of trading, 1959, coincided with six of their books being chosen as 'Best Designed Books of the Year' by the National Book League; three of Phaidon's books were selected. Ninety-seven books were chosen to represent British publishing in the international competition, and it is interesting to note that five of the publishers were refugees and that other imprints – including Penguin, Nicholson and Watson and Max Parrish – were heavily influenced by refugee design.[38] The Neuraths were featured on the cover of *The Bookseller* of 14 March 1959, and a reproduction from

A Concise History of Modern Painting by Herbert Read illustrated the front cover of *The Times Literary Supplement* on 23 October of the same year, which dedicated almost two full pages to a review of the book.[39] The review incidentally gave rise to heated correspondence between the reviewer and the author over the next weeks, regarding interpretations of some of the works.[40] A rapturous review was given to another Thames & Hudson photographic book, this time *Indian Landscape* (1959) with photographs by S. Hausamann: '... her compositions of scenes from the life are good enough to bear compositions of the sculptures she has photographed, wherein awe has not dimmed her photographic eye.'[41] On Thames & Hudson's particular strength, the reviewer adds: 'The printers are to be congratulated.'

As a reflection of the general appeal of Thames & Hudson books (they were, after all, meant for a wide audience, not just a scholarly one), *The Bookseller* published a letter, unedited, that a 14-year-old boy from New Zealand had written to the publisher, expressing his search for books about art:

> I decided the most wonderful book I could find was a book in
> your series called the 'Louvre'. At nights I spend hours looking
> at this most beautiful book. I copy pictures with my little set
> of oil paints. After reading and looking at the book my one
> and only ambition is to get another so I am sloging way at the
> scrub earning my 2s an hour. Within a few weeks I will have my
> hearts desire – another of those books. Will you please send me
> the details of your forthcoming books, if you would I will think
> you are wonderful people, you English. You sure can make
> 'beaut' art books too [*sic*].[42]

Thames & Hudson publications played a special role in the education of young people in general and art students in particular. In their first ten years of publishing, they made such an impact that it was clear to all that they were here to stay.

Phaidon Press

It was during Phaidon's time at 14 St Giles in Oxford – the war years, from 1940 to 1945 – that its scholarly reputation was established, for it was then that crucial relationships were created with English art critics and art historians. But it was thanks to *The Story of Art*, which was translated into many languages and reprinted very many times, that Phaidon became highly profitable.

In 1955, on a company visit to New York (fig. 18), Béla Horovitz had a heart attack and died suddenly. (Asked by the ship's doctor if he was allergic to anything, he answered, 'Yes, America.') His daughter, Elly, and son-in-law, Harvey Miller (figs 19 and 20), took over the company. Elly had read Philosophy, Politics and Economics at Somerville College Oxford and had worked extensively with other publishers, for example at OUP in New York, where she helped research a history of *The Times*. She was interviewed for that job by Stanley Morison, who astounded her by asking why she had left her country – a naïve question which it seems hard to justify. She had also already been working at Phaidon for some time, and so was well acquainted with its practices. Even while a schoolgirl, she had helped Ludwig

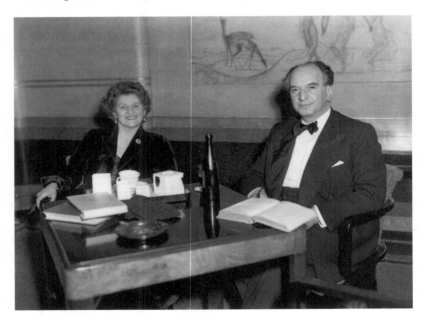

18 Béla Horovitz and his wife Lotte on board the Queen Mary on their way to New York, 1955.

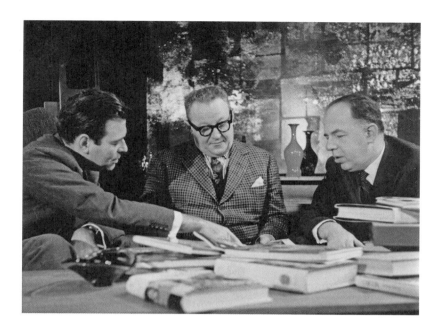

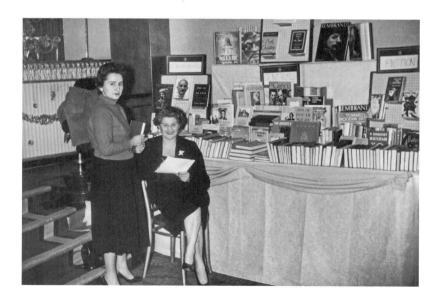

19 Harvey Miller, Béla Horovitz's son-in-law (left), with Douglas Cooper
    and Ernst Gombrich, c. late 1950s.

20 Elly (Horovitz) Miller (left) and her mother, Lotte Horovitz, c. late 1950s.

Goldscheider with paste-ups of proofs and illustrations. After Horovitz's death, the staff stayed on at Phaidon, with Goldscheider and Innozenz Grafe providing important support and continuity. As before, with a staff of only twelve, the employees did many different jobs, which would be very unusual in a modern publishing house.[1] Goldscheider and Lotte Horovitz took over the East and West Library, an imprint focusing on Jewish philosophy and culture that was established by Béla Horovitz in response to the attempted destruction of Jewish traditions.

The company remained 'upmarket' during the Miller period – it produced Otto Benesch's six-volume study of Rembrandt's drawings, for example[2] – but in 1967 Elly and Harvey Miller sold Phaidon to Frederick Amos Praeger of New York. Praeger was himself a Viennese refugee who had escaped to the United States in 1938 and had done well enough with Frederick A. Praeger Inc. to develop Phaidon's potential. The new venture started well, with five Phaidon books being commended in the best-designed book awards in 1970. The firm was then sold to the Encyclopaedia Britannica Company, with which firm Praeger was then working in Chicago. Encyclopaedia Britannica was experiencing financial difficulties, however, and in 1974 Phaidon was sold to Elsevier, a long-established Dutch publishing house. There then followed a period of greater commercialization and, despite continuing a highly respected art list, what might be called a 'dumbing-down' of the company. Elsevier moved to Oxford, and the range of titles produced expanded to include almost any type of book with illustrations. The new, diluted Phaidon list did not thrive, competing as it did with many other cheap illustrated books. A management buyout followed, resulting in the setting up of the Musterlin holding company. The proven formula of large print runs and inexpensive prices was abandoned; in 1988 an edition of Burckhardt's *The Altarpiece in Renaissance Italy*, though of characteristic good quality, retailed for the vast sum of £75. Bankruptcy followed in 1990, and the company was offered for sale in the *Financial Times*.

The advertisement was seen by an entrepreneur named Richard Schlagman. A young businessman who had enjoyed financial success in consumer electronics, he knew nothing about publishing, but he was a collector of modern art and had a large art library, including Phaidon books. He and a partner, Mark Futter, purchased the company, but only Schlagman threw himself into the activity of publishing, immersing himself in the content, design and production of the books, and he soon bought out his colleague. After the purchase, Schlagman invested much time and energy championing and relaunching Ernst Gombrich's books, which over the years had slipped from public conciousness, particularly in the United States, and he and his team reviewed and relicensed every foreign language edition. Schlagman invited Gombrich to update the *The Story of Art*, which author and publisher worked on together; the creation of the revised and expanded sixteenth edition was an experience that Schlagman greatly valued. In a letter to the publisher, Gombrich refers to the book as 'our joint magnum opus'.[3] As well as a good professional relationship, Gombrich and Schlagman enjoyed a close personal friendship, sharing interests such as opera and exhibitions, and in 1994 Schlagman organized an eighty-fifth birthday celebration for Gombrich at the National Portrait Gallery in London. He travelled to New York with Gombrich and his wife, Ilse, to promote the new edition of *The Story of Art*, a journey on which Gombrich was initially reluctant to embark. In the end he was pursuaded, and Schlagman and the Gombrichs thoroughly enjoyed the trip, Gombrich writing to his publisher later, 'Not only did you recreate *The Story of Art* from scratch, you also managed to whisk its former author across the Atlantic, acting as travel agent, impresario, caterer, wheelchair pusher, nurse and last but not least as a welcome travel companion.'[4] Working closely with Gombrich, Schlagman ensured that all his titles remained in print, created a new compilation of essay volumes called *The Essential Gombrich*, and launched a pocket edition of *The Story of Art* in 2006.

When Schlagman discussed his connections with the original Phaidon founders, he questioned any notion of Phaidon's Jewishness, saying that the tradition of culture often attributed to the Jews of 'Mitteleuropa' was more likely a product of central Europe itself. Although he is Jewish, he describes himself as 'anti-religious', sharing Gombrich's view that Jewishness played no role in his professional life. He resumed the Phaidon tradition of producing high-quality books at competitive prices, with the adjustment, perhaps, of placing greater emphasis on modern and avant-garde art than the founders had done.

The company became enormously successful under Schlagman's directorship, with a multi-million-pound turnover of books on the visual arts and a worldwide reputation for excellence. The publications produced over the twenty years of Schlagman's management included a wide list of books on contemporary art, architecture and photography at a full range of prices, but always at good value. But it was the 1994 publication *The Art Book* (pls 24 and 25) that most closely paralleled the success of *The Story of Art,* bringing high-quality reproductions of the world's major paintings to a wide audience, thanks to the low cover price. Although Alan Fletcher, co-founder of the Pentagram design firm and consultant Art Director of Phaidon, may have suggested the idea of reusing transparencies from the enormous Phaidon archives, in the end the project required an entirely new selection and sourcing of images. 'The concept is simple: 500 images, one per page, an A–Z ordering of material.'[5] This book represents a certain symmetry in the development of Phaidon. It topped the bestseller list in 1997, thereby vindicating yet again Horovitz's original theory of successful art publishing: good quality reproduction, good design and a very competitive cover price.

However, the trend in recent Phaidon publishing is not without its critics. Robin Kinross, after drawing attention to publications such as *Century*,[6] which came with its own carrying case, or '*Fresh Cream*, a compilation of new art ... encased within an inflated plastic pillow',[7] noted that it is ironic that Phaidon books have become a victim of their own design success. Referring to Phaidon as Thames & Hudson's rival, he notes, 'Phaidon often gives the impression of having buried content in the desire to amaze with its design radicalism...'[8] Readers disagreed, however, noting that 'the Phaidon Press constantly surprises and delights not only with the content of their art books, but also in their presentation and form'. One reader added,

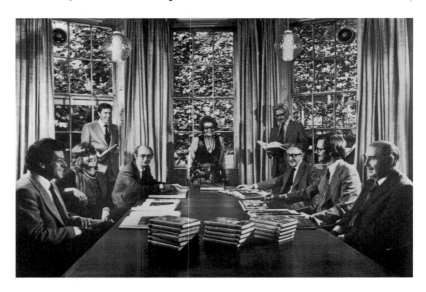

21 Eva Neurath presiding over the Thames & Hudson board of directors, *c.*1970: (left to right) Thomas Neurath and Constance (Neurath) Kaine, Simon Huntley, Eric Bates, Eva Neurath, the production manager Werner Guttmann, the company's chronicler Trevor Craker, Ian Middleton and Ian Carriline.

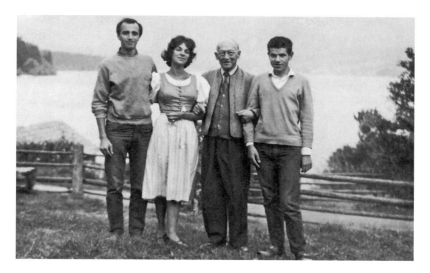

'The book uses itself as a jumping off point for the discussion, closing itself in its invisible plastic wrap as if to illustrate modern art's many facets; impenetrability, transition, meaning, transparency, metaphysics and weightiness.'[9]

In October 2012 Richard Schlagman sold Phaidon Press to the New York financier and art collector Leon Black. Black has stated in interviews that the acquisition is unconnected with his investment firm and that the publishing company was purchased as a family project.

Thames & Hudson

'They were born and raised in England, inherited a lot of their father's talent and do what they do brilliantly. If the *Anschluss* of 1938 hadn't happened, they would probably now be famous publishers in Vienna. So there is hardly a trace of 'Danube' and 'Spree' left in our company, and that is fine with us.'[10] The last part of Eva Neurath's statement in a German newspaper interview when she was 84 can be challenged: there is more than a little trace of Vienna or Berlin at Thames & Hudson (fig. 21). The second generation émigrés show how cultural values are passed on, especially when they chose to work in the publishing house created by their father, as Elly Miller did at Phaidon. Thomas Neurath, born in 1940, expressed his frank amazement at his stepmother's claim, pointing out that the company had always been and, indeed still is, relentlessly continental. The burr of German accents heard in the 1940s is still discernible in the twenty-first-century offices, where many of the employees are German-speaking.

22 Constance (Neurath) Kaine with her husband, John Kaine, her grandfather Artur Müller and her brother, Thomas Neurath, in Austria, 1959.

Thomas Neurath mentioned his mixed heritage in an interview published in the *International Herald Tribune* on the occasion of Thames & Hudson opening a Paris branch.[11] His interviewer, remarking that he was 'Austrian by family', noted that he had studied archaeology at Cambridge, which one might guess would have met with the approval of his father and stepmother. Neurath explained that one reason the company had set up its own office in France was that they had not succeeded in finding a French publisher to take the 'World of Art' series, though 'art paperbacks for students seemed to me something that was really useful.'

He also expressed nostalgia for the sort of company that his father had founded and run, admitting that the publishing house had become 'too big in London' and complaining that 'such a small fraction of the day is devoted to what I like doing most'. He wished for a return to the days when eccentric academics would come into the office with unpublishable manuscripts, which they would defend with single-minded passion. Commenting on the staff at Thames & Hudson, he identified half of the employees as being English and 'restrained', the other half being outspoken and 'given to fits of shouting', a description often made of his father and, indeed, of his colleague and rival Wolfgang Foges.[12] Thomas 'straddles both worlds', again an implicit contradiction of Eva's statement.

Constance Kaine (née Neurath; fig. 22) and her brother joined Thames & Hudson in 1961 and are still involved with the firm. Walter Neurath, who like Horovitz died young, at least witnessed the great success of his company and knew it to be in safe hands. On his father's death, Thomas Neurath took over the running of the company aged only 25, but he was supported completely by Eva Neurath. Constance now appreciates how little Eva interfered once Thomas was in charge, despite having held such an important role herself. Eva Neurath's son, Stephan Feuchtwang, spent some three years at the company but surprised his fellow employees by choosing not to stay in publishing, becoming an academic instead. Members of the third generation of Neuraths are also employed at Thames & Hudson.

Friends and Rivals

Phaidon and Thames & Hudson are both unusual in contemporary British publishing in that they are still independent rather than being owned by newspaper publishing groups. Another point of commonality is 'their active support and promotion of backlist titles that built the identity of the firm and established its reputation'.[13]

In this way both companies maintain strong links with their original refugee publishing origins.

The refugees were a source of support and comfort to each other, both materially and emotionally. But could this cooperation be extended to professional life, particularly in the highly competitive world of publishing? The bitter falling-out between Foges and Neurath (see pp. 159–60 above) suggests that the desire to survive and succeed was paramount, and although both men provided employment for fellow refugees, this was not purely out of sympathy but also a recognition of their fellow Germans' or Austrians' special skills. A shared history and background was not always enough to create solidarity: Joseph Roth was invited by Horovitz to write a book for

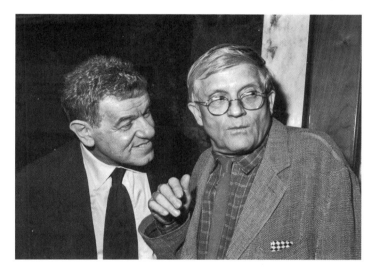

Phaidon, but not only did Roth not produce the commissioned book, he attacked Horovitz in his letters, accusing him of being interested only in money.

The relationship between Béla Horovitz and Walter Neurath was necessarily based on rivalry. Elly Miller recalls that the Horovitzes were taken aback on seeing the first Thames & Hudson books, which looked uncannily like Phaidon volumes. Joseph, Béla's son, also remembers meeting Neurath with his father around 1950 and recalls his father's suspicion that Neurath wanted to copy the Phaidon publishing style. Béla Horovitz and Walter Neurath had known each other in Vienna before they emigrated. They had studied at the same university, were Jewish (although with very different views on their

Jewishness) and shared many friends. However, they both needed to survive in their host country, which meant competing against each other's publishing houses in the market for art books. Elly Miller revealed that there had once been talk of her father joining a publishing venture that Neurath was setting up at the time.

Alice Hammond, the principal secretary at Phaidon for more than 40 years, recalled at least one visit by Neurath to the office, although Thomas Neurath thinks it unlikely that the two met more than once. Hammond speculated that the two publishers might have been negotiating to avoid producing books on the same artists, thereby flooding the market and benefiting neither of them. However, Richard Schlagman, who periodically lunched with Thomas Neurath, later said that cooperation of this kind was highly unlikely, adding that today art books are commissioned by means of individual deals made directly with the artists (fig. 23). According to Schlagman, the two publishing houses developed their lists in slightly different ways and probably would have been meeting primarily for social reasons.

Ernst Gombrich was a link between the two Viennese publishers. No doubt the publication of *The Story of Art* and its unexpected success for both author and Phaidon in material and professional terms was a source of disappointment for Neurath, who had originally discussed the book with Gombrich in Vienna but would not have been in a position to publish it, even had Gombrich completed it at the time (see pp. 91–92 above).

However, a few books by Gombrich did reach the tables of other publishers. *Conversations on Art and Science*, published by Thames & Hudson, came about through the French journalist Didier Eribon, who had interviewed Gombrich and had his own publishing deal.[14] Gombrich's *Little History of the World* was another. Schlagman and Gombrich talked for years about his history of mankind from caveman to the First World War, originally published as *Weltgeschichte von der Urzeit bis zur Gegenwart* (*A World History from Prehistoric Times to the Present*) in 1936, and subsequently as *Eine kurze Weltgeschichte für junge Leser* (*A Short World History for Young Readers*) by DuMont Verlag in 1985. Gombrich had always been reluctant for it to be published in English, saying that it was too Eurocentric, written a long time ago, and that the world had changed. Towards the end of his life he decided to revise it, with the intention of publishing it with Phaidon. Although he had started work, it was unfinished before he died, and his assistant, Caroline Mustill, completed the work after his death. Meanwhile, DuMont was keen to sell the rights to the English language edition and started negotiations with various parties. Richard Schlagman appealed to Gombrich's granddaughter, Leonie (Gombrich's literary executor), to encourage DuMont to license the rights to Phaidon, but the book was published by Yale University Press in 2005.

11 Jostling Imitators

Sharing the costs of book production between publishers was a practice that had its origins in the eighteenth century. Explaining that 'Conger' was the name given to an association of a number of booksellers for trade purposes, one book historian chronicled a further development in the trade, a cooperative system: 'the old custom of cooperative publishing – on the lines of the combined enterprise ... gradually developed into the systematic division of individual books, or series of books, into shares, each shareholder being responsible for his portion of the expenses.'[1] So the idea of sharing the costs and then the profits for publishing was not a new one; it was simply one that the refugee publishers refined and expanded successfully, realizing the potential of such a practice for the expensive production of art books. One immediate effect of Phaidon's successful formula was 'jostling imitators ... Neurath at Thames & Hudson was one such; while across the Atlantic ... Jason Epstein of Doubleday openly acknowledged his emulation of the Phaidon model as bequeathed by Horovitz'.[2]

Walter Neurath might be considered the father of international publishing, simply because of the scale of his operations. He printed thousands of sets of illustrations and sold them to European publishers who added native language texts. The manner in which these large-format publications had been produced lowered unit production costs without reducing image quality. The design of the books enabled the text to be set separately from the colour plates, thereby considerably reducing costs, since the same colour plates could be used in many editions.[3] Neurath was preceeded, however, by William Heinemann, who though not an émigré publisher (his family went to Britain in the nineteenth century) was probably the first publisher to see the economies of scale that could be achieved through co-editions: as early as 1910 he had arranged the simultaneous publication in nine languages of Shackleton's *Heart of the Antarctic*.

Phaidon's practice of publishing co-editions was developed and expanded by Neurath, whose daring gamble – extending sales of one title in different languages to many countries at once – was one that challenged both in-house designers and production managers alike. Moreover, Thames & Hudson invited different publishers to participate in their ventures, rather than merely printing in different languages. Other innovations were to some extent a product of their time: Thames & Hudson had its inception at a time when colour printing was enjoying a period of technical progress, and integrated colour illustration soon became their best-known trademark. The tipped-in plates of the older Phaidon books would soon look old-fashioned.

Walter Neurath was given no English decoration, but he was awarded the *Goldenes Ehrenzeichen*, 'the approximate Austrian equivalent of the Commander of the British Empire'.[4] However, if imitation is indeed the highest form of flattery, the greatest honour was to be bestowed by those publishers, refugees and British, who were to recognize the success of both Phaidon and Thames & Hudson, and build their own on it.

George Rainbird and Ruari McLean

Two British book packagers were quick to credit German-speaking refugees with having given them the impulse to become producers of well-written, well-designed books: George Rainbird and Ruari McLean. Indeed, at the very beginning of his autobiography, Rainbird declares his debt to the refugee publishers. Admitting that there is nothing new under the sun, and that he has been wrongly credited with being the father of packaging, Rainbird points to his predecessor Dr Horovitz of Phaidon, referring to the 'marvellous art books' he published, with the text in many languages arranged round the same pictures, bound in folio size and sold profitably at half a guinea each: 'They meant a lot to me in my formative years, and certainly played their part when I started Rainbird's. Also Adprint ... with their manifold "Britain in Pictures" series through Collins ... I learned what technique I have under the late Walter Neurath and Wolfgang Foges.'[5]

George Rainbird had worked until his middle years in advertising. After setting up a new branch of the advertising company Holden's in London, he started to produce books for some of his clients. Rainbird's interest in book production stemmed from this professional experience and from a parting gift received from a previous employer: 'a small collection of finely printed limited editions'.[6] In his search for someone to put together the first book for his client, Whitbread & Co., Rainbird chose Adprint.[7] Both Neurath and Foges obviously made a great impression on him.

The way in which George Rainbird chanced upon what was to become the first Rainbird, McLean packaged book is almost identical to the way in which Eva Neurath chanced upon what was to be the first book published by the fledgling Thames & Hudson. Both encounters took place in the office of William 'Billy' Collins, where Eva saw the proofs of the Hürlimann photographs for *English Cathedrals*. In Rainbird's case, he saw on the wall of Collins's office a framed print from Thornton's *Temple of Flora*. Billy Collins admitted that he had wanted to publish a book of these prints, but that nobody seemed to know how to go about it. Rainbird discussed the project with McLean, then art director at Rainbird's company, and the two concluded that if the experienced Collins did not know how to publish such a book, 'there must be other publishers in the same situation, and that we could fill the gap'.[8] McLean had already provided the design for several earlier Rainbird projects, including a series of local guide books called 'About Britain'. Now the two became partners in their joint venture of Rainbird, McLean, which lasted some seven years. During this time they packaged illustrated books on subjects ranging from birds to cricket to the Coronation, although Rainbird's particular forte was books on gardens and flowers. In 1958 they went their separate ways, after which Rainbird continued to publish as George Rainbird. In 1965 Rainbird sold a majority interest in his firm to Lord Thomson of Fleet and became chairman of Thomson Book Publishing until his retirement in 1982.[9]

Book packaging required a particular combination of skills. Rainbird, like Foges, was good at bringing the right people together to create a particular book and was, similarly, a great socializer. Much of the packagers' success depended on networking, and the hospitality and sociability of people such as Walter Neurath and Wolfgang Foges were part of that success – all the more impressive for being carried out in English, not their native language. As for the winning formula of the Rainbird books, again it mirrored that of Adprint. Stating the importance of a good text by the best author available, Rainbird also stressed the need for 'well-researched and accurate illustrations, if possible *printed on the same page or opposite the actual text. This gives, in my view, a kind of third dimension to reading, whereby the reader can see the subject about which he is reading at one and the same time.*'[10]

Illustrations were essential to the Rainbird books: 'The authors did not get as high a royalty as they received from their other books because the illustrations were realistically regarded as being as important in sales appeal as the text, but they enjoyed an international sale, the American and German markets being especially important.'[11] It is perhaps difficult to comprehend the importance of these integrated illustrations in an age when photographs are no longer routinely grouped at the centre or end of a book. The Rainbird formula was not groundbreaking; rather, it was the 'scale, imagination and the total involvement of the new concepts which marks them out'.[12] The most striking claim made for the Rainbird books, described as 'documentary books', with their starting point at Adprint, had an even wider-reaching influence: that they 'stimulated and influenced those later responsible for much we have seen of a similar nature on our television screens'. In some ways, the move from the printed page to the moving image on the screen seems a logical step; the Adprint photographer Wolf Suschitzky moved from being a stills photographer to a cameraman with no apparent difficulty. At that time the documentary film was in its infancy, and those involved simply experimented until they found good solutions. So it was that illustrated books can be linked to a more contemporary form of the diffusion of visual information.

Ruari McLean went to work for a printing firm in Weimar before the war, and it was there that he learned some of his printing skills; but his autobiography reveals that even after that early period, his professional life was marked by encounters with Germans and Austrians. An important discovery, made when he was working at Lund Humphries in 1939, was the work of the German typographer Jan Tschichold, then exiled in Switzerland. McLean visited him there and learned a great deal about the 'new typography' – essentially the asymmetrical modernist layout championed by Tschichold at the time. McLean worked as a book designer for Penguin after the war and fully acknowledged his debt to Tschichold.[13] Around 1948 he started to teach at the Royal College of Art in London, where he came into contact with the typographer Berthold Wolpe, whom he chose to design the typeface for *The Eagle*, the children's comic that he was instrumental in creating; later Wolpe would also design the fonts for *Girl* and *Robin*. In 1952 McLean went to work on *Picture Post*, which was essentially the creation of the refugee Stefan Lorant. He worked with the refugee letterer Hans Tisdall in his later professional life.[14] Another refugee friend was the artist Fritz Kredel. The fact that McLean came into contact professionally with so many refugees indicates just how active the German-speaking émigrés were in the field of book and magazine design and typography in Britain. Another enterprise on which McLean worked with a refugee designer was the journal *Motif*, founded by James Shand as a vehicle for good typography.

Kurt Maschler

After the war, there was both a great demand for books and nostalgia for the beauty and lasting values represented by cultured civilization. One response to this nostalgia was FAMA, created by the refugee publisher Kurt Maschler, who had run two publishing companies in pre-war Berlin.[15] Foreseeing the restrictions on publishing once the Nazis rose to power, Maschler transferred his publishing activities to a new enterprise, Atrium, in Switzerland. From there he continued to publish the lucrative writer Erich Kästner, author of *Emil and the Detectives*. Eventually he moved to England. Tom Maschler, born in 1933, recounted his father's attempts to make a living in his host country. He had the 'excellent idea to produce a series of low-priced art books, thus filling a surprising gap in the market'.[16] The 'surprising' element is difficult to account for, unless his arrival just preceded Phaidon's in 1938; and even before then, Stanley Unwin was distributing Phaidon books successfully in Britain on a modest scale. Maschler goes on to explain that his father needed a partner for such an enterprise, both because he was foreign and because he lacked funds. He decided to approach one of the most respected and conservative British publishers, Faber and Faber. Together, they set up FAMA, an acronym composed in equal parts of the names Faber and Maschler. FAMA went on to produce the art book series 'The Faber Gallery'. 'Total sales,' recorded Tom Maschler of his father's enterprise, 'far exceeded a million copies.'[17] A look at one of FAMA's productions, *Raoul Dufy: Poet and Craftsman* by Jean Cassou, shows that the book is credited to the Swiss Editions d'Art Albert Skira and was published in 1947, two years before the founding of Thames & Hudson. It is of the traditional type – folio size, printed on quality art paper, the tipped-in plates without any text, but with an introduction by Jean Cassou. Tom Maschler describes the FAMA books as each containing 'an introduction by one of our leading art historians'. The majority seem to have been produced in the late 1940s and the 1950s. They covered a wide period of art history, ranging from the fifteenth century, represented for example by Sir Kenneth Clark's *Florentine Paintings* (1945), to the nineteenth, exemplified in works such as *Impressionist Paintings* by Elizabeth Rothenstein (1950). No doubt these books met with serious competition once Thames & Hudson and their imitators arrived on the scene.

Paul Hamlyn

Paul Hamburger was born in Berlin in 1926, arriving in Britain as a child in 1933, just before Hitler came to power.[18] He was schooled almost entirely in England, unlike the older Béla Horovitz and Walter Neurath. However, if one accepts the Jesuit saying that a child is formed at an early age, Hamlyn's early days in Berlin must have played a part in shaping the future publisher. His family were assimilated Jews, 'left-wing, middle-class with an academic slant'.[19] His brother, the poet and academic Michael Hamburger, wrote: 'We did not know we were Jewish until Hitler made us Jews', an experience he shared with many of the émigrés. Another familiar theme in his early life is that the Hamburger home in Berlin was 'bookish' but that Paul had preferred music to reading and the natural world to books. (Allen Lane also claimed to be unscholarly.) However, Michael Hamburger was once invited to his brother's West Country estate, where he was shown Paul's collection of rare, illustrated nature books.[20]

Paul Hamburger changed his name to Paul Hamlyn because he had disliked being teased about his surname at school. His publishing career has many of the elements of a rags-to-riches stereotype. He was forced to leave his Quaker boarding school at the age of 15 because of financial difficulties caused by the death of his father. He went to work as an office boy at *Country Life*, and thereafter as a sales assistant at Zwemmer's. With £350 inherited from his grandfather, he set up a bookstall in Camden Market. It was at this point, around 1948, that he turned his attention to the British book market, still buoyant after the war. He realized the possibilities inherent in buying up remaindered books and selling them to department stores and elsewhere. Not content with this hugely successful venture, Hamlyn started to publish his own books in the early 1950s, mostly illustrated general books he had printed in Czechoslovakia. In an article forming part of the series 'The Immigrants' in the publishing journal LOGOS, it was noted that Czechoslovakian printers were then redeveloping their pre-war reputation for fine gravure printing by investing in new four-colour offset machinery. 'It is probably a well-kept secret to this day that Paul was given an elaborate signed and sealed contract granting him exclusive use of Czechoslovak printing for books in the English language.'[21]

Hamlyn thus set a trend that British publishers followed.[22] He subsequently began to deviate from the path beaten by other refugees: he diversified, going into music sales and buying and selling failing publishing companies, amassing a fortune along the way. One of the innovations for which he is responsible is a change in attitude to British bookselling: he noted that British bookshops were intimidating places, but his own bright products helped to make them more accessible.[23] Unlike Béla Horovitz and Walter Neurath, who published high-quality, often highly scholarly art books, Hamlyn aimed for the mass market: brightly coloured, inexpensive art books, low cost and lavishly illustrated, on all sorts of subjects. In the early 1960s, he began to produce art books that were printed in Europe – cheap, but with none of the quality of Phaidon or Thames & Hudson books. Although he later published the series 'Landmarks of the World's Art', well-printed in the Netherlands and of good quality, cheaply printed, colourful books for a wide public were to become the stock-in-trade of one of his major publishing companies, Octopus. They chimed with the 1960s, a time in Britain when goods became cheaper, younger people had more disposable income, and books such as Hamlyn's were bought on impulse for their appealing, colourful appearance and low cover price. They were not meant for serious students of art.

Hamlyn was a maverick in publishing, opening up new markets and sourcing cheaper printers from countries not used before by the British publishing industry, particularly in East Asia. Phaidon and Thames & Hudson were both well established as serious art publishers by the time Hamlyn arrived on the scene, and no doubt perceived Hamlyn books as a watering-down of quality, both in terms of production and scholarship. But someone once worked out that Hamlyn sold in one year more copies of an illustrated book on Rembrandt (the text written over a weekend by a young art historian called Trewin Copplestone) at ten shillings a copy, than all the other British publishers had sold of scholarly books on Rembrandt in five years.[24]

Paul Hamlyn's vision of publishing – bringing highly illustrated, inexpensive books to the mass market – was very profitable, and he repaid his debt to his host country a hundred-fold. In 1987 the Paul Hamlyn Foundation was created, and it is now one of the UK's largest grant-giving organizations. Ten million pounds went to London's Royal Opera House in 2007, just one example of the foundation's work.

Mitchell Beazley and Dorling Kindersley

James Mitchell and John Beazley, described as 'two clever young men', were publishers and packagers of international illustrated books whose success lit up the book world in the 1970s and 1980s. Mitchell was said to be the ideas man and Beazley the steady financial influence, attempting to hold the feet of his erratic and brilliantly creative partner firmly to the floor. Among other titles, they specialized in lavishly illustrated atlases, an inventive way of getting across information, be it Patrick Moore's astronomy books or Hugh Johnson's wine books. Their achievements would not have been possible without the leadership of Béla Horovitz or Walter Neurath – and, even more, the example of Adprint.

Christopher Dorling and Peter Kindersley worked for Mitchell Beazley but broke away in 1974 to found their own company. When asked to comment on any possible influence by the refugee publishers, Kindersley answered that he had not known Wolfgang Foges and neither, as far as he knew, had his partner. Nevertheless, the similarities between the aims of Adprint and those of Dorling Kindersley are too striking to ignore. DK's style of artwork and graphics was instantly recognizable, and their boldness was rewarded. They commissioned John Seymour to write new books on self-sufficiency: his instructions on how to make a loaf of bread began with how to grow a field of wheat. Equally iconic were the 'Eyewitness Guides', useful and innovative travel books showing clever architectural cross-sections of such buildings as cathedrals and castles. Initially Dorling and Kindersley packaged their ideas and sold them to other publishers worldwide; later they had a publishing programme of their own.

Like Thames & Hudson, DK offset the high costs of colour printing against the higher sales afforded through co-editions. DK books, with their minimal text and attractive, clear colour photos, rendered them ideal for the translation market, with profitable results. By the mid-1990s, over 40 per cent of their sales were outside the US and UK.[25] Like Adprint's 'Britain in Pictures' series, DK solicited well-known authorities to write their texts, such as the British Red Cross in 1982 for their *First Aid Manual*. DK continues to produce illustrated books today, having been acquired by the newspaper group Pearson in 2000. They followed where Adprint had led.

André Deutsch and George Weidenfeld

No book on émigré publishers can avoid homage to André Deutsch and George Weidenfeld. However, like Peter Owen and Paul Elek, also émigré publishers, they are not the main focus here because they did not specialize in art books in the way in which Phaidon and Thames & Hudson do. André Deutsch's first experience in pubishing came through a contact with a fellow internee on the Isle of Man, Francis Aldor. Deutsch left Aldor Publications after a few months, moving on to the successful Nicholson and Watson non-fiction publishers. In 1952 he set up his own imprint, specializing in modern fiction, publishing, for example, V. S. Naipaul and Jack Kerouac.

George Weidenfeld is known as a British Establishment figure today, having made his name as a publisher during the second half of the twentieth century. Born in 1919, he came from a privileged family in Vienna and was destined to make a career as an Austrian diplomat. History intervened, and he fled to Britain in 1938, where he became a publisher of general books. As one of the leading lights in the cultural life of his adopted country, he was knighted in 1969 and made a peer in 1976. In his autobiography, *Remembering My Good Friends*, he recalls that he had sensed in around 1943, with the war still far from over, that Britain was experiencing fresh influences on cultural life, for example from the writings of German opponents to the Nazi regime. He wanted to publish a magazine that would reflect this new current, hoping that it would eventually be 'published in several languages in various European capitals by local publishers, with London acting as the coordinating editorial headquarters'.[26] The magazine, entitled *Contact*, was launched through the support of the refugee publisher André Deutsch and with a financial and editorial contribution from the publisher and MP Nigel Nicolson. However, although authors and editors had prepared work, paper restrictions meant that the publication of a new magazine would not be allowed. For this reason – to conform to government regulations – Weidenfeld's legal adviser suggested publishing the contributions in hardback book form. The first was *New Deal for Coal*, by the then relatively unknown young MP, Harold Wilson. The series had an unusual hybrid nature, combining elements of book and magazine. The inside page of *People on the Move: The Fourteenth Contact Book*, with its hard cover and book format, states that '*Contact* Books are edited for the regular rather than the casual reader'.[27] There is a strong refugee presence in articles such as 'German Refugees' by John Midgley and 'Foreign Artists in London' by Edith Hoffmann, as well as articles on 'The Road to Zion' by Nigel Nicolson, reflecting Weidenfeld's own passion for Zionism. Weidenfeld's literary editor on the series was Philip Toynbee, the same critic who had referred to 'Britain in Pictures' as 'non-books for non-people' (see p. 156 above).

However, it was not *Contact* that was to make Weidenfeld's fortune. His success was due instead to the intervention of Israel Sieff, the Marks & Spencer magnate, who persuaded Weidenfeld to produce a series of English children's stories. These would take the place of the 'garish' imported American rivals then on sale at Marks & Spencer. Weidenfeld had the good sense to agree and then to take on the typographer and designer Robert Harling, who in turn commissioned first-rate illustrators. In 1948, George Weidenfeld formalized his publishing partnership with Nigel Nicolson, renaming the firm Weidenfeld and Nicolson.[28]

Lord Weidenfeld freely admitted that he had made use of the practices introduced in Britain by Walter Neurath: although not an art publisher, he published well-designed, beautifully illustrated books. He worked to create links between post-war Germany and Britain, for example by writing a regular column for *Die Welt*. He was paid a compliment that linked him both with British publishing history and his country of origin: 'A cultured man with a strong sense of being European, he could be seen as a late twentieth-century William Heinemann, drawing on the continent in which he was born to bring forth much that was valuable in literature.'[29]

The émigré art publishers engaged with the twin themes of 'education' and 'youth'. Wolfgang Foges's commitment to *Jugend*, Walter Neurath's dedication to revealing cultural history to young people from his very first publication, Teddy Schüller's wish to 'explain the world to people' and Ernst Gombrich with his *The Story of Art* have created some of Britain's most celebrated art publications. This noble aim of teaching young people about art was realized in several ways: through the refugees' publications, through their direct influence on art students as teachers and, finally, through the creation of prizes and awards in their names for excellence in the field of art, photography and illustration.

Gombrich's Legacy

Tom Boase of the Courtauld Institute wrote anonymously in the *Times Literary Supplement* that *The Story of Art* would affect the thought of a generation. This proved to be an underestimate. Many of Britain's art professionals, from gallery directors to artists and principals of art schools, have been profoundly affected by the work of the refugees active in the field of art publishing, whether they were writers, illustrators or teachers. This can be seen in a full-page article in *The Guardian* by Charles Saumarez Smith, then director of the National Gallery, in which he outlines the importance to his own professional development of *The Story of Art*.[1] While acknowledging his appreciation of Phaidon's design of the book and the choice of photographs, many of which would have been selected from the Warburg's photographic archive, Saumarez Smith states that Gombrich's authorial voice is the most powerful element in the book. He makes the point that, although Gombrich claimed he was writing the book for teenagers just discovering art for themselves, these imagined teenagers must have been based on the Viennese youth of the author's own time, who had had an unusually rich and varied cultural life. Gombrich himself, for example, spent time in the company of such friends of his parents as Freud and Schoenberg.

Saumarez Smith looks at Gombrich's comparison of two paintings by Caravaggio, one painted in conditions of complete artistic freedom, the second executed as a commission for the church. Gombrich finds the second less honest and sincere than the first, a reflection of the constraints on the artist. Saumarez Smith comments: 'Given that Gombrich was commissioned to write the book while working as a translator for the BBC's monitoring service, it is impossible not to recognize his profound belief in the moral freedom of the artist from any form of coercion.' He goes on to mention other influences that can be seen in Gombrich's writings, such as his relationship with the art historian and psychoanalyst Ernst Kris, which affected Gombrich's approach to visual observation. The Warburg Institute, where Gombrich worked from 1935, also influenced his research methods. Referring to Gombrich's familiarity with the Warburg Library and the interdisciplinary manner in which it was organized, Saumarez Smith comments that 'this background made him completely comfortable writing about primitive art, classical art, medieval art and Renaissance art, and helped to provide the sense of powerful intellectual confidence that pervades nearly every sentence of the book.' He remembers Gombrich as a man who represented to an extraordinary degree the European tradition of the study of the humanities, which he knew had become deeply unfashionable under the onslaught of postmodernism.

A week after the publication of that article *The Guardian* published a letter from a reader who had attended a lecture by Gombrich in the 1980s on the subject of perspective. The writer, Tim Brown, remembered that Gombrich had asked members of the audience to experiment: to hold a finger in front of their eyes and then to move it away. They would then see that it hid a much smaller area when it was further away. When they looked at the person sitting in the next seat, then at the person sitting at the far end of the row, they were to ask whether they really saw the distant person as smaller than the near one. 'Brilliant!'[2]

A similarly inventive approach was demonstrated in Gombrich's lectures in the 1960s. These were talks on modern art for science and engineering undergraduates at Imperial College London, during which Gombrich invited them to evaluate works of art they did not know. Having given the works marks out of ten, the students were surprised to learn they had all awarded high marks to one of the paintings. Even more surprising was the fact that the painter was Jackson Pollock. The students had been unaware of Pollock's reputation but had unerringly picked it above the very average selection of other paintings, thereby providing Gombrich with the introduction for a lecture on aesthetics.[3]

The Lasting Effects of the Refugee Teachers
This experience is typical of that of many Britons who were taught by the German-speaking refugees. For it was not just the art books produced by the émigrés that influenced young people in Britain;

it was the high-calibre, German-speaking refugees themselves who taught both by example and in the classroom. A large number who worked in book production also took up posts as teachers, anxious to generate additional income. That they succeeded in gaining and holding posts is in itself remarkable, given the competition for teaching art, traditionally a source of reliable income for all artists; there was also the problem of the émigrés' sometimes limited knowledge of English. The list of those who taught, by no means comprehensive, includes the artist Margarete Berger-Hamerschlag; Susan Einzig, an illustrator who taught from 1946 to 1951 at Camberwell Art School and later at the Chelsea School of Art; and the celebrated graphic designer Hans Schleger, who taught at the Central School of Arts and Crafts and later at the Royal College of Art in the 1950s and 1960s. F. H. K. Henrion taught at the London School of Printing; George Him was senior lecturer at the Polytechnic of Leicester from 1969 to 1977; and the great typographer and designer Berthold Wolpe taught for many years at the Royal College of Art.

One of the most eminent refugees whose teaching left a lasting impression on his students and who infected them with a lifelong passion for art history was Nikolaus Pevsner. Magda Czigany, who came to Britain as a Hungarian refugee student, remarked that he was the one teacher who changed the course of her life: he provided her with the skills and interest to become the librarian with responsibility for creating the history of art library when the subject was introduced at University College London in the 1960s.

As the teachers were involved in the process of transferring ideas and skills to young Britons, with their own education and training having taken place in Germany or Austria, one wonders how different they found British young people's art education compared to their own. How were the refugee teachers perceived by these young Britons, and how successful were the teachers in transferring their own cultural values and technical skills to the young British students of art?

Margarete Berger-Hamerschlag, who taught not at an art school but at a youth club just after the war, was horrified not just by the delinquency but by the cultural emptiness of the young people she encountered. In her autobiographical account, *Journey into a Fog* (pl. 26), she describes how she herself had painted from childhood in the art classes of Professor Franz Cižek, the founder of the first art classes for children in Vienna as part of the movement in child development in the 1920s (see p. 30 above). Berger-Hamerschlag learned there that art 'is born of inner freedom and the joy'.[4] Such creative experiences were not only reserved for middle-class children: the Social Democratic initiatives of Red Vienna were to include all classes. The English working-class teenagers with whom Berger-Hamerschlag later worked were not so fortunate. Not only were they technically incompetent, unable to use a pencil or a brush correctly, but they were also embarrassed by the very notion of art other than as a form of technical reproduction. Berger-Hamerschlag singled out their attitude to nudity as an example of their cultural poverty. Why, she wondered, were children not taught about ancient Greece?[5] She explained that on the continent children in elementary school knew about Greek gods and had seen Classical sculpture. To them, nudity was not connected with sex. The English children looked on pictures of nudes as obscene, and life drawing would have been impossible, such was their unruly behaviour.

Berger-Hamerschlag also touched on an issue at the heart of British and German cultural values: the dichotomy between arts and crafts. She had noticed that boys learning a trade behaved better than the others. In 1930s' central Europe a more enlightened attitude towards the crafts prevailed, whereas in Britain crafts had been undervalued from the Victorian period on. The troubled history of the schools of design has been chronicled by Quentin Bell,[6] whose account covers the tension between the Royal Academy, with its devotion to the Renaissance tradition, and the School of Design, founded in London in 1837 to supply Victorian manufacturers with artisans to create design and decoration for their goods. The separation of arts and crafts in this way was not a success, and the School of Design closed in 1851.

The School of Design had been founded partly in response to the excellent imported designs from abroad, notably from France, Prussia and Bavaria.[7] The schools in Bavaria were long established, and their success was due to two guiding principles: first, they made sure that their students had a well-rounded education before their design school training; second, they geared students' design training to the real needs of industry. Both of these principles were lacking in the British system. William Morris and the Arts and Crafts movement had tried to address the problem of British craftsmanship in the industrial age but with only partial success, and had had little to say about art education.[8]

One of the most impressive artists and teachers to graduate from the Leipzig Academy was Hellmuth Weissenborn (fig. 24), who studied there at a time when the tension between the arts and crafts concerned academics. On page 6 of an Academy manual he owned (pl. 27), published in 1912, the author calls on German artists to respect the craft tradition rather than to treat it as less important than aesthetics. Such overvaluing of pure art would be less marked in Germany than in England, but it is nevertheless noteworthy that the manual draws attention to the danger. The author goes on to stress the importance of redressing the balance between the aesthetic and technical sides of the creative process. Great emphasis was placed on students' involvement in the whole work of art, designing for a print and then actually learning all the skills necessary to produce the finished object. Otherwise, the manual warned, students' designs could be unsuitable for printing and there would be a mismatch between the art and the craft.

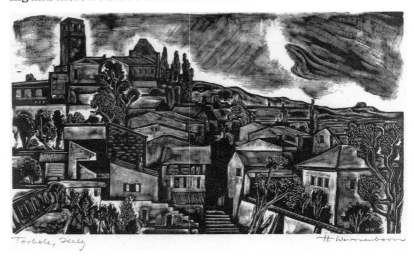

The refugee art historian Klaus Hinrichsen refers fleetingly to the refugee artists as being 'slowly absorbed into British life, some as successful artists and many as influential teachers, notably [Peter] Midgely and Weissenborn at Ravensbourne College of Art'.[9] Midgely, born Fleischmann, had been interned in Hutchinson Camp on the Isle of Man along with Hellmuth Weissenborn. During the war, Weissenborn was offered a teaching post at the Beckenham School of Art, Kent, which later became the Ravensbourne College of Art, on the recommendation of the British painter Carel Weight.

Weissenborn took his teaching duties seriously. He noted, 'I taught two days a week and later once a week, enough to remain in touch with young people interested in the arts, and I stayed there teaching thirty years.'[10] His own father had been an educational reformer

24 Perspex print by Hellmuth Weissenborn, *c.*1970s.

and artist, and Hellmuth himself had studied psychology as part of his anthropology studies at Leipzig. His colleague Wolf Kassemoff-Cohen remembered that the boys they taught were on day release from Beckenham Technical School for Boys, next door to the art school. Weissenborn was a kind and thoughtful teacher, with nevertheless a very rigorous approach.

Former students of Weissenborn give testimonials that bring to mind the letter about Gombrich's perspective lessons. Michael Edser, now a professional artist, was taught perspective by Weissenborn one day a week. On entering the classroom, he found that Weissenborn had constructed a spiral staircase, on top of which he added a candle. The students had to sketch the shadows that would be cast as the candle was moved. Onto this technically correct background, Weissenborn had superimposed a layer of the natural environment – trees, grass and so on – so that the boys could see that the laws of perspective applied everywhere. Edser said that he had applied this principle ever since in his career as a professional artist.

Another former student, Cailean MacKirdy, spoke movingly of the enormous impact that Weissenborn had had on the lives of the mostly working-class boys from Kent.[11] He had gone beyond teaching them the skills they needed to paint and had introduced them to great European and Asian art, lending them books where necessary. He had even taken them from provincial Beckenham to that most continental of London neighbourhoods, Hampstead, to see European films. Art, theatre, music and film were all part of the learning experience, as a result of which MacKirdy was inspired eventually to gain a doctorate. He still remembers vividly his teacher with the strong German accent and the difference he made to many lives.

Prizes Continue the Émigrés' Influence

That the refugee publishers were committed to democratizing art books and to bringing well-printed reproduction and design to books published in Britain is clear. In the twenty-first century, art publishing is still a flourishing business, with the international leaders still including Phaidon and Thames & Hudson, as well as more recent German arrivals such as Taschen, Te Neues and Prestel, who have followed on from the refugees' successes. The origins of Taschen can surely be traced back to the Hamlyn model, for Taschen produces even cheaper, more colourful books on art, architecture, cinema and photography. Some titles dilute the concept of 'art' to include soft pornography, no doubt an excellent genre with which to generate

213

high sales. It seems that despite the ease with which digital images can be downloaded via the internet, millions of people still feel a need to own books that represent the canon of the visual arts, for pleasure and for reference. This continuing interest is reflected in the practice of awarding prizes for illustrated books. Some of these, bearing the names of refugee publishers, are another way of keeping their names alive and celebrating their ideas and high standards.

Thomas Neurath recalled the origins of the prizes awarded by Thames & Hudson. In the 1950s the Summerson Committee was set up to look into the conversion of art school diplomas into degrees. It was agreed that there should be an art history component in these degree courses. Sitting on the committee was Bryan Robertson, an artist, art critic and later Thames & Hudson author, who eventually became director of the prestigious Whitechapel Gallery. Robertson was a close friend of both Walter and Eva Neurath. Through this link the Neuraths went to see student degree shows in the 1960s, participating first-hand in the discovery of new talent in Britain. Keen to encourage this talent, the Neuraths, in conjunction with the Summerson Committee, worked out a list of some 20 art schools the students of which would be eligible to receive prizes in the form of Thames & Hudson books.

The sculptor Wendy Taylor was awarded one of these prizes and explained what it meant to her. At the time she was a student at St Martin's School of Art and had very limited funds. The prize was a sum of money to be spent on books at Thames & Hudson on a particular day. Until then she had only looked longingly at such books, 'but to actually open them and walk away with the books under your arm was something else'. She made the choice with difficulty in the stockroom of Thames & Hudson, opting for *A Time of Gods* by R. Beny (1962); an edition of *Kandinsky*; *Precious Stones* by R. Metz (1964); and a paperback book on twentieth-century art (probably the 'World of Art' volume). She still possesses these books, and said: 'I chose books that in my wildest dreams I would never have been able to afford to buy, but that would give me pleasure and mark the occasion of winning the prize. In retrospect I am extremely glad the prize was something so tangible. Clearly a lasting reminder of the time and event.'

The artist David Carr was awarded a prize for a painting in 1964, when he was a student at the Slade. Commenting on his prize, he pointed out that there had been not one single art book in his home nor indeed any at his grammar school in the late 1950s, until the arrival of a new, younger art master who created an art library.

The Slade had a good library, but Carr implied that he did not make use of it: 'As young painters it was the fashion to sneer at the art history department and art historians in general.'

On 15 January 1969 Tom Rosenthal wrote from Thames & Hudson to the secretary of Birkbeck College, A. J. Caraffi, suggesting collaboration on a new initiative: 'We wish to establish an annual lecture in the area of the fine arts, architecture, archaeology or history as a memorial to Walter Neurath, the founder of Thames & Hudson, under the auspices of Birkbeck College.'[12] The choice of Birkbeck would have been a deliberate one: as a college open to working adults, many of whom had unconventional educational backgrounds, Birkbeck chimed with Neurath's own history: he did not complete his own university studies, and much of his publishing was intended to educate the general reader. The suggestion fell on fertile ground: on 30 August 1968 the Clerk of Birkbeck wrote to the Deputy Chairman recommending that the college accept, noting that Neurath was a 'respected and liberal-minded man'. He underlined the benefits to the college: 'The lecture will draw greater attention to the College and will help in that we shall be supplementing "general cultural activities".'[13]

The lectures, which took place between 1969 and 1999, were open to the general public. Invitations were sent to leading figures in the arts, publishing and related areas. The guest list from the 1988 lecture included Frank Auerbach, Francis Bacon, Robert Harling and Charles Saumarez Smith, the latter two of whom had refugee connections. On the same evening, a formal dinner was held at the college for friends and family of the Neuraths and the speaker. Initially, the speakers were all Thames & Hudson authors, with Nikolaus Pevsner giving the first lecture, on 'Ruskin and Viollet-le-Duc', on 3 March 1969. Other noted speakers included Ernst Gombrich, Kenneth Clark and Eric Hobsbawm. Each chose his own topic, which had to be approved by the head of the Department of the History of Art at Birkbeck. The lecture was subsequently published by Thames & Hudson and given to friends of the publishers as a Christmas gift. A press release outlined one desirable element of both the lectures and the books: 'It is hoped that each lecture will have some visual associations; it is expected that the ensuing volume will contain as many illustrations as each lecturer shall need to document his subject.'[14]

The lectures seem to have been well received. The Master of the college wrote to Thames & Hudson on 13 March 1972: 'We all look forward to seeing it as Thames & Hudson alone can present it.'[15] In 1990

215

an article in the *Hampstead and Highgate Express* referred to the talks, noting a lecturer's view that Prince Charles had picked 'the wrong target in attacking architects for destroying Britain's city centres'.[16] Summarizing the importance of the lectures, Eva Neurath wrote to Ernst Gombrich to thank him for giving the annual lecture: 'There is nothing that I could think of which would do greater honour to the memory of Walter.'[17]

The coveted Jan Mitchell Prize for art history had been the result of negotiations by George Weidenfeld, who admitted in an interview with the author that he had a passion for bringing people together and setting up worthwhile projects. A website dedicated to one of the winners describes the importance of the prize: 'Scholarly and well-written art history illuminates the artist's true intention and brings us into closer understanding of his or her creation. Among the distinguished past recipients are Francis Haskell, Meyer Schapiro and John Pope-Hennessy.'[18]

The Hungarian refugee Andor Krazsna-Krausz ('KK') had made his mark as the creator of the most important photography publishing house in Britain, following a career in Austria and Germany writing mainly about film. Nowadays the Focal Press is administered by the publishing giant Elsevier. Six years before his death, Krazsna-Krausz donated his huge library to the National Media Museum in Bradford. In a circular letter sent to publishers in 2006, the coordinator for the KK Awards, Margaret Brown, outlined the scope and origin of the awards, worth up to £10,000:

> The Awards recognize publications about film, television and photography and will from now on be presented annually ... to books about still or moving images. Over the years, the awards have attracted a high calibre of entries and have been presented at annual ceremonies by such big names from the worlds of film and photography as Mike Leigh, Don McCullin and Miklos Jancso. ... Books in English, which advance the understanding and appreciation of the art, history, practice and technology of photography and the moving image, are eligible.'[19]

Recent winners of the KK Book Awards Photography Prize include, in 2004, *Family Business* by Mitch Epstein, published by Steidl, and in 2002, *The Photographic Art of William Henry Fox Talbot* by Larry J. Schaaf, published by Princeton University Press. Schaaf, who has won the prize three times, acknowledged the different roles it had played in his professional life: 'The first time I won a major award was for my

book, *Out of the Shadows: Herschel, Talbot & the Invention of Photography*.[20]
I would have to say that the award probably had the most direct
influence on my work. As a freelancer then, money was very tight,
and the award made it possible for me to make some choices about
time and travel that directly inspired my subsequent publication
work.' The three different functions of the Kraszna-Krausz prize
were, at least as far as Larry Schaaf saw it, financing research, bringing recognition to a project and acknowledging the achievements of
the scholar.

Walter Trier, illustrator of *Emil and the Detectives*, was born in
Prague and made his name in Berlin. As a Jew, he fled to Britain but
later emigrated to Canada. His illustrations influenced generations
of children, among whom was Fritz Wegner.[21] Wegner, born in
Vienna in 1924, was only 13 when he went to Britain in 1938 without
his parents. At the 'inspired suggestion' of one of the refugee com-
mittees, it was agreed that Wegner should go to art school rather than
conventional school because he did not then speak English; so he
attended St Martin's School of Art from 1939 to 1942. During the war,
when he was engaged in agricultural war work, he decided to become
a graphic artist, starting by designing posters for the Buckingham
War Agricultural Committee. The war over, he established a career in
design and illustration. In his work for children's books he was able
to reconnect with his childhood in Vienna, for example when illustrating Michael Rosen's version of *Till Eulenspiegel* ('*The Wicked Tricks
of Till Owlyglass*').[22] His inclusion of a stork nesting on a roof shows
his familiarity with central European life. Wegner supplemented
his freelance income from graphic work by returning to St Martin's
as a tutor. Here he taught several future illustrators, notably Patrick
Benson, who was awarded the Kurt Maschler Prize.

It happens that two of the refugees in whose names prizes are
awarded had been colleagues in Berlin: Erich Kästner and Andor
Kraszna-Krausz. Both men had worked on the magazine *Die Weltbühne* ('*The World Stage*'), known as 'the most important weekly newspaper of the left-wing bourgeois opposition in the German Weimar
Republic'.[23] The link between them was a mutual friend: Rudolf
Arnheim. Film reviews and film theory in the 1920s were relatively
new and exciting topics for the magazine, at home in the city of the
film company UFA. Arnheim lists his contacts in his cv, including his
friendship with Andor Kraszna-Krausz, who had published books
and journals for Wilhelm Knapp-Verlag before founding the Focal
Press in London. Arnheim wrote a positive review for *Die Weltbühne*

of Kästner's novel *Fabian*, which was held by more conservative readers to be immoral because of its treatment of homosexuality, abortion and promiscuity.[24] Arnheim, Kästner and Kraszna-Krausz all shared an interest in film, albeit in different aspects. Erich Kästner is, of course, famous as the author of the classic children's book *Emil and the Detectives*. It was first published in German by Kurt Maschler.[25]

One of the many lasting contributions made by Kurt Maschler was his creation of a prize that was awarded until the year 2000. Tom Maschler described the background: 'My father had found the perfect illustrator for Kästner's work – Trier. This relationship inspired him to found his prize, which is given for the best combination of illustration and text in a picture book. The winner receives a bronze "Emil" replica of Trier's drawing, plus a cheque for £1,000.'[26] The awards 'were established in 1982, and are given annually to honor [*sic*] "a work of imagination for children, in which text and illustration are integrated so that each enhances and balances the other"'.[27] The integration of text and image was a *leitmotif* in the work of the refugee publishers, and it seems fitting that the award was created to celebrate successful examples of such work. The last winner was the artist Helen Oxenbury for her work on Lewis Carroll's *Alice in Wonderland*; other winners had illustrated contemporary publications such as Anthony Browne's *Gorilla*, published by Julia MacRae in 1983. Helen Oxenbury noted the special kudos associated with the Emil prize, after remarking that she had been more delighted to receive this award than any other. The distinguishing element of the prize, the little statue of Emil in bronze, is a tangible symbol of the surviving values of the refugee publishers.

Conclusion

The prizes that the refugees set up themselves, as well as the awards created in their names, have perpetuated their achievements. They ensure not just that names live on, but that the special abilities of the publishers, book artists and others do so as well. When, in 1979, Kraszna-Krausz was awarded the prestigious *Kulturpreis* by the Photographic Society of Germany, he said: 'We are only a link in the chain – never just the beginning and we hope not the end of everything that we started ourselves.'[1]

It is impossible to know if British books would have been the same had it not been for the impact of the refugee publishers: improvements in printing, design and production would undoubtedly have been introduced after the war, and in any case better communications would eventually have allowed non-British influences to be felt. As it was, however, existing links between British and Austrian and German book production pre-dating emigration meant that the new links in the chain were easily forged when extended to Britain by the refugees.

The starting point of the exile story is sadness: persecution, loss and alienation were experienced by most of the refugees. Nevertheless, an account of an incident in Hellmuth Weissenborn's life can be used to symbolize the positive side of the refugee experience: the creativity that springs from adversity. In Hutchinson Camp on the Isle of Man, where he was interned in 1940, the windows of the boarding house where he was lodged were painted blue to create a blackout effect. Weissenborn set about them with a razor blade, initially, as his fellow refugee and art historian Klaus Hinrichsen reported, 'to let the light in but thereafter to exploit the graphic potential of the new technique'.[2] He went on to create a hunting group: Artemis and centaurs followed, until soon a whole mythological landscape emerged from the window panes.

In a way, this is what the refugee publishers did: they changed their visual landscape. Through the books they published, they also changed the visual landscape for British readers.

Endnotes

Appendices

Bibliography

Acknowledgements

Endnotes

INTRODUCTION

1 Mayfair bookshop Heywood Hill asked
  100 customers – from Anna Wintour
  to Stephen Fry – to nominate the book
  that meant the most to them since the
  shop opened in 1936.

1

PORTRAITS

1 For more information on the history
  of Phaidon, see also V. Holman (ed.),
  *Visual Resources: An International
  Journal of Documentation, Special Issue
  on The Early History of the Phaidon Press
  1923–1967*, vol. 15, no. 3, 1999.
2 'Gehilfen- und Lehrlingstellen', *Das
  Börsenblatt*, no. 119, 23 May 1922, p. 5949.
3 Information on Ludwig Goldscheider
  based on interviews with Gaby
  Goldscheider, 2003.
4 L. Goldscheider to Le Brooay, 1 June
  1962, Getty Research Institute [GRI]
  (840066), Box 1, Folder 5.
5 Alice Hammond in an interview
  with the author, October 2002.
6 E. Fischer, 'The Phaidon Press in
  Vienna, 1923–1938', in V. Holman
  (ed.), op. cit., p. 293.
7 V. Dahm, 'Jüdische Verleger, 1933–1938',
  in A. Paucker, S. Gilchrist, B. Suchy
  (eds.), *Die Juden im Nationalsozialistischen
  Deutschland*, Tübingen: J. C. B. Mohr,
  1986, p. 273.
8 On this, see M. G. Hall, *Österreichische
  Verlagsgeschichte 1918–1938, Geschichte
  des österreichischen Verlagswesens*, vol. 1,
  Vienna, Cologne, Graz: Böhlau, 1985,
  p. 287.
9 http://books.google.co.uk/books?id=V
  RpFAvD7vAsC&pg=PA3&lpg=PA3&dq
  =%22peter+
  smolka%22+ministry+of+informa-
  tion&source=web&ots=I2easT3Zb
  R&sig=Cs88m8FNaLOYYxo2N9X
  beeXqrS8&hl=en&sa=X&oi=book–
  result&resnum=1&ct=result#PPA3,
  M1, accessed 27 November 2008. See
  also R. Philby et al., *The Private Life of
  Kim Philby: The Moscow Years*, London:
  St Ermin's Press, 1999, p. 349.

10 *Der Neuen Jugend*, no. 1, March 1930, p. 14.

11 Or possibly *Moderne Welt*. It has not proved possible to find a copy. See U. Westphal, 'German, Czech and Austrian Jews in English Publishing', in W. Mosse (ed.), *Second Chance: Two Centuries of German-speaking Jews in the United Kingdom*, Tübingen: J. C. B. Mohr, 1991, p. 197.

12 Alice Harrap in a letter to Michael Carney, undated, replying to a letter from Carney, 13 July 1994.

13 M. Seaton, 'A Family Affair', *The Telegraph Magazine*, 5 June 1999, pp. 50–53.

14 H. Read, *The Times*, 5 October 1967, p. 12.

15 Entry for Walter Neurath, Archiv der Universität Wien, UA Z1. 1434-2/2002 lö/do.

16 M. Seaton, op. cit., p. 52.

17 T. Rosenthal, op. cit., p. 12. On the *Kunststelle*, see for example, W. Madethaner, 'Austro-Marxism: Mass Culture and Anticipatory Socialism' *Austrian Studies: Culture and Politics in Red Vienna*, vol. 14, 2006, pp. 21–37.

18 M. Seaton, op. cit., p. 52.

19 T. Rosenthal, op. cit., p. 13.

20 E. H. Gombrich in D. Eribon, *E. H. Gombrich, A Lifelong Interest: Conversations on Art and Science with Didier Eribon*, London: Thames & Hudson, 1993, p. 43.

21 Ibid., p. 44.

22 Information on Harry Fischer from an interview between Fischer's son Wolfgang and the author, March 2008.

23 O. Schürer, *Prag: Kultur, Kunst, Geschichte*, Munich: G. W. D. Callwey, 1935.

24 H. Kralik, *Die Wiener Philharmoniker: Monographie eines Orchesters*, Vienna, Leipzig and Olten: Frick, 1938.

25 T. Rosenthal, op.cit., p. 13.

26 See, for example, *The Independent*, 3 January 2000, p. 5; *The Daily Telegraph*, 14 January 2000, p. 5; *Die Zeit*, 26 June 1992, p. 79. The German television programme referred to is Mitteldeutscher Rundfunk, 'Zeugen der Zeit', interview with Elke Wendt Kummer, 15 January 1995.

2
ROOTS

1 K. Adler, 'What I Found in the English Book Trade', *The Bookseller*, no. 1697, 9 June 1938, pp. 228–29.

2 'Petrel' [Hubert Wilson], 'Notes by the Way', *The Bookseller*, no. 1693, 12 May 1938, pp. 34–35.

3 C. Schorske, *Fin-de-siècle Vienna: Politics and Culture*, London: Weidenfeld & Nicolson, 1980.

4 S. Zweig, *Die Welt von Gestern: Erinnerungen eines Europäers*, London and Stockholm: Hamish Hamilton / Bermann Fischer, 1941; C. Schorske, op. cit.

5 G. Bing, 'Fritz Saxl (1980-1948)', in D. J. Gordon (ed.), *Fritz Saxl 1890–1948: A Volume of Memorial Essays from his Friends in England*, London: Thomas Nelson and Sons Ltd, 1957, p. 2.

6 G. Weidenfeld, *Remembering My Good Friends: An Autobiography*, London: HarperCollins, 1994, p. 33.

7 *Menschen am Sonntag*, 1929, was directed by Curt and Robert Siodmak, with screenplay by Billy Wilder.

8 D. Snowman, *The Hitler Emigrés: The Cultural Impact on Britain of Refugees from Nazism*, London: Chatto & Windus, 2002, p.14.

9 M. Papo, *In Memoriam Béla Horovitz 1898–1955*, in A. Altman (ed.), *Between East and West: Essays Dedicated to the Memory of Béla Horovitz*, London: East and West Library, 1958, p. 3.

10 S. Zweig, op. cit., p. 37.

11 Daniel Snowman, op. cit., p. 32.

12 T. Rosenthal, op. cit., p. 12. On the *Kunststelle*, see for example, W. Madethaner, 'Austro-Marxism: Mass Culture and Anticipatory Socialism', *Austrian Studies: Culture and Politics in Red Vienna*, vol. 14, 2006, pp. 21–37.

13 M. G. Hall, op. cit., vol. II, p. 328.

14 The relationship between the RIKOLA companies is shown in a diagram in M. G. Hall, vol. II, p. 320.

15 M. G. Hall, op. cit., vol. 1, p. 48.

16 Interview with Milein Cosman, 23 March 2006, for *Refugee Voices: The Association of Jewish Refugee Audio-Visual History Collection*.

17 R. Wittmann, *Geschichte des deutschen Buchhandels: Ein Überblick*, Munich: C. H. Beck, 1991, p. 323.

18 Ibid., p. 300.

19 Elon, Amos, *The Pity of it all: A Portrait of Jews in Germany 1743–1933*, London: Penguin Books, 2002, p. 165.

20 A. Strubel, *The People of the Book: Jews in German Publishing 1871–1933*, New York: Leo Baeck Institute, 1990, p. 3.

21 On Schocken, see for example David, Anthony, *The Patron: A Life of Salman Schocken 1877–1959*, New York: Metropolitan Books, Henry Holt and Company, 2003.

22 See for example, *Der Börsenverein des Deutschen Buchhandels 1825–2000: Ein geschichtlicher Aufriss,* Frankfurt am Main: Buchhändler-Vereinigung, 2000.

23 A. Strubel, op. cit., p. 13.

24 Ibid.

25 H. Schwab-Felisch, 'Bücher bei Ullstein', in W. Joachim Freyburg and Hans Wallenberg (eds.), *Hundert Jahre Ullstein 1877–1977 in vier Bänden*, Frankfurt am Main, Berlin and Vienna: Ullstein, 1977, vol. I, p.186.

26 Ibid., p. 203.

27 R. Feilchenfeldt, *Paul Cassirer Verlag 1898–1933: Eine kommentierte Bibliographie, Bruno und Paul Cassirer Verlag 1898–1901, Paul Cassirer Verlag 1908–1933*, Munich: K. G. Saur, 2002, p. 11.

28 Von Marees reproductions from Piper were sold at Zwemmer's bookshop in the 1920s.

29 E. Piper and B. Raab, *90 Jahre Piper: Die Geschichte des Verlags von der Gründung bis heute*, Munich and Zurich: Piper, 1994, p. 80.

30 F. Uhlman, *The Making of an Englishman,* London: Victor Gollancz, 1960, p. 54.

31 Ibid., pp. 196–97.

32 A. J. p. Taylor, *English History 1914-1945*, London: Book Club Associates, 1965, p. 311.

33 T. Mowl, *Stylistic Cold Wars: Betjeman versus Pevsner*, London: John Murray, 2000.

34 On the Royal Academy see for example http://www.geocities.com/eyre–crowe/royal–academy.html, accessed 6 February 2008.

35 http://www.asiamap.ac.uk/collections/institution.php?ID=24&Query=%22Victoria+and+Albert+Museum+National+Art+Library%22, accessed 6 February 2008.

36 N. Vaux Halliday, *More than a Bookshop: Zwemmer's and Art in the 20th Century*, London: Philip Wilson, 1991, p. 80.

37 'Modern German Art', *The Studio: An Illustrated Magazine of the Fine Arts. Contemporary Design, Furnishings, Decoration*, vol. 116, July–December 1938, pp. 160–63.

38 S. Zweig, op. cit., p.47.

39 M. Secrest, *Kenneth Clark: A Biography*, London: Weidenfeld and Nicolson, 1984, p. 91.

40 Ibid.

41 Ibid., p. 26.

42 Ibid., p. 71.

43 Ibid., p.151.

44 Ibid., pp.183–84.

45 Hilde Kurz to Ilse Mintz, 6 May 1939, Hilde Kurz folder, Erica Barrett Archive.

46 J. King, *The Last Modern: A Life of Herbert Read*, London: Weidenfeld and Nicolson, 1990, p.xv.

47 On the Warburg, see D. McEwan, 'A Tale of One Institute and Two Cities: The Warburg Institute', in Wallace, Ian (ed.), *German-speaking Exiles in Great Britain: Yearbook of the Research Centre for German and Austrian Exile Studies*, vol. 1, 1999, pp. 25–42.

48 See for example, S. Harries, *Nikolaus Pevsner: The Life*, London: Random House, 2011.

49 M. Carter, *Anthony Blunt: His Lives*, London: Macmillan, 2001, pp. 142–43 .

50 A. Blunt, 'Sleepers Awake', *The Spectator*, 11 October 1935, p. 548. The artist is named Joseph van Ripper, but this is supposed to be a pseudonym.

51 M. Carter, op. cit., p. 196.

52 Ibid., p. 140.

53 Ibid., p. 89.

54 I. Norrie, *Mumby's Publishing and Bookselling in the Twentieth Century*, London: Bell and Hyman, 1982, pp. 22–23.

55 Ibid., p. 220.

56 V. Holman, *Print for Victory: Book Publishing in England 1939–1945*, London: The British Library, 2008, pp. 6, 8–9.

57 H. Bolitho (ed.), *A Batsford Century: The Record of a Hundred Years of Publishing and Bookselling 1843–1943*, London: B. T. Batsford, 1943.

58 Ibid., p. 65–66.

59 Ibid., p. 67.

60 J. Baker, 'Eyes on Promotion', *The Bookseller*, no. 1703, 21 July 1938, p. 458.

3
FLIGHT FROM NAZI EUROPE

1 3 September 1964, Getty Research Institute, Los Angeles [GRI], (840066), Goldscheider's unpublished poems, Box 1, Folder 5.

2 Louise London, *Whitehall and the Jews 1933–1948*, Cambridge: Cambridge University Press, 2000, p. 11.

3 Steven Beller, *Vienna and the Jews 1867–1938: A Cultural History*, Cambridge: Cambridge University Press, 1989, p. 188.

4 A. Elon, *The Pity of it all: A Portrait of Jews in Germany 1743–1933*, London: Penguin Books, 2003, p. 165.

5 S. Beller, op. cit., pp. 89, 93.

6 M. Berghahn, *Continental Britons: German Jewish Refugees from Nazi Germany*, Oxford, Hamburg, and New York: Berg, 1984, p. 74.

7 See for example '*Ausgrenzung, Verfolgung, Vertreibung: Nationalsozialistische Politik gegen Unerwünschte*', in W. Benz, *Flucht aus Deutschland: Zum Exil im 20. Jahrhundert*, Munich: dtv, 2001, pp. 43–84.

8 See for example B. Wasserstein, *Britain and the Jews of Europe 1939–1945*, London: Institute of Jewish Affairs, 1979, pp. 57–58.

9 E. Fischer, *Buchgestaltung im Exil 1933–1950: Eine Ausstellung des Deutschen Exilarchivs 1933–1945 der Deutschen Bibliothek*, Wiesbaden: Harrosowitz, 2003, p. 205.

10 Ibid., p. 24.

11 See for example, H. Ullstein, *The Rise and Fall of the House of Ullstein,* London: Nicholson and Watson, 1944.

12 On how the company was 'Aryanized', see H. Ullstein, op. cit., pp. 226–27.

13 Ruth Rosenberg, interviewed by Cathy Courtney, 1992, *Book Trade Lives*, British Library catalogue reference C872/03 /01-07, tape 5674, side A.

14 Gottfried Bermann Fischer, *Bedroht – Bewahrt: Weg eines Verlegers*, Frankfurt am Main: Fischer Taschenbuch Verlag, 1991, p. 110.

15 Ibid., p. 119.

16 This and the following details are from M. G. Hall, op. cit., vol. I, especially pp. 108–243.

17 Ibid., p. 287.

18 Ibid., p. 423.

19 Ibid., p. 287.

20 Ibid., p. 423.

21 S. Friedländer, *Nazi Germany and the Jews: The Years of Persecution 1933–1939*, London: Weidenfeld and Nicholson, 1997, p. 62.

22 A. J. Sherman, *Island Refuge: Britain and the Refugees from the Third Reich 1833–1939*, London: Frank Cass, 1994, pp. 24–25.

23 T. Herzl, *Der Judenstaat*, Vienna: Breitenstein, 1896. See for example, R. Wistrich, *The Jews of Vienna in the Age of Franz Joseph*, Oxford and Portland, Oregon: The Litman Library of Jewish Civilisation, 1990, pp. 85–88.

24 On Schocken's life and career, see for example A. David, *The Patron: A Life of Salman Schocken 1877–1959*, New York: Metropolitan Books, Henry Holt and Company, 2003; V. Dahm, 'Jüdische Verleger, 1933–1938', in A. Paucker, S. Gilchrist and B. Suchy (eds.), *Die Juden im Nationalsozialistischen Deutschland*, Tübingen: J. C. B. Mohr, 1986, pp. 273–82.

25 L. London, *Whitehall and the Jews 1933–1948*, Cambridge: Cambridge University Press, 2000, p. 9.

26 On the 1919 Act (which Sherman refers to as that of 1920), see A. J. Sherman, op. cit., p. 273.

27 See for example A. J. Sherman, op. cit. and L. London, op. cit.

28 National Archives, CAB. 27 (33), Conclusion 8, 12 April 1933.

29 A. J. Sherman, op. cit., p. 270.

30 F. Lafitte, *The Internment of Aliens*, Harmondsworth: Penguin Special, 1940, pp. 37–39.

31 See for example L. London, op. cit., p. 97.

32 Ibid., p. 65.

33 See for example M. Malet and A. Grenville (eds.), *Changing Countries: The Experience and Achievement of German-speaking Exiles from Hitler in Britain from 1933 to Today*, op. cit., pp. 90–93.

34 On refugee academics, see for example C. Brinson, 'Science in Exile: Imperial College and the Refuges from Nazism – A Case Study', *Leo Baeck Institute Yearbook*, 2006, vol. 51, pp. 133–51.

35 F. Lafitte, op. cit., p. 35.

36 See for example, C. Brinson, *The Strange Case of Dora Fabian und Mathilde Wurm: A Study of Political Exiles in London during the 1930s*, Berne: Peter Lang, 1997, pp. 185–209; C. Brinson in the foreword to Y. Kapp and M. Mynatt, *British Policy and the Refugees, 1933–1941*, London and Portland, Oregon: Frank Cass, 1997, p. xi.

37 Other refugees stayed there too, for example the musician Fritz Spiegel; see D. Snowman, op. cit., p. 244.

38 Stanley Unwin, *The Truth about a Publisher*, London: Allen and Unwin, 1960, p. 69.

39 Horovitz to Unwin, 23 February 1927, University of Reading, Publishers' Archive [URPA], Special Collections, AUC 9/4.

40 Foyle to Unwin, 30 March 1937, URPA, Special Collections, AUC 54/5.

41 Horovitz to Unwin, November 1936, URPA, Special Collections, AUC 19/4.

42 Stanley Unwin, op. cit., p. 223.

43 Harvey Miller, '*Phaidon and the Business of Art Book Publishing 1923–1967*', in V. Holman (ed.), *Visual Resources*, op. cit., p. 349. Harvey Miller claimed that the interview took place in 1935.

44 From Home Office Aliens Department to Unwin, 1938 [sic], URPA, Special Collections, AUC 62/17.

45 In a film *Facing the Anschluss* made by Dorothea McEwan at the Warburg Institute in 1988 to commemorate the Exhibition of the same name by the London Board of Deputies of British Jews.

46 Horovitz to Unwin, 27 March 1938, URPA, Special Collections, AUC 54/5.

47 Goldscheider to Belgian Minister for Justice, GRI (840066), Box 1, Folder 1.

4
ARRIVAL AND WAR

1 U. A. Fanthorpe, *Collected Poems, 1978–2003*, Cornwall: Peterloo Poets, 2005, p. 468. Reproduced by kind permission of R. V. Bailey.

2 Political activities by refugees were officially banned, although many political refugees did manage to be active during their asylum, often under cover of organizations claiming to be social or cultural. See for example, C. Brinson, '"*Ein sehr ambitioniertes Projekt*": Die Anfänge des Austrian Centre', in M. Bearman, C. Brinson, R. Dove, A. Grenville and J. Taylor, *Wien – London, hin und retour: Das Austrian Centre in London 1939–1947*, Vienna: Czernin Verlag, 2004, pp. 15–28.

3 See for example, C. Holmes, *Anti-Semitism in British Society 1876–1939*, New York: Holmes and Meier, 1979.

4 Ibid., p. 176.

5 Ibid., p. 229.

6 See for example the essay written in 1945 by G. Orwell, 'Anti-Semitism in Britain', in *Collected Essays*, London: Secker and Warburg, 1961, pp. 288–98.

7 A. J. P. Taylor, *English History 1914–1945*, London: Book Club Associates, 1965, p. 311.

8 On Hilde Kurz, see A. Nyburg, '"*Dein großer Brief war ein Ereignis*": the Private and Professional Correspondence of the Refugee Art Historians Hilde and Otto Kurz', in A. Hammel and A. Grenville (eds.), *Refugee Archives: Theory and Practice, The Yearbook of the Research Centre for German and Austrian Exile Studies*, vol. 9, 2007, pp. 123–39.

9 An account of the Schüller family is given in M. Perloff, *The Vienna Paradox: A Memoir*: New York: New Directions Paperback, 2004.

10 H. Kurz to I. Mintz, 27 September 1938, Erica Barrett Archive [EBA] Hilde Kurz folder, 1938.

11 Information on Innozenz Grafe from his daughter Denise, 2013.

12 C. M. Bowra, *Memories, 1898–1939*, London: Weidenfeld and Nicolson, 1966, p. 354.

13 http://uk.phaidon.com/resource/ phaidon-history.pdf

14 Kenneth Clark to Goldscheider, 17 March 1943, GRI (840066), Box 1, Folder 2.

15 *Helpful Information and Guidance for Every Refugee*, London: German Jewish Aid Committee and Board of Deputies, 1939.

16 L. London, op. cit., p. 170.

17 On internees, see for example C. Brinson, '"In the exile of internment" or "Von Versuchen aus seiner Not eine Tugend zu machen": German-speaking Women Interned by the British during the Second World War', in W. Niven and J. Jordan (eds.), *Politics and Culture in Twentieth Century Germany*, Rochester, N.Y.: Camden House, 2003, pp. 63-87; M. Kochan, *Britain's Internees in the Second World War*, London: Macmillan, 1983; D. Cesarani and T. Kushner (eds.), *The Internment of Aliens in Twentieth Century Britain*, London: Frank Cass, 1993; *Politics and Culture in Twentieth-Century Germany*, Camden House, 2003, pp. 63–87; F. Lafitte, *The Internment of Aliens*, Harmondsworth: Penguin, 1940.

18 On activities in internment, see for example, K. Hinrichsen, 'Visual Art behind Barbed Wire', in D. Cesarani and T. Kushner (eds.), op. cit., pp. 188–209.

19 On internment art, see for example, F. Schwartz, 'Kulturarbeit in den englischen Internierungscamps', in H. Krug and M. Nungesser (eds.), *Kunst im Exil in Großbritannien 1933–1945*, Berlin: Frölich & Kaufmann, 1986, pp. 283–88.

20 Stephan Feuchtwang, in an interview with the author, August 2003.

21 Parliamentary Papers: *Cmd. 6217, German and Austrian Civilian Internees: Categories of Persons Eligible for Release from Internment and Procedure to be Followed in Applying for Release*, July 1940; *Cmd. 6223, Civilian Internees of Enemy Nationality: Categories of Persons Eligible for Release from Internment and Procedure to be followed in Applying for Release*, August 1940; *Cmd. 6233, Civilian Internees of Enemy Nationality (revised)*, October 1940.

22 Wolfgang Fischer, Harry's son, in an interview with the author, 5 March 2008.

23 Alien members joining the British armed forces were encouraged to change their names, in case they fell into enemy hands and were subjected to reprisals. See H. Fry, *Jews in North Devon during the Second World War: The Escape from Nazi Germany and the Establishment of the Pioneer Corps*, Tiverton: Halsgrove, 2005, p. 17.

24 From Unwin, 12 December 1939, GRI (940066), Box 1, Folder 1.

25 H. J. Stenning to Goldscheider, 9 August 1940, GRI (840066), Box 1, Folder 4.

26 K. Clarke to L. Goldscheider , 15 October 1941, GRI, (840066), Box 1, Folder 2.

27 Valerie Holman, *Print for Victory: Book Publishing 1939–1945*, London: British Library, 2008, p. 41.

28 On this and the following section see
   I. Norrie, op. cit., pp. 85–91; V. Holman,
   op. cit.; J. Gardiner, *Wartime Britain
   1939–1945*, London: Headline Book
   Publishing, 2004, pp. 483–94. See also
   individual publishers' accounts, for
   example F. Warburg, *All Authors are
   Equal*, London: Hutchinson, 1973;
   J. Joos, *Trustees for the Public? Britische
   Buchverlage im Spannungsfeld von intelle-
   ktueller Selbständigkeit, wirtschaftlichem
   Interesse und patriotischer Verpflichtung im
   Vorfeld und während des Zweiten Weltkriegs*,
   Wiesbaden: Harrassowitz, 2008.

29 V. Holman, op. cit., pp. 72–74.

30 P. Ziegler, *London at War 1939–1945*,
   London: Pimlico, 2002, p. 72.

31 V. Holman, op. cit., pp. 158, 161.

32 J. Brophy, *Britain Needs Books*, London:
   National Book Council, 1941, p. 46.

33 T. Borenius to L. Goldscheider, 27 April
   1943, Getty Research Institute [GRI]
   Box 1, Folder 2.

34 V. Holman., op. cit., pp. 63–130.

35 F. Warburg, *All Authors are Equal:
   The Publishing Life of Frederic Warburg
   1936–1971*, London: Hutchinson, 1973,
   p. 22.

36 V. Holman, op. cit., p. 82.

37 Gombrich's letter of 26 September 1938
   to Esther Simpson indicating his will-
   ingness to assist the war effort, MS SPSL
   187/3 folders 234–388, SPSL Archive,
   Bodleian Library, University of Oxford.

38 Erica Barratt (née Kurz) in a letter to
   the author, 2011.

39 M. Kerr, *As Far as I Remember*, Oxford
   and Portland, Oregon: Hart
   Publishing, 2006, p. 164.

40 D. Snowman, *The Hitler Emigrés*, London:
   Chatto and Windus, 2002, p. 140.

41 See for example E. Howe, *The Black
   Game: British Subversive Operations against
   the Germans during the Second World War*,
   London: Michael Joseph, 1982.

42 Ibid., p. 196.

43 Ibid., p. 128.

44 On Hellmuth Weissenborn, see Anna
   Nyburg, *From Leipzig to London: The Life
   and Work of the Émigré Artist Hellmuth
   Weissenborn*, Delaware: Oak Knoll, 2012.

5
A NEW START

1 N. Vaux Halliday, *More than a Bookshop:
   Zwemmer's and Art in the 20th* Century,
   London: Philip Wilson, 1991, p. 79.

2 Ibid., p. 13.

3 Miranda Carter, *Anthony Blunt: His Lives*,
   London: Macmillan, 2001, p. 28.

4 N. Vaux Halliday, *op. cit.*, p.13

5 Ibid., pp. 181–84.

6 Ibid., pp. 43–45.

7 Valerie Holman, 'Albert Skira and
   Art Publishing in France 1928–48',
   unpublished Ph. D. thesis, University
   of London, 1987.

8 N. Vaux Halliday, op. cit., p.76.

9 Ibid., p. 102.

10 Ibid., p. 127. On Bilbo, see also J. Vincent,
   'Muteness as Utterance of a Forced
   Reality – Jack Bilbo's Modern Art
   Gallery (1941–1948)' in S. Behr and
   M. Malet (eds.), *Arts in Exile in Britain
   1933–1945: Yearbook of the Research Centre
   for German and Austrian Exile Studies*,
   vol. 6, 2004, pp. 301–37.

11 N. Vaux Halliday, op. cit., p. 65.

12 Ibid., p. 130.

13 This was the 37-volume German dictionary of artists published between
   1907 and 1951; see N. Vaux Halliday,
   op. cit., p. 54.

14 Wilfred Blunt, letter of 17 December
   1938, Oxford University Press Archive,
   OCA 1951 O/p 3/01.

15 G. F. J. Cumberlege in a letter to
   Wilfred Blunt, Oxford University Press
   Archive, OCA 1951, O/p 3/01.

16 A. Norrington in a letter to Wilfred
   Blunt, 21 May 1951, Oxford University
   Press Archive, OCA 1951, O/p 3/01.

17 Memories of T. Schüller from his son
   Andrew Schuller, 2013. The family stopped using the umlaut after
   emigration.

18 Memo from T. Schüller, Oxford
   University Press Archive, OCA 1951,
   O/p 3/01.

19 T. Schüller in a letter to E. Gombrich,
   16 November 1951, Oxford University
   Press Archive, OCA 1951, O/p 3/01.

20 Benedict Nicolson in a letter to T. Schüller undated but in the 1952–1955 file, Oxford University Press Archive, BLA/115/00464, o/p 3/01.

21 Internal memo from T. Schüller, Oxford University Press Archive, OCA 1951, o/p 3/01.

22 E. Gombrich in a letter to T. Schüller, 31 March 1950, Oxford University Press Archive, OCA 1950 o/p 3/01.

23 H. Buchthal, 'New Books', *Journal of Education*, Oxford University Press, vol. 86, no. 1016, March 1954, pp. 130–32.

24 Horovitz to Unwin, 3 November 1936, Reading University Publishers Archive, Allen Unwin Correspondence [ACU] 54/4.

25 Unwin to Jacques Schupf, 20 December 1938, [URPA], Special Collections, AUC 54/4.

26 Unwin to Horovitz, URPA, Special Collections, AUC 52/5.

27 Unwin to Horovitz, 10 October 1940, URPA, Special Collections, AUC 94/8.

28 Horovitz to Unwin, 29 June 1949, URPA, Special Collections, AUC 418/12.

29 Allen and Unwin to Horovitz, 30 June 1949, URPA, Special Collections, AUC 418/12.

30 Unwin to Goldscheider, 22 April 1960, Getty Research Institute [GRI] (840066), Box 1, Folder 5.

31 Unwin to Goldscheider, 2 May 1960, GRI (840066), Box 1, Folder 5.

32 Didier Eribon, *E. H. Gombrich, A Lifelong Interest: Conversations on Art and Science with Didier Eribon*, London: Thames & Hudson, 1994.

33 Archive of E. H. Gombrich, Warburg Institute. © the Literary Estate of E. H. Gombrich, [hereafter GAWI], courtesy of Leonie Gombrich.

34 Horovitz to Gombrich, 19 February 1942, GAWI.

35 Gombrich to Horovitz, 10 April 1945, GAWI. The story that Gombrich wrote *The Story of Art* during six weeks of dictation to his secretary is a myth.

36 Contract between Gombrich and Phaidon in the GAWI. Gombrich occasionally felt that Phaidon's owners were not as generous as they might have been, given his contribution to the publisher's success. He mentioned the matter to the art historian Hilde Kurz and her husband, Otto, with whom he had daily contact as a fellow employee at the Warburg. See letter from Hilde Kurz to her sister Ilse, 3 February 1939, in the possession of Erica Barrett.

37 Goldscheider to Gombrich [no date], 1948, GAWI.

38 Goldscheider to Gombrich, 5 September 1948, GAWI.

39 'The History of Art', *The Times Literary Supplement*, 27 January 1950, p. 51.

40 Goldscheider to Le Brooay, 1 June 1962, GRI (840066), Box 1, Folder 5.

41 Goldscheider to Witsch (in German), 1 June 1959, GRI (840066), Box 1, Folder 9.

42 Irving Stone to B. Cumming of the New York Graphic Society, 12 June 1962, GRI, (840066), Box 1, Folder 5.

43 Fritz Ungar to Goldscheider, 19 August 1966, GRI (840066), Box 1, Folder 6.

44 Goldscheider to Witsch (in German), 4 June 1959, GRI (084066), Box 1, Folder 4.

6
BETWEEN THE PAGES

1 R. McLean, *How Typography Happens*, London and Delaware: British Library and Oak Knoll Press, 2000, p. 38.

2 See for example, E. Cummings and W. Kaplan, *The Arts and Craft Movement*, London: Thames & Hudson, 1991; L. Parry, *William Morris and the Arts and Crafts Movement: A Source Book*, London: Studio Editions, 1989.

3 W. Peterson (ed.), *The Ideal Book: Essays and Lectures on the Arts of the Book by William Morris*, Berkeley: University of California Press, 1982.

4 J. Aynsley, *Graphic Design in Germany 1890–1945*, London: Thames & Hudson, 2000, p. 30.

5 See for example, S. Wishmann, *Jugendstil, Art Nouveau: Floral and Functional forms*, Boston: Little, Brown and Co., 1984.

6 See R. Brewer, 'A Man and His Work' *British Printer*, December 1982, pp. 32–35; J. Mosley, 'Eric Gill and the Golden Cockerell Type', *Matrix: A Review for Printers and Bibliophiles*, no. 2, 1982, pp. 19–27; E. Gill, *Eric Gill: A Bibliography*, Winchester and Detroit: St Paul's Bibliographies, 1991; F. MacCarthy, *Eric Gill*, London: Faber & Faber, 1990, pp. 61, 193–95.

7 See R. Healy, 'Germany's First Private Press', *Matrix: A Review for Printers and Bibliophiles*, no. 27, Winter 2007.

8 Ibid., p. 117.

9 R. McLean, *How Typography Happens*, London and Delaware: British Library and Oak Knoll, 2000, p. 52.

10 G. Cinamon, *Rudolf Koch, Letterer, Type Designer, Teacher*, Delaware and London: Oak Knoll, 2000, p. 78.

11 Georg Schauer, 'The Art of the Book in Germany', in K. Day (ed.), *Book Typography in Europe and the United States of America*, London: Ernest Benn Ltd, 1966, p. 101.

12 R. Kinross, *Modern Typography: an Essay in Critical History*, London: Hyphen Press, 1992, p. 101; see also J. Howes and p. Paucker, 'German Jews and the Graphic Arts', in *Leo Baeck Yearbook*, vol. 34, 1989, pp. 443–73.

13 R. Kinross, *Modern Typography*, p. 101.

14 Ibid.

15 J. Eyssen, op. cit., p. 66.

16 See for example, A. Windisch, *Professor Dr. L. C. Walter Tiemann*, Mainz: Gutenberg Gesellschaft, 1953.

17 S. Morison, *Philobiblion*, vol. X, no. 6, 1938, p. 261. On Koch see also S. Guggenheim, 'Rudolf Koch: His Work and the Offenbach Workshop', *Print: A Quarterly Journal of the Graphic Arts*, vol. v, no. 1, 1947, p. 7; A. Windisch, 'The Work of Rudolf Koch', in S. Morison (ed.), *The Fleuron, A Journal of Typography*, no. vi, Cambridge and New York: Greenwood Reprint Corporation, 1928, pp. 1–34.

18 E. Fischer (ed.), *Buchgestaltung im Exil, 1933–1950: Eine Ausstellung des deutschen Exilarchivs 1933–1945 der Deutschen Bibliothek*, Wiesbaden: Harrassowitz, 2003, p. 214.

19 G. Cinamon, *Rudolf Koch*, op. cit., p. 36

20 Ibid., p. 147.

21 Ibid., p. 172.

22 *100 Jahre Insel Verlag 1899–1999: Begleitbuch zur Ausstellung*, Frankfurt am Main and Leipzig: Insel Verlag, 1999, p. 159.

23 Ibid., p. 102.

24 F. Whitford, *Bauhaus*, London: Thames & Hudson, 1984, p. 157.

25 See for example D. Evans and S. Gohl, *Photomontage: A Political Weapon*, London: Gordon Fraser, 1986; C. Müller, *Typofoto: Wege der Typographie zur Foto-Text-Montage bei László Moholy-Nagy*, Berlin: Gebr. Mann Verlag, 1994; L. Becker, 'Dynamic City Design and Montage', in *Avant-Garde Graphics 1918–1934*, London: Hayward Gallery Publishing, 2004, p. 11.

26 E. Fischer (ed.), op. cit., pp. 100–04.

27 P. Baines, *Penguin by Design: A Cover Story 1935–2005*, London: Allen Lane, 2005.

28 J. Lewis, *Penguin Special: The Life and Times of Allen Lane*, London: Viking, 2005, p. 280.

29 N. Games, C. Moriarty and J. Rose, *Abram Games: His Life and Work*, New York: Princeton University Press, 2003, p. 25.

30 In a telephone conversation, 9 May 1988, referred to in J. Howes and P. Paucker, op. cit., p. 464.

31 V. Holman, op. cit., p. 113.

32 Cambridge University Library, MS Add. 9812/Francis Meynell to Oliver Simon, 9 December 1936, Stanley Morison Archive [SMA], Morison Papers, Box XV1.1.

33 F. Meynell, *My Lives*, London: The Bodley Head, 1971, pp. 160–61.

34 P. Paucker, 'Two Typographer-calligraphers', in Brinson, Charmian, Dove, Richard *et al.* (eds.), *Keine Klage über England? Deutsche und österreichische Exilerfahrungen in Großbritannien*, Munich: Iudicium, 1998, pp. 200–14.

35 Werner Guttmann in an interview with the author, November 2005.

36 R. Kinross, 'Emigré Graphic Designers in Britain around the Second World War and Afterwards', *Journal of Design History*, vol. 3, no. 1, 1990, p. 52.

37 Recorded interview in the *Book Trade Lives* series, (British Library), Tanya Schmoller, F14744–46.

38 *Oxford Illustrated Encyclopedia*, vol. 6, Oxford: Oxford University Press, 1993, p. 232.

39 'Civilian Internment in Britain 1939–1945', transcribed interview, Imperial War Museum, Department of Sound Archives, Accession No. 003771/04, 16 June 1978.

40 P. Schleger, *Zero, Hans Schleger: A Life of Design*, Aldershot, New York: Lund Humphries, 2001, p. 21.

41 F. MacCarthy, Introduction to ibid., p. 11.

42 Ibid., p. 16.

43 See T. Christoph, 'Henrion, Ludlow and Schmidt (GBR)', *Novum Gebrauchsgraphik*, vol. 60, no. 3, March 1989, pp. 6–13; C. Ludlow, obituary in *Creative Review*, vol. 10, no. 9, September 1990, pp. 57–58; [n. a.]' How F. H. K. Henrion, Designer, Became HAD International', *Designer,* May 1979, pp. 14–16.

44 See C. Rosner, 'George Him', *Graphis*, no. 94, March/April 1961, p. 146; F. H. K. Henrion, 'George Him', *Design*, no. 403, July, 1982, p. 9.

45 F. H. K. Henrion, 'How FHK Henrion, Designer, Became HAD International', op. cit., p. 15.

46 I. Norrie, *Mumby's Publishing and Bookselling in the Twentieth Century*, sixth edition, London: Bell and Hyman, 1982, p. 160.

47 Ibid., p. 37.

48 H. Schmoller, 'The Paperback Revolution' in A. Briggs (ed.), *Essays in the History of Publishing in Celebration of the 250th Anniversary of the House of Longman 1724–1974*, London: Longman, 1974, p. 289.

49 J. Lewis, *Penguin Special: The Life and Times of Allen Lane*, Viking, London: 2005, p. 77; see also S. Hare (ed.), *Penguin Portrait: Allen Lane and the Penguin editors 1935–1970*, London: Penguin Books, 1995; J. Morpurgo, *Allen Lane: King Penguin*, London: Hutchinson, 1979.

50 E. Fischer, op. cit., p. 68.

51 J. Lewis, op. cit., pp. 76–79.

52 J. Feather, *A History of British Publishing*, London and New York: Routledge, 1988, p. 211.

53 F. Lafitte, *The Internment of Aliens*, Harmondsworth: Penguin Special, 1940.

54 J. Lewis, op. cit., p. 95.

55 Allen Lane to Oliver Simon, 10 September 1946, in Cambridge University Library, Stanley Morison Archive [SMA], Oliver Simon papers, Box XXI.22.

56 E. Fischer (ed.), op. cit., p. 81.

57 C. Burke, *Paul Renner: The Art of Typography*, London: Hyphen Press, 1998, p. 177.

58 Allen Lane to Oliver Simon, 25 February 1952, Cambridge University Library, SMA, Oliver Simon Papers, Box XXI.22.

59 For example Lotte Koch-Reiniger, who illustrated R. Lancelyn-Green, *King Arthur and the Knights of the Round Table*, Harmondsworth: Puffin Books, Penguin, 1953.

60 E. Fischer (ed.), op. cit., p. 150.

61 See Susan Einzig's recorded interview for *Refugee Voices,* Association of Jewish Refugees. She illustrated P. Pearce, *Tom's Midnight Garden*, London: The Bodley Head, 1958.

62 G. Lathey, 'Eulenspiegel to Owlyglass: The Impact of Work of the Exiled Illustrators Walter Trier and Fritz Wegner on British Children's Literature', in A. Grenville (ed.), *Refugees from the Third Reich, Yearbook of the Research Centre for German and Austrian Exile Studies*, vol. 4, 2002, pp. 97–116.

63 E. Mordaunt, *Blitz Kids*, London: Oxford University Press, 1941.

64 G. Lathey, op. cit., p. 98.

65 J. Farleigh, *It Never Dies: A Collection of Notes and Essays 1940-1946*, London: Sylvan Press, 1946.

66 R. Koch, *Soldatenstiefel*, n. pl.,
Rudolfinische Drucke, 1919 [1920].

67 G. Cinamon, op. cit., p. 61.

68 W. E. Butler (ed.), 'Geometrical
Typographical Bookplate design by
Hellmuth Weissenborn', *The Bookplate
Journal*, vol. 1, no. 1, March 1983, p. 19.

69 Adrian and Sylvie Marston in an interview with the author, September 2005.

70 'Both Sides of the Line', *Arena, Art
and Design*, BBC 1, 6 April 1977; and
'The Whittington Press', *In the Making*,
BBC 1, 18 May 1977.

71 M. Hove, *Autumn Fields*, London:
Methuen, 1944.

72 Max Parrish, formerly a director at
the Ministry of Information, worked
at Adprint before setting up his own
publishing house, Max Parrish Ltd.,
where he employed Ruth Rosenberg
for many years. He and Rosenberg later
both went to work for W. Neurath at
Thames & Hudson. On Max Parrish,
see also V. Holman, *Print for Victory*,
op. cit., and Chapter 5.

73 Ruth Rosenberg, interviewed by Cathy
Courtney, 1992, *Book Trade Lives* British
Library catalogue reference C872/03/
01-07, tape F5674 side A.

7

PHOTOGRAPHY AND PRINTING

1 See for example D. Mellor, 'London-
Berlin-London: A Cultural History:
The Reception and Influence of the
New German Photography in Britain
1927–33', in D. Mellor (ed.), *Germany:
The New Photography 1927-33*, London:
The Arts Council of Great Britain,
1978, pp. 113–30; A. Hamber,
'Communicating Colour', in V. Holman
(ed.), *Visual Resources, An International
Journal of Documentation, Special Issue
on the Early History of the Phaidon Press
1923-1967*, vol. 15, no. 3, 1999, pp. 355–70.

2 J. Winckler, 'Gesprach mit Wolfgang
Suschitzky', in C.-D. Krohn,
E. Rotermund et al. (eds), *Film
und Fotografie: Exilforschung, Ein
Internationales Jahrbuch*, vol. 21, 2003,
p. 257.

3 D. Mellor, op. cit., p. 115.

4 K. Honnef, 'Fotografen im Exil',
in ibid., p. 175.

5 G. Graham, 'Only a Link in the Chain:
A Tribute to a Great Publisher', *The
Bookseller*, no. 3858, 1 December 1979,
p. 2454.

6 Ibid.

7 This monthly journal was edited by
Kenneth MacPherson and published
in Switzerland by the collective
known as POOL. On this, see http://
www.screenonline.org.uk/film/crit-
icism/criticism5.html, accessed 12
December 2007.

8 U. Westphal, 'German, Czech and
Austrian Jews in English Publishing',
in W. Mosse (ed.), *Second Chance:
Two Centuries of German-speaking Jews
in the United Kingdom*, Tübingen:
J. C. B. Mohr, 1991, p. 203.

9 G. Graham, op. cit., p. 2454.

10 J. Dorner, 'Andor Kraszna-Krausz:
Pioneering Publisher in Photography',
LOGOS: *Forum of the World Book
Community*, no. 15/1, 2004, pp. 118–25.

11 J. Chittock, 'Focal Press Founder Dies',
British Journal of Photography, no. 6752,
18 January 1990, p. 6.

12 C. Douglas Milner, *Mountain
Photography: Its Art and Technique
in Britain and Abroad*, London and
New York: The Focal Press, 1945, p. 10.

13 All of this supporting correspondence
is held in the Kraszna-Krausz Archive
in the National Media Museum,
Bradford.

14 Joseph Horovitz in an interview
with the author, July 2012.

8

THE RISE AND FALL OF ADPRINT

1 See for example R. Calvocoressi,
'Oskar Kokoschka, Red Vienna and
the Education of the Child', J. Beniston
and R. Vilain (eds), *Austrian Studies:
Culture and Politics in Red Vienna*, vol. 14,
2006, pp. 215–27.

2 Alice Harrap in a letter to Brian Mills
(author of an article on Adprint),
6 November 1986.

3 B. Mills, 'Some Notes on the Story of Adprint', *Antiquarian Book Monthly Review*, vol. 13, 1981, p. 372.

4 M. Carney, *Britain in Pictures: A History and Bibliography*, London: Werner Shaw Ltd, 1995, p. 29.

5 C. Ridler, *Out-House Publishing*, Oxford: Oxford Polytechnic Press, 1976, p. 9.

6 On Bettina Ehrlich see Z. Fuss Phillips, *German Children's and Youth Literature in Exile 1933–1950*, Munich: 2001. On Katarina Wilczynski see H. Krug and M. Nungesser (eds.), *Kunst im Exil in Großbritannien 1933–1945*, Berlin: Frölich und Kaufmann, 1986, p.161.

7 V. Holman, 'Albert Skira and Art Publishing in France 1928–1948', unpublished Ph. D. thesis, University of London, 1987, p. 2.

8 Ruth Rosenberg, interviewed by Cathy Courtney, 1992, *Book Trade Lives*, British Library catalogue reference C872/03/01-07, tape F5674 side A.

9 F. Luft (ed.), *Facsimile Querschnitte durch die Berliner Illustrirte*, Berne/Munich: Scherz, 1965, p. 6.

10 Shalom Schotten in an interview with the author, 26 July 2006.

11 On Suschitzky see J. Winckler, 'Gespräch mit Wolf Suschitzky', in C.- D. Krohn, E. Rotermund et al. (eds), *Film und Fotografie*: Exilforschung: Ein Internationales Jahrbuch, vol. 21, 2003, pp. 254–80. Suschitzky was also later published by Thames & Hudson.

12 Wolfgang Suschitzky in an interview with the author, 28 March 2006.

13 B. Mills, op. cit., p. 369.

14 J. E. Morpurgo, *Allen Lane: King Penguin*, London: Hutchinson & Co, 1979, p. 144.

15 Ibid., p. 149.

16 M. Carney, op. cit., p. 49.

17 J. Morpurgo, op. cit., p. 149

18 J. Harley, 'The King Penguin Series: An Historical Survey', *Matrix* 5, no. 5, Winter 1985, p. 144.

19 Ibid., p. 153.

20 See also V. Holman, *Print for Victory: Book Publishing in England 1939–1945*, London: The British Library, 2008, pp. 108–11.

21 M. Carney, op. cit., p. 21.

22 S. Conradt, 'Die Fotobildbandreihen des Karl Robert Langewieschen Verlages 1902 bis 1931 am Beispiel ausgewählter Kunst- und Naturbände', unpublished Ph. D. thesis, Georg August Universität, Erlangen, July 1999, p. 70.

23 M. Carney, op. cit., p. 29.

24 Ibid., p. 60.

25 T. Rosenthal, 'Walter and Eva Neurath: Their Books Married Words with Pictures', LOGOS: *The Journal of the World Book Community*, vol. 15, no. 1, 2004, pp. 12–19.

26 Letter from J. Betjeman to O. Stonor, 17 March 1943, in C. Lycett-Green (ed.), *John Betjeman Letters, Volume One: 1926 to 1951*, London: Methuen, 1994, p. 313.

27 See T. Mowl, *Stylistic Cold Wars: Betjeman versus Pevsner*, London: Murray, 2000.

28 M. Carney, op. cit., p. 57.

29 Peter Foges in an interview with the author, June 2006.

30 See for example G. Hofner-Kulenkamp, 'Versprengte Europäerinnen: Deutschsprachige Kunsthistorikerinnen im Exil', in C.- D. Krohn, E. Rotermund et al. (eds.), *Frauen und Exil: Zwischen Anpassung und Selbstbehauptung: Exilforschung: Ein Internationales Jahrbuch*, vol. 11, 1993, pp. 190–203.

31 An unpublished, undated account of Alice Kun's life, in possession of Christopher Foyle.

32 P. Mountain with C. Foyle, *Foyles: A Celebration*, London: Foyles Books, 2003.

33 For Isoytpes, see R. Kinross, *Graphic Communication through* ISOTYPE, exhibition catalogue, University of Reading, 1976.

34 Information courtesy of Robin Kinross. The museum had formerly been known as the Siedlungsmuseum.

35 R. Kinross, 'Emigré Graphic Designers', *Journal of Design History*, vol. 3, no. 1, 1990, p. 43.

36 Marion Wesel, widow of F. H. K. Henrion, in an interview with the author, 13 April 2006.

37 Recorded interview in the *Book Trade Lives* series (British Library), Ruth Rosenberg, F6570–F6576.
38 *The Bookseller*, 28 March 1959, no. 2779, p. 1314.
39 B. Mills, op. cit., p. 370.
40 Norman McKenzie, in an interview with the author in 2012.

9
THE BIRTH OF THAMES & HUDSON

1 N. Hawkes, 'Bright Visions in Wartime: A Study of *British Women go to War* (1943)', *The Journal of the J. B. Priestley Society*, vol. 2, 2001, pp. 20–30.
2 B. Hürlimann, *Seven Houses: My Life with Books*, London, Sydney and Toronto: Bodley Head, 1976.
3 T. Craker, *Opening Accounts and Closing Memories: Thirty Years with Thames and Hudson*, London: Thames & Hudson, 1985, p. 14.
4 Ibid., p. 11.
5 *The Times Literary Supplement*, no. 2534, 25 August 1950, p. 565.
6 *The Times Literary Supplement*, no. 2858, 7 December 1956, p. 726.
7 *The Bookseller*, 12 March 1955, no. 2568, p. 981.
8 *The Bookseller*, 2 February 1952, no. 2407, p. 232.
9 *The Bookseller*, 5 April 1952, no. 2415, p. 940.
10 *The Bookseller*, 26 April, 1952, no. 2418, p. 1064.
11 K. Pearl (ed.), in the introduction to W. Bergengruen, *Der Teufel im Winterpalast*, London: Macmillan, 1964, p. v.
12 T. Craker, op. cit., pp. 30–31.
13 J. King, *The Last Modern: A Life of Herbert Read*, London: Weidenfeld & Nicolson, 1990, pp. xv–xvi.
14 Ibid., p. xvii.
15 Ibid., p. 296.
16 Ibid., p. 174.
17 *The Eastern Daily Press*, 7 June 1961, p. 9.
18 Norfolk Record Office [NRO], ACC 2001/208 box n, M. Oliver typescript, M. Oliver, *Jarrold 1770–1970*, n.d., uncatalogued Jarrold Archive.
19 T. Craker, op. cit., p. 55.
20 NRO, Acc 2001/208 box n, *The Jarrold Magazine: 125th Anniversary Number, 1823–1948*, referred to in the informal history, see above.
21 Another example of the close links between Adprint and Jarrolds can be seen from one of the Adprint staff, Mr J. B. Warren, joining Jarrolds as a sales representative, mentioned in 'News and Chatter', *The Jarrold Magazine*, vol. 3, no. 7, October 1949 [back page].
22 I am grateful to Desmond Field for this information.
23 NRO, ACC 2001/208 box n, H. H., in *The Jarrold Magazine*, vol. 3, no. 6, September 1949, [p. 2].
24 Jarrold Informal History, op. cit.
25 NRO, ACC 2001/208 box n, H. J. Jarrold, in *The Jarrold Magazine*, vol. 3, no. 7, October 1949, [p. 1].
26 NRO, ACC 2001/208 box n, *The Jarrold Magazine*, vol. 4, no. 4, July 1950, [p. 2].
27 Untitled article, *The Financial Times*, 30 November 1964, p. 9, by 'F. T. Reporter'.
28 Thomas Neurath, in an interview with the author, 24 January 2007.
29 Anon, 'Client Should Discuss His Printing with Both Designer and Printer as Early as Possible', *Printing World*, 13 June 1962, p. 711.
30 Information based on an interview with Werner Guttmann, November 2005.
31 Werner Guttmann, interviewed by Jenny Simmons, 2001, Book Trade Lives, British Library Catalogue Reference C872/64/01-07, tapes F9089–F9190.
32 T. Craker, op. cit., p. 54.
33 Ibid., p. 19.
34 *The Bookseller*, no. 3223, 30 September 1967, p. 186.
35 *The Bookseller*, no. 2571, 2 April 1955, p. 1157.
36 *The Bookseller*, no. 2574, 23 April 1955, p. 1283.
37 Letter apparently to Dan Davin, Secretary to the Oxford University Press, probably from a senior member of the Courtauld Institute, O. U. P archive, 1965–66, O/P310 866107.

38 *The Bookseller*, 14 March 1959, no. 2777,
   pp. 1180, 1188.
39 'Private View', in *The Times Literary
   Supplement*, 23 October 1959, no. 3008,
   pp. 601–02.
40 *The Times Literary Supplement*, 30
   October 1959, no. 3009, p. 625; *The Times
   Literary Supplement*, 13 November 1959,
   no. 3011, p. 661.
41 *The Times Literary Supplement*, 24 April
   1959, no. 2982, p. 243.
42 *The Bookseller*, 7 March 1959, pp. 1111–12.

10

PHAIDON AND THAMES & HUDSON
COME OF AGE

1 Information on Phaidon in this section
   from N. Spivey, 'A Short History of the
   Phaidon Press, 1923–1998', in V. Holman
   (ed.), *Visual Resources: An International
   Journal of Documentation. Special Issue
   on The Early History of the Phaidon Press
   1923–1967*, vol. 15, no. 3, 1999, p. 287. The
   second version is the online account
   www.phaidon.com/phaidon/about-
   frame.asp?m=a/c, accessed May 2007.
2 O. Benesch, *A Catalogue of Rembrandt's
   Drawings*, London: Phaidon, 1947.
3 Letter from Gombrich to Schlagman,
   25 July 1995, in the possession of
   Richard Schlagman.
4 Letter from Gombrich to Schlagman,
   29 September 1995, in the possession of
   Richard Schlagman.
5 R. Kinross, www.hyphenpress.co.uk/
   column/column–6.htlm, accessed
   April 2002.
6 B. Bernard, *Century: One Hundred Years
   of Human Progress, Regression, Suffering
   and Hope*, London: Phaidon, 1999.
7 *Fresh Cream: Contemporary Art in Culture*,
   London, Phaidon Press, 1998.
8 R. Kinross, op. cit., p. 9, accessed 10
   April 2004.
9 http://www.amazon.com/Fresh-
   Cream-Editors-Phaidon-Press/
   dp/0714839248.
10 W. Draeger, 'Berlinerin noch immer',
   in *Die Zeit*, 26 June 1992, p. 79.

11 Remarks by Neurath are from
   M. Blume, 'An Art Publisher and
   His Paris Dream', *International Herald
   Tribune*, 12 June 1989, p. 20.
12 For example in T. Craker, op. cit.,
   1985, p. 11.
13 R. Kinross, http://www.hyphenpress.
   co.uk/journal/2002/05/22/architects–
   of–the–book., p. 9.
14 D. Eribon, *E. H. Gombrich: A Lifelong
   Interest. Conversations on Art and Science
   with Didier Eribon*, London: Thames
   & Hudson, 1994.

11

JOSTLING IMITATORS

1 I. Norrie, F. Mumby, op. cit., pp. 129–30.
2 N. Spivey, op. cit., p. 286.
3 A. Hamber, 'Communicating Colour',
   in V. Holman (ed.), *Visual Resources*,
   op. cit., p. 359.
4 T. Rosenthal, 'Walter and Eva Neurath:
   Their Books Married Words with
   Pictures', LOGOS: *The Journal of the World
   Book Community*, vol. 15, no. 1, 2004, p. 17.
5 G. Rainbird, *The Rainbird Archive:
   An Autobiographical Bibliography*,
   London: Rainbird, 1985, p. xiii.
6 R. McLean, *True to Type*, London and
   Delaware: Oak Knoll Press and Werner
   Shaw, 2000, p. 87.
7 G. Rainbird, *Inns of Kent*, Whitbread
   Library, London: Whitbread & Co., 1948.
8 G. Rainbird, *The Rainbird Archive*, op.
   cit., p. xiv.
9 Ibid., p. xxx.
10 Ibid.
11 Ian Norrie in F. A. Mumby and I.
   Norrie, *Publishing and Bookselling*,
   London: Jonathan Cape, 1974, p. 504.
12 R. Lusty in G. Rainbird, *The Rainbird
   Archive*, op. cit., p. x.
13 R. McLean, op. cit., p. 52.
14 R. McLean, op. cit., p. 174. On Tisdall,
   whose surname was originally
   Aufseeser, see Valerie Holman, *Print
   for Victory, Book Publishing 1939–1945*,
   London: British Library, 2008, p. 112.
15 T. Maschler, *Publisher*, London:
   Picador, 2005, p. 26.
16 Ibid.

17 Ibid.

18 On Hamlyn see E. de Bellaigue, *British Book Publishing as a Business since the 1960s: Selected Essays*, London: British Library, 2004, pp. 31–32.

19 Ian Norrie, unpublished memoir, provisionally titled '*Mentors and Friends: Short Lives of Leading Publishers and Booksellers I Have Known*', lent to the author by Lord Gavron, p. 164.

20 Ibid., p. 176.

21 P. Jarvis and S. Thompson, 'Paul Hamlyn: "There must be another way …", The Immigrants', LOGOS, vol. 14, issue 3, 2003, p. 124.

22 Ian Norrie in F. Mumby and I. Norrie, op. cit., p. 492.

23 Ibid., p. 493.

24 P. Jarvis and S. Thompson, op. cit., p. 124.

25 http://www.fundinguniverse. com/company-histories/Dorling-Kindersley-Holdings-plc-Company-History.html, accessed February 2007.

26 G. Weidenfeld, *Remembering My Good Friends: An Autobiography*, London: HarperCollins, 1995, p. 16.

27 *People on the Move: The Fourteenth Contact Book*, London: Contact Publications, February 1949.

28 G. Weidenfeld, op. cit., pp. 137–38.

29 I. Norrie and F. Mumby, op. cit., p. 128.

12
RIPPLE EFFECT

1 C. Saumarez Smith, 'Old Master', *The Guardian*, 2 December 2006, p. 22.

2 Tim Brown, 'Far Sighted', letter in *The Guardian*, 9 December 2006, p. 15.

3 H. Gay, *The History of Imperial College London 1907–2007: Higher Education and Research in Science, Technology and Medicine*, London: Imperial College Press, 2007, p. 586.

4 M. Berger-Hamerschlag, *Journey into a Fog*, London: Victor Gollancz , 1955, p. 10.

5 Ibid., p. 58.

6 Q. Bell, *The Schools of Design*, London: Routledge and Kegan Paul, 1963.

7 Ibid., p. 59.

8 C. Frayling, *The Royal College of Art: One Hundred and Fifty Years of Art and Design*, London: Barrie and Jenkins, 1987, p. 70.

9 K. Hinrichsen, 'Visual Art behind Barbed Wire', in D. Cesarani and T. Kushner (eds.), *The Internment of Aliens in Twentieth Century Britain*, London and Portland: Frank Cass, 1993, p. 199.

10 Hellmuth Weissenborn, 'Civilian Internment in Britain 1939–1945', transcribed interview, Imperial War Museum, Department of Sound Archives, Accession No. 003771/04, 16 June 1978.

11 At the launch of the Hellmuth Weissenborn biography, *From Leipzig to London: The Life and Work of the Émigré Artist Hellmuth Weissenborn*, at Ravensbourne, 30 November 2012.

12 T. Rosenthal to A. Caraffi, Birkbeck College Archive, Walter Neurath Memorial Lecture file [BCA, WNML], 1968/69.

13 The Clerk of Birkbeck College to B. Chibnell, 30 August 1968, BCA, WNML, 1968/69.

14 Press release from Thames & Hudson, n. d. BCA, WNML, 1968/69.

15 R. Tress to E. Neurath, 13 March 1972, BCA, WNML, 1972.

16 Undated newspaper article in BCA, WNML.

17 E. Neurath to E. Gombrich, 17 March 1976, BCA, WNML.

18 http://www.oxalumny.org/blog/ archives/2005/04/colin–bailey–aw.html, last accessed 8 June 2007.

19 Letter from M. Brown to Head of Publicity, Impact Books, 20 July 2006, in the possession of the author.

20 Yale University Press, 1992.

21 G. Lathey, 'Eulenspiegel to Owlyglass: The Impact of Work of the Exiled Illustrators Walter Trier and Fritz Wegner on British Children's Literature', in A. Grenville (ed.), *Refugees from the Third Reich in Britain: Yearbook of the Research Centre for German and Austrian Exile Studies*, vol. 4, 2002, pp. 97–116.

22 M. Rosen, *The Wicked Tricks of Till Owlyglass*, London: Walker Books, 1990.

23 On *Die Weltbühne*, see also R. von Soldenhoff (ed.), *Carl von Ossietzky 1889–1938: Ein Lebensbild, 'Von mir ist weiter nichts zu sagen'*, Weinheim and Berlin: Quadriga, 1988.

24 R. Arnheim, 'Moralische Prosa', *Die Weltbühne*, vol. 27, no. 47, 24 November 1931, pp. 787–90.

25 First published as *Emil und die Detektive*, Zürich: Atrium Verlag, 1928. Tom Maschler, Kurt Maschler's son, made a considerable impression on British writers of fiction and non-fiction as the man behind the creation of the Booker Prize, to be the British version of the *Prix Goncourt*.

26 T. Maschler, op. cit., p. 173.

27 http://www.bookawards.bizland.com/kurt-maschler-award-for-children.htm, accessed 5 June 2007.

CONCLUSION

1 J. Dorner, 'Andor Kraszna-Krausz: Pioneering Publisher in Photography', LOGOS, no. 15/1, 2004, p. 125.

2 K. Hinrichsen, 'Nail, Knife and Razor-Blade (The Windows of the Camp)', *The Camp*, 6, 27 October 1940, p. 3.

Appendices

Appendix A lists Phaidon's publications from 1932, the year when the publishing house became established as an important publisher of books on cultural history in Vienna, to 1955, the year Béla Horovitz died. From 1938 onwards, Phaidon books were produced in England.

Appendix B lists titles published by Thames & Hudson in their first decade of trading, from 1949 to 1959; the first books appeared in 1950. The years 1950–55 offer a direct comparison between the two companies' publishing lists. Both lists are based on records provided by the publishing companies but may be incomplete.

APPENDIX A
Books Published by Phaidon 1932–55

1932

Englisch, P., *Sittengeschichte Europas; Sittengeschichte des Orients* (2 vols.)
Goldscheider, L. (ed.), *Die schönsten deutschen Gedichte*
Kayser, R., *Spinoza*
Klabund, *Bracke: Ein Eulenspiegelroman*
Lennhoff, E., *Die Freimaurer*
Maurois, A., *Verzicht auf das Absolute*
Mommsen, T., *Römische Geschichte*

1933

Breasted, J., *Geschichte Aegyptens*
Frobenius, L., *Kulturgeschichte Afrikas*
Goldscheider, L. (ed.), *Die schönsten Gedichte der Weltliteratur*
Gregor, J., *Weltgeschichte des Theaters*
Grimm, H., *Das Leben Michelangelos*
Justi, C., *Diego Velazquez und sein Jahrhundert*
Mommsen, T., *Das Weltreich der Caesaren*
de Unamuno, M., *Abel Sanchez.*
de Unamuno, M., *Das Leben Don Quijotes und Sanchez*
de Unamuno, M., *Der Spiegel des Todes.*
de Unamuno, M., *Tante Tula*
Waetzoldt, W., *Dürer und seine Zeit*

1934

Friedländer, L., *Sittengeschichte Roms*
Goldscheider, L., *Zeitlose Kunst*
Grimm, H., *Das Leben Raphaels*
Machiavelli, W., *Geschichte von Florenz*
von Ranke, L., *Deutsche Geschichte im Zeitalter der Reformation*
Thode, H., *Franz von Assisi*
Winckelmann, J., *Geschichte der Kunst des Altertums*

1935

Bredius, A., *Rembrandts Gemälde*
Horaz, *Oden*
Kayser, R., *Kant*
Petrarca, F., *Die Triumphe*
von Ranke, L., *Die Päpste*
von Scheffer, T., *Die Kultur der Griechen*
Schröder, R. A., *Die Gedichte des Horaz*
von Seidlitz, W., *Leonardo da Vinci*
von Sydow, E., *Dichtungen der Naturvölker*
Tacitus, *Sämtliche Werke*
Tietze, H., *Meisterwerke europäischer Malerei in Amerika*

242

1936
Borchardt, R., *Englische Dichter*
Burckhardt, J., *Die Zeit Constantins
des Grossen*
Chesterton, G. K., *Dickens*
Friedell, E., *Kulturgeschichte des
Altertums: Äegypten und Vorderasien*
Hesiod, *Sämtliche Werke*
de Maupassant, G., *Novellen*
Ranke, H., *The Art of Ancient Egypt*
Tietze, H., *Tizian*
Vossler, K., *Romanische Dichter*

1937
Burckhardt, J., *Die Kultur der
Renaissance in Italien*
Buschbeck, H., *Goya: Die
Schrecknisse des Krieges*
Goldscheider, L., *Fünfhundert
Selbstporträts*
Novotny, F., *Cézanne*
Uhde, W., *Impressionisten*
Uhde, W., *Vincent van Gogh*
Venturi, L., *Botticelli*

1938
Goldscheider, L., *El Greco*

1939
Buckley, W., *The Art of Glass*
Goldscheider, L., *The Paintings
of Michelangelo*
Goldscheider, L., *The Sculptures
of Michelangelo*
Stevenson, R. A. M., *Rubens
Paintings and Drawings*
Story, S., *Rodin*

1940
Bodkin, T., *The Paintings of Jan Vermeer*
Goldscheider, L., *Roman Portraits*

1941
Goldscheider, L., *Donatello*
Goldscheider, L., *Etruscan Scultpure*
Suida, W., *Raphael*
Trivas, N. S., *The Paintings of Frans Hals*

1942
Borenius, T., *Rembrandt: Selected Paintings*
Puyvelde, L. van, *Flemish Drawings
at Windsor Castle*

1943
Goldscheider, L., *Leonardo da Vinci*
Ironside, R., *Wilson Steer*
Lafuente, E., *Velazquez*
van Puyvelde, L., *Dutch Drawings
at Windsor Castle*
Rothenstein, J., *Augustus John*

1945
Blunt, A., *French Drawings at Windsor Castle*
Buchanan, D. W., *Canadian Painters*
Hendy, P. and Goldscheider, L.,
Giovanni Bellini
Parker, K. T., *Holbein Drawings
at Windsor Castle*
Rothenstein, E., *Stanley Spencer*

1947
Benesch, O., *Rembrandt: Selected Drawings.
Plates and Catalogue*
Clark, J. M., *Holbein: Dance of Death*
Friedell, E., *Kulturgeschichte Ägyptens
und des Alten Orients*
Oppé, A. P., *Sandby Drawings
at Windsor Castle*
Pope-Hennessy, J., *A Sienese Codex
of the Divine Comedy*
Pope-Hennessy, J., *Sienese
Quattrocento Painting*
Redgrave, S. and R., *A Century
of British Painters*

1948
Cohn, W., *Chinese Painting*
Fromentin, E., *The Masters of Past Time*
de Goncourt, E. and J., *French Eighteenth
Century Painters*
Gregorovius, F., *Lucrezia Borgia*
Ironside, R. and Gere, J., *Pre-Raphaelite
Painters*
Oppé, A. P., *The Drawings of William Hogarth*
Parker, K. T., *Canaletto Drawings
at Windsor Castle*
Pope-Hennessy, J., *Domenichino
Drawings at Windor Castle*
Tietze, H., *Tintoretto*

243

1949

Cellini, B., *The Life of Benvenuto Cellini, Written by Himself*
Friedell, E., *Kulturgeschichte Griechenlands*
Goldscheider, L., *Ghiberti*
Popham, A. E., and Wilde, J., *Italian Drawings of the XV and XVI Centuries at Windsor Castle*
van Puyvelde, L., *The Genius of Flemish Art*
Ring, G., *A Century of French Painting, 1400–1500*

1950

Burckhardt, J., *Recollections of Rubens*
Ganz, P., *The Paintings of Hans Holbein*
Gernsheim, H., *Beautiful London*
Gombrich, E. H., *The Story of Art*
Oppé, A. P., *English Drawings at Windsor Castle, Stuart and Georgian Periods*
Pope-Hennessy, J., *Paolo Uccello*
Valentiner, W. R., *Studies of Italian Renaissance Sculpture*
Waetzoldt, W., *Dürer and his Times*

1951

Bell, C., *French Impressionists*
Clark, K., *Piero della Francesca*
Delacroix, E., *The Journal of Eugène Delacroix*
Gernsheim, H., *Masterpieces of Victorian Photography*
Goldscheider, L., *Michelangelo: Drawings*
Goldscheider, L., *Towards Modern Art*
Leslie, C. R., *Memoirs of the Life of John Constable*
Morshead, O., *Windsor Castle*
Uhde, W., *Van Gogh*

1952

Baldass, L., *Jan van Eyck*
Berenson, B., *The Italian Painters of the Renaissance*
Gaunt, W., *Renoir*
Goldscheider, L., *Unknown Renaissance Portraits*
Goldscheider, L., *Leonardo da Vinci: Landscapes and Plants*
Huizinga, J., *Erasmus of Rotterdam*
Münz, L., *Rembrandt: Etchings*
Pope-Hennessy, J., *Fra Angelico*
Wittkower, R., *Carracci: Drawings at Windsor Castle*
Wölfflin, H., *Classic Art*

1953

Goldscheider, L., *Michelangelo: Paintings, Sculptures, Architecture*
Hillier, J., *Japanese Masters of the Colour Print*
Soria, M. S., *Zurbaran*

1954

Benesch, O., *The Drawings of Rembrandt* (vols I and II)
Blunt, A., *Castiglione and Stefano della Bella: Drawings at Windsor Castle*
Clark, C., *Leonardo da Vinci: Selected Drawings from Windsor Castle*
Kramrisch, S., *The Art of India*
Parker, K. T., *Holbein: Selected Drawings from Windsor Castle*
Wildenstein, G., *Ingres*

1955

Baudelaire, C., *The Mirror of Art*
Benesch, O., *The Drawings of Rembrandt* (vols. III and IV)
Bluemel, C., *Greek Sculptors at Work*
Dos Santos, R., *Nuno Gonçalves*
Grossmann, F., *Bruegel: Complete Edition of the Paintings*
Hillier, J., *Hokusai*
Kurz, O., *Bolognese Drawings at Windsor Castle*
Morassi, A., *Tiepolo: His Life and Work*
Pope-Hennessy, J., *Italian Gothic Sculpture*
Scherer, M., *Marvels of Ancient Rome*
de Silva-Vigier, A., *The Life of Buddha*
Tietze-Conrat, E., *Mantegna*
Tietze, H., *Treasures of the Great National Galleries*
Wittkower, R., *Gian Lorenzo Bernini*

Books Published by Thames & Hudson
1950–1959

1950

Amiot, P., *Bijou, the Little Bear*
Einstein, A., *Out of My Later Years*
Ernst, M., *Max Ernst Frottages*
Griaule, M., *Arts of the African Native*
Grigson, G., *Horse and Rider*
Hoetzsch, O., *Evolution of Russia*
Hürlimann, M., *Children's Portraits*
Hürlimann, M., *English Cathedrals*
Leenhardt, M., *Arts of the Oceanic Peoples*
Michel. p. H., *Romanesque Wall Paintings in France*
Newmark, M., *Dictionary of Foreign Words and Phrases*
Van Moe, E. A., *Illuminated Initials in Medieval Manuscripts*
Verlaine, P., *Confessions of a Poet*

1951

Cane, F., *The Artist in Each of Us*
Englebert, O., *The Lives of the Saints*
Hamburger, M. (ed.), *Beethoven: Letters, Journals and Conversations*
Hürlimann, M. and Spender, S., *Europe in Photographs*
Kerényi, C., *The Gods of the Greeks*
Lum, P., *The Stars in Our Heaven*
Stypulkowski, Z. F., *Invitation to Moscow*
Taylor, B., *French Painting*
Thesleff, H., *Farewell Windjammer*
Valéry, P., *Reflections on the World Today*

1952

Abegg, L., *The Mind of East Asia*
Acker, W., *T'ao the Hermit*
Barker, E., *Golden Ages of the Great Cities*
Bergenguen, W., *Matter of Conscience*
Cook, O., *English Parish Churches*
Huyghe, R., *Art Treasures of the Louvre*
Hyams, E., *Soil and Civilisation*
Johnson, E., *Return to Ithaca*
Lenormand, H.- R., *The Rising*
Lethbridge, T. C., *Boats and Boatmen*
Lum, P., *Fabulous Beasts*
Phillips, D., *The Phillips Collection*
Richardson, J., *Fanny Brawne*
Wyatt, C., *The Call of the Mountains*

1953

Bergengruen, W., *The Last Captain of Horse*
Cassou, J., *The Female Form in Painting*
Cole, W. H., *America Laughs at Punch*
Edlin, H. R., *The Forester's Handbook*
Englebert, J. O., *The Wisdom of Father Pecquet*
Fazakerley, G. R., *Shadow in Saffron*
Gilbert, G. H. J., *Have Pity for the Damned*
Graham Balcarres, C., *Art Treasures for the Nation*
Graham, F. A., *Catholicism and the World Today*
Hürlimann , M., *Switzerland*
Hürlimann, M., *Italy*
Lynch, J., *How to Make Mobiles*
Massingham, H. J., *Prophecy of Famine*
Monelli, P., *Mussolini*
Peyrefitte, R., *Diplomatic Diversions*
Proust, M., *Letters to Antoine Bibesco*
Soloviev, M., *When the Gods are Silent*
Taubes, F., *The Mastery of Oil Painting*
Taylor, R., *Sex in History*
Warner, R., *Eternal Greece*
White, B., *Teen-age Dance Book*
Wingert, p. S., *Art of the South Pacific Islands*

1954

Adams, G. A., *The Playbook Library*
Ambrose, E., *Know Your House*
Burling, J., *Chinese Art*
Burton, H., *The City Fights Back*
Burton, M., *Living Fossils*
Cleugh, J., *Secret Enemy*
Cook, O., *English Cottages and Farmhouses*
De Ong, E. R., *Insect, Fungus and Weed Control*
Dow, E. R., *How to Make Dolls' Clothes*
Ellsworth, L. R., *Halibut Schooner*
Fremantle, A. J., *Europe*
Gregoire, J. A., *Best Wheel Forward*
Groth-Kimball, I., *The Art of Ancient Mexico*
Hildebrand, D. V., *Christian Ethics*
Hürlimann, M., *Rome*
Hürlimann, M., *Spain*
Lyons, C. L., *Antiquity and Photography*
McNeil, I., *Hydraulic Operation and Control of Machines*
Peyrefitte, R., *South from Naples*
Stamm, A. J., *Chemical Processing of Wood*
Tischner, F., *Oceanic Art*
Viollet, R., *Greece in Photographs*

Watts, A. W., *Myth and Ritual in Christianity*
White, B., *Dancing Made Easy*

1955
Comben, N., *Dogs, Cats and People*
Cowell, F. C., *History, Civilisation and Culture*
Fazakerley, G. R., *Kongoni*
Ingersoll, L. R., *Heat Conduction*
Joubert de la Ferté, p. B., *The Third Service*
Pfister, P., *Pius XII: The Life and Work of a Great Pope*
Wehle, H. B., *Art Treasures of Prado*
Zaborszky, J., *Electric Power Transmission*

1956
Acton, J. E. E. D., *Essays on Freedom and Power*
Arthaud, C., *The Andes*
Aubier, D. B., *Fiesta in Seville*
Baum, J., *German Cathedrals*
Bechtel, E. D. T., *Jacques Callot*
Bellew, H., *Ballet in Moscow Today*
Borsig, A. V., *Tuscany*
Buber, M., *Tales of the Hasidim*
Bultmann, R. C., *Primitive Christianity in its Contemporary Setting*
Cartier-Bresson, H., *China in Transition*
Cassou, J., *French Drawing of the XXth century*
Catullus, C. V., *The Poems of Catullus*
Christensen, E. O., *Primitive Art*
Coggin, P. A., *Drama and Education*
Decker, H., *The Italian Lakes*
Dehn, A. A., *Water Color, Goache and Casein Painting*
Doisneau, R., *Paris Parade*
Elgar, F., *Picasso*
Eustis, M. H., *The Home Decorator's Guide*
Finck, J. L., *Thermodynamics from the Classic and Generalized Standpoints*
Frantz, J. B., *The American Cowboy*
de la Fere, N., *Italian Bouquet*
de la Fuye, M., *The Apostle of Liberty*
Gantner, J., *Romanesque Art in France*
Gilbert, K. E., *A History of Esthetics*
Grant, P., *The Good Old Days*
Grover, H. J., *Fatigue of Metals and Structures*
Grzimek, B., *No Room for Wild Animals*
Hackenbroch, Y., *Chelsea and Other English Porcelain, Pottery and Enamel in the Irwin Untermeyer Collection*

Hackenbroch, Y., *Meissen and other Continental Porcelain, Faience and Enamel in the Irwin Untermeyer Collection*
von Hayek, C. M. F., *Beetles*
Herda, H., *Fairy Tales from Many Lands*
Hürlimann, M., *Athens*
Hürlimann, M., *Germany*
Hürlimann, M., *London*
Huxley, G., *Talking of Tea*
Huxley, J., *Kingdom of the Beasts*
Huyghe, R., *French Drawing of the 19th Century*
James, E. O., *The Nature and Function of Priesthood*
von Koenigswald, G. H. R., *Meeting Prehistoric Man*
Lorca, F. G., *Poet in New York*
Merton, T., *Silence in Heaven*
Nawrath, E. A., *Sicily*
Pittaluga, M., *Raphael Panel Paintings*
Rébuffat, G., *From Mont Blanc to Everest*
Schwankl, A., *Bark*
Seltman, C., *Women in Antiquity*
Shenfield, M., *Bernard Shaw*
Sitwell, S., *Austria*
Smith, F. S., *Know-How Books*
Smithsonian Institution, *National Gallery of Art, Washington, DC*
Soloviev, M., *My Nine Lives in the Red Army*
Tate, J. O. A., *The Man of Letters in the Modern World*
Taubes, F., *Pictorial Anatomy of the Human Figure*
Tillich, P., *The Religious Situation*
Vallance, A. T., *The Summer King*
Wilson, W., *Congressional Government*
Wolfe, B. D., *Three Who Made a Revolution*

1957
Aston, R. L., *The Diesel Locomotive*
Bazin, G., *Impressionist Paintings in the Louvre*
Bernabó Brea, L., *Sicily*
Boehmer, H., *Martin Luther: The Road to Reformation*
Bottineau, Y., *Portugal*
Boule, M., *Fossil Men*
Burrows, M., *What Mean These Stones?*
Cali, F., *Architecture of Truth*
Costa, A., *Persia*
Daiken, L. H., *London Pleasures for Young People*
Decker, H., *Venice*

246

Degas, E., *Degas Sculpture*
Djilas, M., *The New Class*
Edlin, H. L., *Tree Injuries*
Erben, W., *Marc Chagall*
Grigson, G., *Art Treasures of the British Museum*
Grigson, G., *England*
Grigson, G., *The Wiltshire Book*
Groslier, B. P., *Angkor*
Haftmann, W., *Paul Klee*
Henle, F., *A New Guide to Rollei Photography*
Hürlimann, M., *Asia*
Hürlimann, M., *Europe*
James, E. O., *Prehistoric Religion*
James, H., *William Wetmore Story and his Friends*
Kaufmann, W., *Existentialism from Dostoevsky to Sartre*
Keene, D., *Modern Japanese Literature*
Kerényi, K., *Greece in Colour*
Klindt-Jensen, O., *Denmark Before the Vikings*
Krutch, J. W., *The American Drama Since 1918*
Lieberman, W. S., *Matisse: 50 Years of his Graphic Art*
Lullies, R., *Greek Sculpture*
Lynch, J., *Metal Sculpture*
Macku, A., *Vienna*
Maine, R., *Trafalgar*
Mann, H., *South America*
Mann, M., *Peacetime Uses of Atomic Energy*
Marchini, G., *Italian Stained Glass Windows*
Marnau, A., *The Guest*
Metz, P., *The Golden Gospels of Echternach*
Moyer, J. W., *Practical Taxidermy*
Müller-Alfeld, T., *The World is Full of Wonders*
Munsterberg, H., *The Arts of Japan*
Musgrave, C., *The Sussex Book*
Palme, P., *Triumph of Peace*
Peyrefitte, R., *Diplomatic Conclusions*
Pinakothek, Munich staff, *The Munich Pinakothek*
Piper, D. T., *The English Face*
Plattner, F. A., *Christian India*
Rambach, P., *Expedition Tortoise*
Rice, T. T., *The Scythians*
Rossi, F., *Art Treasures of the Uffizi and Pitti*
San Larazzo, G. D., *Klee*
Schindler, O., *Freshwater Fishes*
Schindlmayr, A., *Useful Plants*
Séjourne, L., *Burning Water*
Seuphor, M., *Piet Mondrian*

Smith, E., *English Parish Churches*
Spiegelberg, F. H., *Living Religions of the World*
Starr, C. H., *The Specification and Management of Materials in Industry*
Steingraeber, E., *Antique Jewellery: Its History in Europe from 800 to 1900*
Stern, F., *The Varieties of History*
Suschitzky, W., *Animal Babies*
Taine, H., *Taine's Notes on England*
Thorwald, J., *The Century of the Surgeon*
Vayer, L., *Master Drawings from the Collection of the Budapest Museum of Fine Arts*
Viollet, R., *Egypt*
Watts, A., *The Spirit of Zen*
Widmann, W., *Stars*
Zigrosser, C. D., *The Expressionists*

1958
Ballo, G., *Modern Italian Painting*
Bazin, G., *Impressionist Paintings in the Louvre*
Beny, R., *The Thrones of Earth and Heaven*
Bloch, R., *The Etruscans*
Brion, M., *Art Since 1945*
Brion, M., *Modern Painting from Impressionism to Abstract Art*
Cabanne, P., *Van Gogh*
Carter, G. M., *The Politics of Inequality*
Ceram, C. W., *A Picture History of Archaeology*
Courthion, P., *Flemish Painting*
Descargues, P., *German Painting from the 14th to the 16th Centuries*
Edlin, H. L., *The Living Forest*
Elgar, F., *Van Gogh*
Elisofon, E., *The Sculpture of Africa*
Flanagan, G. A., *How To Understand Modern Art*
Gloag, J., *English Furniture*
Glück, G., *Peter Bruegel the Elder*
Grünewald, M., *Grünewald*
Henle, F., *The Caribbean*
Herberts, K., *The Complete Book of Artists' Techniques*
Hürlimann, M., *Istanbul*
James, E. O., *Myth and Ritual in the Ancient Near East*
Kaufmann, F., *Methodology of the Social Sciences*
Keusen, H., *South Asia*
Knox, I., *The Aesthetic Theories of Kant, Hegel and Schopenhauer*

Kramer, S. N., *History Begins at Sumer*
Laet, S. J. D., *The Low Countries*
Lannoy, R., *Israel*
McNeil, I., *Trouble-free Hydraulics*
Oswald, M., *Asia Minor*
de Paor, M., *Early Christian Ireland*
Paz, O., *An Anthology of Mexican Poetry*
Pearce, B., *Brett Whitely*
Powell, T. G. E., *The Celts*
Robinson, F., *Caruso: His Life in Pictures*
Rothenstein, J., *A Brief History of
  the Tate Gallery*
Roubier, J., *Benelux*
Sells, A. L., *Animal Poetry*
Sotriffer, K., *Printmaking: History
  and Technique*
Steinert, H., *The Atom Rush*
Sterling, C., *Great French Painting
  in the Hermitage*
Stone, J. F. S., *Wessex Before the Celts*
Valentin, E., *Beethoven: A Pictorial Biography*
Vaudoyer, J. L., *Venetian Painting*
Verster, A. J. G., *Old European Pewter*
Watts, A. W., *Nature, Man and Woman*
Yashiro, Y., *2000 Years of Japanese Art*

1959
Babelon, J., *Great Coins and Medals*
Bidder, I., *Lalibela*
Bloch, R., *Etruscan Art*
Buchheim, L. G., *Picasso*
Canaday, J., *The Mainstreams of Modern Art*
Cowell, F. R., *Culture in Private and Public Life*
Decker, H., *Romanesque Art in Italy*
Descargues, P., *Dutch Painting*
Dhingra, B., *Asia through Asian Eyes*
Djilas, M., *Anatomy of a Moral*
Evans, J. D., *Malta*
Fernau, J., *Encyclopaedia of Old Masters*
Flincker, K., *Afghanistan*
Gelder, J. G. V., *Dutch Drawings and Prints*
Godfrey, D. E. R., *Theoretical Elasticity
  and Plasticity for Engineers*
Grohmann, W., *Wassily Kandinsky*
Haesaerts, P., *James Ensor*
Hausammann, S., *India in Colour*
Hunter, S., *Joan Miró: His Graphic Work*
Hürlimann, M., *Masterpieces of
  European Sculpture*
Huyghe, R., *The Discovery of Art*
James, E. O., *The Cult of the Mother-Goddess*
Jardot, M., *Pablo Picasso: Drawings*

Kerényi, K., *The Heroes of the Greeks*
Kidder, J. E., *Japan before Buddhism*
Langui, E., *50 Years of Modern Art*
Levenson, J. R., *Liang Ch'i-ch'ao
  and the Mind of Modern China*
Levy, R., *The Tales of Marzuban*
Masson, G., *Italian Villas and Palaces*
Méray, T., *Thirteen Days that Shook
  the Kremlin*
Morice, P. B., *Linear Structural Analysis*
Ogrizek, D., *France Observed*
Pecher, E., *Pope John XXIII*
Read, H. E., *A Concise History of
  Modern Painting*
Rice, D. T., *The Art of Byzantium*
Rorimer, J. J., *Les Belles heures de Jean
  de France, Duc de Berry*
Roskill, M., *English Painting from
  1500 to 1865*
Ruge, G., *Pasternak*
Russoli, F., *Modigliani*
Sanchez-Canton, F. J., *The Prado*
Schott, R., *Florentine Painting*
Signorelli, O., *Eleonora Duse*
Stillman, E. O., *Bitter Harvest*
Tralbaut, M. E., *Van Gogh*
Tuulse, A., *Castles of the Western World*
Unterecker, J. E., *A Reader's Guide
  to William Butler Yeats*
Willemsen, C. A., *Apulia*

Acknowledgements

My special thanks are due to Charmian Brinson for her constant support and to Richard Schlagman, who thought this story was worth telling. I am grateful to Penny Hoare for her patience, good humour and skill. Special thanks are also due to John Trotter, my family and to my friends for their unflagging support. I am indebted to all the following for their interviews and correspondence: Erica Barrett, Ernie Braun, Peter-Michael Braunwarth, David Carr, Magda Czigany, Peran Dachinger, Michael Edser, Stephan Feuchtwang, Wolfgang Fischer, Peter Foges, Christopher Foyle, Lord Gavron, Gaby Goldscheider, Leonie Gombrich, Denise Grafe, Werner Guttmann, Michael Hall, Alice Hammond, Joseph Horovitz, Elspeth Juda, Constance Kaine, Wolf Kassemoff-Cohen, Peter Kindersley, Henry Kuttner, Adrian and Sylvie Marston, Dorothea McEwan, Tom Meinhard, Elly Miller, Lord Moser, Julia Neuberger, Thomas Neurath, Tom Rosenthal, Larry Schaaf, Shalom Schotten, Andrew Schuller, Audley Southcote, Luisa Stigol, Wolfgang Suschitzky, Wendy Taylor, Eric Thomas, Heather Wegner, Lord Weidenfeld, Odile Weissenborn and Marion Wesel.

I am also very grateful to the following people for their advice or other help: Sylvia Asmus, Pauline Baines, Jean-Luc Barbanneau, Alexandre Barbanneau, Thomas Barbanneau, Chiara Barbieri, Michael Burke, Peter Collin, Peter Dannheisser, Bernard Dod, Angela English, Rahel Feilchenfeldt, Ernst Fischer, Colin Ford, Hannah Gay, Anthony Grenville, Nick Grindle, Valerie Holman, Oliver House, Robin Kinross, Henry Kuttner, Gillian Lathey, Sheila Lecoeur, Bea Lewkowicz, Brian Liddy, Miren Lopategui, Julia MacKenzie, Marian Malet, Martin Maw, Emily Mayhew, Ros Miller, Gabrielle Morton, Norman MacKenzie, Pauline Paucker, Naomi Pritchard, Paul Rennie, Bryan Ryder, Ursula Seeber, Christine Terrey, Liam Watson, Geoff White, Ian Willison, Julia Winkler and Sally Wood.

In addition, I would like to thank staff at the following archives, which were consulted for this study, especially for allowing me access to unpublished material: Andor Kraszna-Krausz Archive, National Media Museum, Bradford; Belsize Square Synagogue Archive; Birkbeck College Archive, Birkbeck College Library; Cambridge University Library; The Getty Research Institute, Los Angeles; Institute of Germanic and Romance Studies Library, London; Leo Baeck College Library; National Art Library, London; Norfolk Record Office; Österreichische Nationalbibliothek, Vienna; University of Oxford, Bodleian Library; University of Oxford, The SPSL Archive; Phaidon Archive, London; Public Records Office, London; Reading University Publishers' Archive, Special Collections; Stanley Morison Archive, University of Cambridge; The Wiener Library, London. My thanks also to Erica Barrett, Leonie Gombrich and Andrew Schuller for kindly allowing me access to their private archives.

All translations are the author's own.

Bibliography

100 Jahre Insel Verlag 1899–1999, Begleitbuch zur Ausstellung, Frankfurt am Main and Leipzig: Insel Verlag, 1999

Abbey, W., Brinson, C. et al. (eds.), *Between Two Languages: German-speaking Exiles in Great Britain 1933–45*, Stuttgart: Verlag Hans-Dieter Heinz Akademischer Verlag, 1995

Adler, K., 'What I Found in the English Book Trade', *The Bookseller*, no. 1697, 9 June 1938, pp. 228–29

Adunka, E. and Roessler, p. (eds.), *Die Rezeption des Exils: Geschichte und Perspektiven der österreichischen Exilforschung*, Vienna: Mandelbaum Verlag, 2003

Altman, A. (ed.), *Between East and West: Essays Dedicated to the Memory of Béla Horovitz*, London: East and West Library, 1958

Ambrose, T., *Hitler's Loss: What Britain and America Gained from Europe's Cultural Exiles*, London: Peter Owen, 2001

Anderson, P., 'Components of the National Culture', *New Left Review*, no. 50, July–August 1968, pp. 3–57

Angell, N., and Baxton, D., *You and the Refugee: The Morals and the Economics of the Problem*, Harmondsworth: Penguin Special, 1939

Arnheim, R., *Art and Visual Perception: A Psychology of the Creative Eye*, London: Faber, 1956;

— 'Moralische Prosa', in *Die Weltbühne*, vol. 27, no. 47, 24 November 1931, pp. 787–90

Athill, D., *Stet: A Memoir*, London: Granta, 2000

Aynsley, J., *Graphic Design in Germany 1890–1945*, London: Thames & Hudson, 2000

Baines, P., *Penguin by Design: A Cover Story 1935–2005*, London: Allen Lane, 2005

Barea, I., *Vienna, Legend and Reality*, London: Secker & Warburg, 1966

Barron, S. (ed.), *Exiles and Emigrés: The Flight of European Artists from Hitler*, Los Angeles: Los Angeles County Museum of Art, 1997

Bearman, M., and Brinson, C., '"Jugend voran": Sieben Jahre Junges Österreich in Großbritannien', in Krohn, C.-D. et al. (eds.), *Kindheit und Jugend im Exil – ein Generationenthema: Exilforschung, ein Internationales Jahrbuch*, vol. 24, 2006, pp. 150–67

Béchard-Léauté, A., *The Contribution of Emigré Art Historians to the British Art World after 1933*, unpublished Ph. D. thesis, University of Cambridge, 1999

Becker, L. and Hollis, R. (eds.), *Avant Garde Graphics 1918–1934, from the Merrill C. Berman Collection*, London: Hayward Gallery Publishing, 2004

Behr, S. and Malet, M. (eds.), *Arts in Exile in Britain 1939–1945: Politics and Cultural Identity: Yearbook of the Research Centre for German and Austrian Exile Studies*, vol. 6, 2004

Bell, Q., *The Schools of Design*, London: Routledge & Kegan Paul, 1963

de Bellaigue, E., *British Book Publishing as a Business since the 1960s: Selected Essays*, London: The British Library, 2004

Beller, S., *A Concise History of Austria*, Cambridge: Cambridge University Press, 2006

— *Vienna and the Jews 1867–1938: A Cultural History*, Cambridge: Cambridge University Press, 1989

Beniston, J. and Vilain, R. (eds.), *Culture and Politics in Red Vienna, Austrian Studies*, vol. 14, 2006

Benjamin, W., 'The Work of Art in the Age of Mechanical Reproduction', in *Illuminations*, London: Pimlico, 1999, pp. 211–44

Bentwich, N., *The Rescue and Achievement of Refugee Scholars: The Story of Displaced Scholars and Scientists, 1933–1952*, The Hague: Martinus Nijhoff, 1953

Benz, W., *Flucht aus Deutschland: Zum Exil im 20. Jahrhundert*, Munich: DTV, 2000

Berendsohn, W., *Die Humanistische Front: Einführung in die deutsche Emigranten-Literatur, Erster Teil: Von 1933 bis zum Kriegsausbruch 1939*, Zürich: Europa Verlag, 1946

— *Zweiter Teil: Vom Kriegsausbruch 1939 bis Ende 1946*, Worms: Verlag Georg Heintz, 1976

Berger, J., *Ways of Seeing: Based on the Television Series with John Berger*, London: BBC, Harmondsworth: Penguin Books, 1972

Berger-Hamerschlag, M., *Journey into a Fog*, London: Victor Gollancz, 1955

Berghahn, M., *Continental Britons: German Jewish Refugees from Nazi Germany*, Oxford, Hamburg etc.: Berg, 1984

Bermann-Fischer, B., *Sie schrieben mir oder: Was aus meinem Poesiealbum wurde*, Munich: DTV, 1981

Bermann-Fischer, G., *Bedroht – Bewahrt, Weg eines Verlegers*, Frankfurt am Main: Fischer Taschenbuch Verlag, 1971

Berry, T., Johnson, A. and Jaspert, W. (eds.), *The Encyclopedia of Type Faces*, London: Blandford Press, 1953

Bing, G., 'Fritz Saxl (1890–1948)', in Gordon, D. J. (ed.), *Fritz Saxl 1890–1948: A Volume of Memorial Essays from his Friends in England*, London: Thomas Nelson & Sons Ltd, 1957, pp. 1–46

Bisanz, H., 'Franz Cizek: Kunstpädagogik für das Jahrhundert des Kindes', in *Franz Cizek: Pionier der Kunsterziehung (1865–1946)*, Vienna: Museen der Stadt, 1985

Black, J., *The Making of Modern Britain: The Age of Empire to the New Millennium*, Stroud: Sutton Publishing, 2001

Blau, E., 'Isotype and Architecture in Red Vienna: The Modern Projects of Otto Neurath and Josef Frank', in Beniston, Judith and Vilain, Robert (eds.), *Culture and Politics in Red Vienna, Austrian Studies*, vol. 14, 2006, pp. 227–57

Blume, M., 'An Art Publisher and His Paris Dream', *International Herald Tribune*, 12 June 1989, p. 20

Blunt, A., 'Sleepers Awake', *The Spectator*, 11 October 1935, p. 548

Bolitho, Hector (ed.), *A Batsford Century: The Record of a Hundred Years of Publishing and Bookselling 1843–1943*, London: B. T. Batsford Ltd, 1943

Börsenblatt für den deutschen Buchhandel, 100. Jahrgang 1834–1933, [Leipzig], [1933]

Bott, G. (ed.), *Von Morris zum Bauhaus: Eine Kunst gegründet auf Einfachkeit*, Würzburg: Peters Verlag, 1977

Bowra, C. M., *Memories 1898–1939*, London: Weidenfeld & Nicolson, 1966

Brandstätter, C. (ed.), *Vienna 1900 and the Heroes of Modernism*, London: Thames & Hudson, 2005

Brendon, P., *The Dark Valley: A Panorama of the 1930s*, London: Jonathan Cape, 2000

Briggs, A. (ed.), *Essays in the History of Publishing: In Celebration of the 250th Anniversary of the House of Longman, 1724–1974*, London: Longman, 1974

Brinson, C., 'A Woman's Place ...? German-speaking Women in Exile in Britain, 1933–1945', *German Life and Letters*, no. 51, 2 April 1998, pp. 205–24

— '"Ein sehr ambitioniertes Projekt": Die Anfänge des Austrian Centre', in Bearman, M., Brinson, C. et al. (eds.), *Wien – London, hin und retour: Das Austrian Centre in London 1939–1947*, Vienna: Czernin Verlag, 2004, pp. 5–28

— '"In the Exile of Internment" or "Von Versuchen aus einer Not eine Tugend zu machen": German-speaking Women Interned by the British during the Second World War', in Niven, W. and Jordan, J. (eds.), *Politics and Culture in Twentieth Century Germany*, Rochester, N.Y.: Camden House, 2003, pp. 63–87

— 'Science in Exile: Imperial College and the Refugees from Nazism – A Case Study', in *Leo Baeck Institute Year Book*, no. 51, 2006, pp. 133–51

— *The Strange Case of Dora Fabian and Mathilde Wurm: A Study of German Political Exiles in London during the 1930s*, Berne, Berlin etc.: Peter Lang, 1996

— and Dove, R., *Politics by Other Means: The Free German League of Culture in London 1939–1946*, London: Vallentine Mitchell, 2010

— and Dove, R. (eds.), *'Stimme der Wahrheit': German-language Broadcasting by the BBC, Yearbook of the Research Centre of the German and Austrian Exile Studies*, vol. 5, 2003

—, Dove, R. and Taylor, J., *'Immortal Austria?' Austrians in Exile in Great Britain, Yearbook of the Research Centre of the German and Austrian Exile Studies*, vol. 8, 2007

—, Dove, R. et al. (eds.), *England? Aber wo liegt es?: Deutsche und österreichische Emigranten in Großbritannien*, Munich: iudicium, 1996

—, Dove, R. et al. (eds.), *'Keine Klage über England?: Deutsche und österreichische Exilerfahrungen in Großbritannien*, Munich: iudicium, 1998

Brophy, J., *Britain Needs Books*, London: National Book Council, 1941

Buchthal, H., 'New Books', *Journal of Education*, vol. 86, no. 1016, March 1954, pp. 130–32

Burke, C., *Paul Renner: The Art of Typography*, London: Hyphen Press, 1998

Buruma, I., *Voltaire's Coconuts: Or Anglomania in Europe*, London: Weidenfeld & Nicolson, 1999

Butler, W. (ed.), 'Geometrical Typographical Bookplate Design by Hellmuth Weissenborn', *The Bookplate Journal*, vol. 1, no. 1, March 1983, p. 19

Calvocoressi, R., 'Oskar Kokoschka, Red Vienna and the Education of the Child', in Beniston, J. and Vilain, R. (eds.), *Culture and Politics in Red Vienna, Austrian Studies*, vol. 14, 2006, pp. 215–27

Carney, M., *Britain in Pictures: A History and Bibliography*, London: Werner Shaw Ltd, 1995

— *Stoker: The Life of Hilda Matheson* OBE, *1888–1940*, Llangygnog: private publ., 1999

Carter, M., *Anthony Blunt: His Lives*, London: Macmillan, 2001

Carter, S., 'A Little World made Cunningly', *Matrix: A Review for Printers and Bibliophiles*, no. 5, Winter 1985, pp. 51–54

Cazden, R. E., *German Exile Literature in America, 1933–1950: A History of the Free German Press and Book Trade*, Chicago: American Library Association, 1970

Cesarani, D., *Britain and the Holocaust*, London: The Holocaust Educational Trust, 1998

— and Kushner, T. (eds.), *The Internment of Aliens in Twentieth Century Britain*, London: Frank Cass, 1993

Chandler, A., Stokłosa, K. et al. (eds.), *Exile and Patronage: Cross-cultural Negotiations beyond the Third Reich*, Münster: LIT Verlag, 2006

254

Chappell, C., *Island of Barbed Wire: Internment on the Isle of Man in World War Two*, London: Corgi Books, 1984

Christoph, T., 'Henrion, Ludlow and Schmidt (GBR)', *Novum Gebrauchsgraphik*, vol. 60, no. 3, March 1989, pp. 6–13

Cinamon, G., 'Hans Schmoller 1916–1985', in *Hans Schmoller, Typographer: His Life and Work, A Special Issue of The Monotype Recorder*, no. 6, April 1987, pp. 1–13;

— *Rudolf Koch: Letterer, Type Designer, Teacher*, Delaware and London: Oak Knoll Press, 2000

Clare, G., *Last Waltz in Vienna: The Destruction of a Family, 1842–1942*, London: Pan Books, 1982

Clark, K., *Another Part of the Woods: A Self-portrait*, London: Coronet Books, 1976

— (ed.), *Penguin Modern Painters*, Harmondsworth: Penguin, 1943

Conradt, S., *Die Fotobildbandreihen des Karl Robert Langewieschen Verlages 1902 bis 1931 am Beispiel ausgewählter Kunst- und Naturbände*, unpublished Ph. D. thesis, Georg August Universität, Göttingen, July 1999

Craker, T., *Opening Accounts and Closing Memories: Thirty Years with Thames and Hudson*, London: Thames & Hudson, 1985

Cummings, E., and Kaplan, W., *The Arts and Craft Movement*, London: Thames & Hudson, 1991

Dahm, V., *Das Jüdische Buch im dritten Reich, Teil 1*, Munich: Buchhändler-Vereinigung, 1979

— 'Jüdische Verleger, 1933–1938', in Paucker, A., Gilchrist, S. and Suchy, B. (eds.), *Die Juden im Nationalsozialistischen Deutschland*, Tübingen: J. C. B. Mohr, 1986, pp. 273–82

David, A., *The Patron: A Life of Salman Schocken 1877–1959*, New York: Metropolitan Books, Henry Holt and Company, 2003

Day, K. (ed.), *Book Typography in Europe and the United States of America, 1815–1965*, London: Ernest Benn, 1966

Day, L., *Alphabets Old and New*, London: Batsford, 1902

Delmer, S., *An Autobiography: Black Boomerang*, London: Secker and Warburg, 1962

Der Börsenverein des Deutschen Buchhandels 1825–2000: Ein geschichtlicher Aufriss, Frankfurt am Main: Buchhändler-Vereinigung, 2000

Dorner, J., 'Andor Kraszna-Krausz: Pioneering Publisher in Photography', *LOGOS, Forum of the World Book Community*, vol. 15, no. 1, 2004, pp. 118–25

Dove, R., *Journey of No Return: Five German-speaking Exiles in Britain, 1933–1945*, London: Libris, 2000

Draeger, W., 'Berlinerin noch immer', *Die Zeit*, 26 June 1992

Droste, M., *Bauhaus 1919–1933*, Cologne: Taschen, 1990

Dube, W.-D., *The Expressionists*, London: Thames & Hudson, 1972

Eisler, C., 'Kunstgeschichte American Style: A Study in Migration', in Fleming, D. and Bailyn, B. (eds.), *The Intellectual Migration: Europe and America 1930–1960*, Cambridge, Mass.: The Belknap Press, 1969, pp. 544–629

Elon, A., *The Pity of It All: A Portrait of Jews in Germany 1743–1933*, London: Penguin Books, 2002

Emanuel, M., and Gissing, V., *Nicholas Winton and the Rescued Generation*, London: Vallentine Mitchell, 2002

Eribon, D., *E. H. Gombrich: A Lifelong Interest. Conversations on Art and Science with Didier Eribon*, London: Thames & Hudson, 1994

Ermarth, M. (ed.), *Kurt Wolff: A Portrait in Essays and Letters*, Chicago and London: University of Chicago Press, 1991

Evans, D. and Gohl, S., *Photomontage: A Political Weapon*, London: Gordon Fraser, 1986

Eyssen, J., *Buchkunst in Deutschland: Vom Jugendstil zum Malerbuch*, Hanover: Schlütersche Verlagsanstalt und Druckerei, 1980

Farleigh, J., *It Never Dies: A Collection of Notes and Essays, 1940–1946*, London: Sylvan Press, 1946

Feather, J., *A History of British Publishing*, London and New York: Routledge, 1988

Feilchenfeldt, R., *Paul Cassirer Verlag, 1898–1933: Eine kommentierte Bibliographie, Bruno und Paul Cassirer Verlag 1898–1901, Paul Cassirer Verlag 1908–1933*, Munich: K. G. Saur, 2002

Fer, B., Batchelor, D., and Wood, p. (eds.), *Realism, Rationalism, Surrealism: Art between the Wars*, New Haven and London: Yale University Press, 1993

Fischer, E. (ed.), *Buchgestaltung im Exil 1933–1950: Eine Ausstellung des deutschen Exilarchivs 1933–1945 der Deutschen Bibliothek*, Wiesbaden: Harrassowitz, 2003

— 'The Phaidon Press in Vienna, 1923–1938', in Holman, Valerie (ed.), *Visual Resources: An International Journal of Documentation, Special Issue on The Early History of the Phaidon Press 1923–1967*, vol. 15, no. 3, 1999, pp. 289–309

Fleming, D. and Bailyn, B. (eds.), *The Intellectual Migration: Europe and America 1930–1960*, Cambridge Mass.: The Belknap Press, 1969

Franz Cizek: Pionier der Kunsterziehung (1865–1946), exhibition catalogue, Historisches Museum der Stadt Wien, Vienna: Eigenverlag der Stadt Wien, 1985

Frayling, C., *The Royal College of Art: One Hundred and Fifty Years of Art and Design*, London: Barrie and Jenkins, 1987

Fresh Cream: Contemporary Art in Culture, London, Phaidon Press, 1998

Freyburg, W. J. and Wallenberg, H. (eds.), *Hundert Jahre Ullstein 1877–1977 in vier Bänden*, Frankfurt am Main, Berlin and Vienna: Ullstein, 1977

Friedländer, S., *Nazi Germany and the Jews: The Years of Persecution 1933–39*, London: Weidenfeld & Nicolson, 1997

Fry, H., *Jews in North Devon during the Second World War: The Escape from Nazi Germany and the Establishment of the Pioneer Corps*, Tiverton: Halsgrove, 2005

Fuss P., Zlata, *German Children's and Youth Literature in Exile 1933–50*, Munich: K. G. Saur, 2001

Füssel, S., Jäger, G., and Staub, H., *Der Börsenverein des Deutschen Buchhandels 1825–2000: Ein geschichtlicher Aufriss*, Frankfurt am Main: Buchhändler-Vereinigung, 2000

Games, N., Moriarty, C., and Rose, J., *Abram Games: His Life and Work*, New York: Princeton University Press, 2003

Gardiner, J., *Wartime Britain 1939–1945*, London: Headline Book Publishing, 2004

Gay, H., *The History of Imperial College London 1907–2007: Higher Education and Research in Science, Technology and Medicine*, London: Imperial College Press, 2007

Gay, P., *My German Question: Growing up in Nazi Berlin*, New York: Yale University Press, 1998

— *Die Republik der Außenseiter: Geist und Kultur in der Weimarer Zeit 1918–1933*, Frankfurt am Main: Fischer, 1970

Gill, Eric, *Last Essays*, London: Jonathan Cape, 1942

Gill, Evan, *Eric Gill: A Bibliography*, Winchester and Detroit: St Paul's Bibliographies, 1991

Gillman, L., and Gillman, P., *Collar the Lot!: How Britain Interned and Expelled its Wartime Refugees*, London: Quartet Books, 1980

Gölner, R., 'Hauptstadt des Kindes und des Antisemitismus: Die pädagogische Reformbestrebung und der steinige Weg zum neuen Menschen', in Riedl, Joachim (ed.), *Wien, Stadt der Juden: Die Welt der Tante Jolesch*, Vienna: Paul Zsolnay Verlag, 2004, pp. 130–32

Gordon, D., *Fritz Saxl 1890–1948: A Volume of Memorial Essays from his Friends in England*, London: Thomas Nelson, 1957

Gombrich, E. H., *A Little History of the World*, New Haven and London: Yale University Press, 2005

— *Art and Illusion: A Study in the Psychology of Pictorial Representation*, New York: Pantheon Books, 1960

— *Meditations on a Hobby Horse and Other Essays on the Theory of Art*, London: Phaidon, 1963

— *The Story of Art*, London: Phaidon, 1950

— *The Uses of Image: Studies in the Social Function of Art and Visual Communications*, London: Phaidon, 1999

— *Weltgeschichte für Kinder*, Vienna and Leipzig: Steyrermühl Verlag, 1936

Graham, G., 'Only a Link in the Chain:
A Tribute to a Great Publisher',
The Bookseller, 1 December 1979,
no. 3858, p. 2454

Grenville, A. (ed.), *Refugees from the Third
Reich in Britain, Yearbook of the Research
Centre for German and Austrian Exile
Studies*, vol. 5, 2003

Gross, G. (ed.), *Publishers on Publishing*,
London: Secker & Warburg, 1961

Haffner, S., *Germany: Jekyll and Hyde*,
London: Secker & Warburg, 1945

Hahn, p. (ed.), *Bauhaus Berlin: Auflösung
Dessau 1932, Schließung Berlin 1933:
Bauhäuser und Drittes Reich*, Berlin:
Weingarten, 1985

Hall, M. G., *Österreichische Verlagsgeschichte
1918–1938*, vol. 1, *Geschichte des österreichischen Verlagswesens*; vol. 2, *Belletristische
Verlage der Ersten Republik*, Vienna/
Cologne/Graz: Böhlau, 1985

Hamber, A., 'Communicating Colour', in
Holman, Valerie (ed.), *Visual Resources:
An International Journal of Documentation.
Special Issue on The Early History of the
Phaidon Press 1923-1967*, vol. 15, no. 3,
1999, pp. 355–70

Hammel, A., 'Jack Pritchard, Refugees
from Nazism and Isokon Design', in
Chandler, A., Stokłosa, K., and Vinzent,
J., (eds.), *Exile and Patronage: Cross-
cultural Negotiations beyond the Third
Reich*, Munster: LIT Verlag, 2006,
pp. 23–32

— and Grenville, A. (eds.), *Refugee Archives,
Theory and Practice: Yearbook of the
Research Centre of the German and Austrian
Exile Studies*, vol. 9, 2007

Hare, S. (ed.), *Penguin Portrait: Allen Lane
and the Penguin Editors*,
Harmondsworth: Penguin, 1995

Harley, B., *The Curwen Press: A Short History*,
London: Curwen Press, 1970

Harley, J., 'The King Penguin Series:
An Historical Survey', in *Matrix:
A Review for Printers and Bibliophiles*, no. 5,
Winter 1985, pp. 143–50

Harris, M. J., and Oppenheimer, D.,
Into the Arms of Strangers, London:
Bloomsbury, 2000

Hawkes, N., 'Bright Visions in Wartime:
A Study of *British Women Go to War*
(1943)', *The Journal of the J. B. Priestley
Society*, vol. 2, 2001, pp. 20–30

Healy, R., 'Germany's First Private
Press', *Matrix: A Review for Printers
and Bibliophiles, no. 27, Winter 2007*

*Hellmuth Weissenborn 1898–1982: Painter
and Graphic Artist*, London: Bachman
and Turner, 1976

Herzfelde, W., *Immergrün: Merkwürdige
Erlebnisse und Erfahrungen eines fröhlichen
Waisenknaben*, Berlin and Weimar:
Aufbau-Verlag, 1969

— *John Heartfield*, Dresden: Fundus, 1986

Herzl, T., *Der Judenstaat*, Vienna:
Breitenstein, 1896

Hinrichsen, K., 'Visual Art behind Barbed
Wire', in Cesarani, D., and Kushner,
T. (eds.), *The Internment of Aliens in
Twentieth Century Britain*, London:
Frank Cass, 1993, pp. 188–209

Hirschfeld, G., (ed.), *Exile in Great Britain:
Refugees from Hitler's Germany*,
Leamington Spa: Berg for the German
Historical Institute, 1984

Hodges, S., *Gollancz – The Story of a Publishing
House 1928–1978*, London: Gollancz, 1978

Hoffmann, L., et al. (eds.), *Kunst und Literatur
im antifaschistischen Exil 1933–1945*, 7
vols., Leipzig: Verlag Reclam, 1980–87;
esp. vol. 5, *Exil in der Tschechoslowakei,
in Großbritannien, Skandinavien und
Palästina*, 1987 (section on Great Britain
by Birgid Leske and Marion Reinisch,
pp. 159–324)

Hoffmann, P., *The Viennese: Splendor,
Twilight, Exile*, New York, London etc.:
Anchor Press Doubleday, 1988

Hofner-Keulenkamp, G., 'Versprengte
Europäerinnnen: Deutschsprachige
Kunsthistorikerinnen im Exil',
in Krohn, Claus-Dieter, Rotermund,
Erwin et al. (eds.), *Frauen und
Exil: Zwischen Anpassung und
Selbstbehauptung: Exilforschung,
Ein Internationales Jahrbuch*, vol. 11,
1993, pp. 190–203

Holman, V. *Albert Skira and Art Publishing
in France, 1928-48*, unpublished Ph.D.
thesis, University of London, 1987

— 'Art Books Against the Odds: Phaidon in England, 1938–1960', in Holman, Valerie (ed.), *Visual Resources: An International Journal of Documentation. Special Issue on the Early History of the Phaidon Press 1923–1967*, vol. 15, no. 3, 1999, pp. 311–29

— *Print for Victory: Book Publishing 1939–1945*, London: British Library, 2008

— (ed.), *Visual Resources: An International Journal of Documentation, Special issue on the Early History of the Phaidon Press 1923–1967*, vol. 15, no. 3, 1999

Holmes, C., *Anti-Semitism in British Society, 1876–1939*, New York: Holmes and Meier, 1979

Honnef, K., 'Fotografen im Exil', in Krohn, Claus-Dieter, Rotermund, Erwin et al. (eds.), *Film und Fotografie: Exilforschung: Ein Internationales Jahrbuch*, vol. 21, 2003, pp. 170–82

Howe, E., *The Black Game: British Subversive Operations against the Germans during the Second World War*, London: Michael Joseph, 1982

Howes, J., and Paucker, P., 'German Jews and the Graphic Arts', *Leo Baeck Yearbook*, vol. 34, 1989, pp. 443–73

Hürlimann, B., *Seven Houses: My Life with Books*, London, Sydney and Toronto: The Bodley Head, 1976

Isherwood, C., *Goodbye to Berlin*, London: The Hogarth Press, 1939

Jackman, J., and Borden, C. (eds.), *The Muses Flee Hitler: Cultural Transfer and Adaptation 1930–1945*, Washington, DC: Smithsonian Institution Press, 1983

James, C., 'On the Library Coffee-Table', in Holman, Valerie (ed.), *Visual Resources: An International Journal of Documentation. Special Issue on the Early History of the Phaidon Press 1923–1967*, vol. 15, no. 3, 1999, pp. 371–77

— *Unreliable Memoirs*, London: Picador, 1980

Jarvis, P. and Thompson, S., 'Paul Hamlyn: "There must be another way…", The Immigrants', LOGOS: *Forum of the World Book Community*, vol. 14, no. 3, 2003, pp. 120–29

Jeffrey, I., *Photography: A Concise History*, London: Thames & Hudson, 1981

Joos, J., *Trustees for the Public? Britische Buchverlage im Spannungsfeld von intellektueller Selbständigkeit, wirtschaftlichem Interesse und patriotischer Verpflichtung im Vorfeld und während des Zweiten Weltkriegs*, Wiesbaden: Harrassowitz, 2008

Joseph, R., *Master of Words*, Southampton: Ashford Press Publishing, 1986

Kallir, J., *Viennese Design and the Wiener Werkstätte*, London: Thames & Hudson, 1986

Kapp, Y., and Mynatt, M., *British Policy and the Refugees, 1933–1941*, London and Portland, Oregon: Frank Cass, 1997

Karpfen, F., *Österreichische Kunst: Gegenwartskunst*, vol. 3, Leipzig/Vienna: Literaria Verlag, 1923

Kerr, M., *As Far as I Remember*, Oxford and Portland, Oregon: Hart Publishing, 2006

Key, E., *The Century of the Child*, New York and London: G. P. Putnam, 1909

King, J., *The Last Modern: A Life of Herbert Read*, London: Weidenfeld & Nicolson, 1990

Kinross, R., 'Emigré Graphic Designers in Britain: Around the Second World War and Afterwards', *Journal of Design History*, vol. 3, no. 1, 1990, pp. 35–57

— *Graphic Communication through Isotype*, exhibition catalogue, University of Reading, 1976

— *Modern Typography: An Essay in Critical History*, London: Hyphen Press, 1992

— *Otto Neurath's Contribution to Visual Communication*, unpublished Ph.D. thesis, University of Reading, 1976

— and Hochuli, J., *Designing Books: Practice and Theory*, London: Hyphen Press, 1996

Koch, E. and Trapp, F. (eds.), *Exil: Forschung, Erkenntnisse, Ergebnisse*, no. 2, 2007

Koch, R., *Soldatenstiefel*, Rudolfinische Drucke, 1919 [1920]

Kochan, M., *Britain's Internees in the Second World War*, London: Macmillan, 1983

Kokoschka, O., *My Life*, New York: Macmillan, 1974

Kralik, H., *Die Wiener Philharmoniker: Monographie eines Orchesters*, Vienna, Leipzig and Olten: Frick, 1938

Krohn, C.-D., Koepke, W., et al. (eds.),
 *Film und Fotografie, Exilforschung: Ein
 Internationales Jahrbuch*, vol. 21, 2003
Krohn, C.-D., Rotermund, E., et al. (eds.),
 *Bücher, Verlage, Medien: Exilforschung: Ein
 Internationales Jahrbuch*, Munich: vol. 22
— *Autobiographie und Wissenschaftliche
 Biografik: Exilforschung: Ein
 Internationales Jahrbuch*, vol. 23, 2005
— *Kindheit und Jugend im Exil, Ein
 Generationsthema: Exilforschung: Ein
 Internationales Jahrbuch*, vol. 24, 2006
Krug, H. and Nungesser, M. (eds.), *Kunst im
 Exil in Großbritannien 1933–1945*, Berlin:
 Frölich & Kaufmann, 1986
Lafitte, F., *The Internment of Aliens*,
 Harmondsworth: Penguin Special, 1940
Landshoff, F., *Amsterdam Keizersgracht 333,
 Querido, Erinnerungen eines Verlegers*,
 Berlin: Aufbau Verlag, 1991
Laqueur, W., *Generation Exodus: The Fate of
 Young Jewish Refugees from Nazi Germany*,
 London: I. B. Tauris, 2004
Lathey, G., 'Eulenspiegel to Owlyglass:
 The Impact of the Work of the
 Exiled Illustrators Walter Trier and
 Fritz Wegner on British Children's
 Literature', in Grenville, Anthony (ed.),
 Refugees from the Third Reich in Britain,
 Yearbook of the Research Centre for German
 and Austrian Exile Studies, vol. 5, 2003,
 pp. 97–116
Lee, C., *The Hidden Life of Anne Frank*,
 London: Viking Penguin Books, 2002
Levey, M., *A Brief History of the National Gallery*,
 London: Pitkin Pictorials Ltd, 1959
Lewis, J., *Penguin Special: The Life and Times of
 Allen Lane*, London: Viking, 2005
Löb, K., *Exilgestalten: Deutsche Buchgestalter
 in den Niederlanden 1932–1956*, Arnheim:
 Gonda Quint, 1995
London, L., *Whitehall and the Jews 1933–1948*,
 Cambridge: Cambridge University
 Press, 2000
Luft, F. (ed.), *Facsimile Querschnitte durch die
 Berliner Illustrirte*, Berne and Munich:
 Scherz, 1965
MacCarthy, F., *Eric Gill*, London: Faber &
 Faber, 1990
Macdonald, L. (ed.), *Hellmuth Weissenborn:
 Painter and Artist*, London: Bachman
 and Turner, 1976

Madethaner, W., 'Austro-Marxism: Mass
 Culture and Anticipatory Socialism',
 in Beniston, J., and Vilain, R. (eds.),
 *Culture and Politics in Red Vienna, Austrian
 Studies*, vol. 14, 2006, pp. 21–37
Malet, M., and Grenville, A. (eds.), *Changing
 Countries: The Experience and Achievement
 of German-speaking Exiles from Hitler
 in Britain from 1933 to Today*, London:
 Libris, 2002
Maschler, T., *Publisher*, London: Picador, 2005
McEwan, D., 'A Tale of One Institute and
 Two Cities: The Warburg Institute',
 in Wallace, Ian (ed.), *German-speaking
 Exiles in Great Britain*, Yearbook of the
 Research Centre for German and Austrian
 Exile Studies, vol. 1, 1999, pp. 25–42
— 'Mapping the Trade Routes of the Mind:
 The Warburg Institute', in Timms,
 E., and Hughes, J. (eds.), *Intellectual
 Migration and Cultural Transformation:
 Refugees from National Socialism in the
 English-speaking world*, Vienna: Springer,
 2003, pp. 37–50
McLaine, I., *Ministry of Morale: Home Front
 Morale and the Ministry of Information
 in World War II*, London: George Allen
 and Unwin, 1979
McLean, R., *How Typography Happens*,
 London and Delaware: British Library
 and Oak Knoll Press, 2000
— *Jan Tschichold: Typographer*, London: Lund
 Humphries, 1975.
— 'The Life and Death of *Picture Post*',
 Antiquarian Book Monthly Review, vol. 12,
 no. 9, September 1985, pp. 336–41
— *The Thames & Hudson Manual of Typography*,
 London: Thames & Hudson, 1980
— *True to Type*, Delaware and London:
 Oak Knoll Press and Werner Shaw, 2000
Medawar, J., and Pyke, D., *Hitler's Gift:
 Scientists who Fled Nazi Germany*,
 London: Pitkus, 2001
Mellor, D., 'London–Berlin–London,
 A Cultural History: The Reception
 and Influence of the New German
 Photography in Britain, 1927–33',
 in Mellor, D. (ed.), *Germany: The New
 Photography 1927–33*, London: The Arts
 Council of Great Britain, 1978,
 pp. 113–30

Mellor, D. (ed.), *Germany: The New Photography 1927–33*, London: The Arts Council of Great Britain, 1978

de Mendelssohn, P., *S. Fischer und sein Verlag*, Frankfurt am Main: Fischer, 1970

Michel, W., *Rudolf Koch: Ein Deutscher Meister*, Cassel: Bärenreiter Verlag, 1938

Miller, E., 'Goldscheider: A Memoir', in Holman, V. (ed.), *Visual Resources: An International Journal of Documentation, Special Issue on the Early History of the Phaidon Press 1923–1967*, vol. 15, no. 3, 1999, pp. 331–42

Miller, H., 'Phaidon and the Business of Art Book Publishing, 1923–1967', in Holman, Valerie (ed.), *Visual Resources: An International Journal of Documentation, Special Issue on The Early History of the Phaidon Press 1923–1967*, vol. 15, no. 3, 1999, pp. 343–53

Mills, B., 'Pictures in the Fire', *Antiquarian Book Monthly Review*, vol. 13, no. 10, issue 150, October 1986, pp. 368–73

— 'Some Notes on the Story of Adprint', *Antiquarian Book Monthly Review*, vol. 13, no. 10, October 1986, pp. 368–73

Milner, C. D., *Mountain Photography: Its Art and Technique in Britain and Abroad*, London and New York: Focal Press, 1945

Morison, S. (ed.), *The Fleuron: A Journal of Typography*, Cambridge: The University Press and New York: Doubleday Page & Co., 1926

Morpurgo, J. E., *Allen Lane: King Penguin*, London: Hutchinson & Co., 1979

Morris, W., *The Ideal Book: Essays and Lectures on the Arts of the Book*, ed. W. Peterson, Berkeley and London: University of California Press, 1982

Mosse, W., Carlebach, J., et al. (eds.), *Second Chance: Two Centuries of German-speaking Jews in the United Kingdom*, Tübingen: J. C. B. Mohr, 1991

Mowl, T., *Stylistic Cold Wars: Betjeman versus Pevsner*, London: John Murray, 2000

Müller, C., *Typofoto: Wege der Typographie zur Foto-Text-Montage bei Làszlò Moholy-Nagy*, Berlin: Gebr. Mann Verlag, 1994

Müller, H.-A., *Woodcuts and Wood Engravings: How I Make Them*, New York: Pynson Printers, 1939

Müller-Härlin, A., 'It All Happened in this Street, Downshire Hill', in Behr, S., and Malet, M. (eds.), *Arts in Exile in Britain 1933–1945: Politics and Cultural Identity, Yearbook of the Research Centre for German and Austrian Exile Studies*, vol. 6, 2004, pp. 241–65

Mumby, F., *A History of British Publishing*, London: Jonathan Cape, 1956

— and Norrie, I., *Publishing and Bookselling*, London: Jonathan Cape, 1974

Neugebauer, R. (ed.), *Zeichnen im Exil – Zeichen des Exils? Handzeichnungen und Druckgraphik deutschsprachiger Emigranten ab 1933*, Weimar: VDG, 2003

Norrie, I., *Mumby's Publishing and Bookselling in the Twentieth Century*, London: Bell and Hyman, 1982

Nyburg, A., '"Dein großer Brief war ein Ereignis": the Private and Professional Correspondence of the Refugee Art Historians Hilde and Otto Kurz', in Hammel, A., and Grenville, A. (eds.), *Refugee Archives: Theory and Practice, The Yearbook of the Research Centre for German and Austrian Exile Studies*, vol. 9, 2007, pp. 123–39

— 'Hardly a Trace Left of Danube or Spree?': *A Contribution to the Study of Art Book Publishing and Illustrated Book Production in Britain by German-speaking Exiles from National Socialism*, unpublished Ph. D. thesis, University of London, 2009

— *From Leipzig to London: The Life and Work of the Émigré Artist Hellmuth Weissenborn*, Delaware: Oak Knoll, 2012

Omasta, M., Mayr, B., et al. (eds.), *Wolf Suschitzky Photos*, Vienna: SYNEMA, 2006

Orwell, G., 'Anti-Semitism in Britain', in *George Orwell: Collected Essays*, London: Secker & Warburg, 1961, pp. 288–98

Osley, A., *Berthold Wolpe: A Retrospective Survey*, exhibition catalogue, London: The Merrion Press, 2005

Papo, M., 'In Memoriam Bela Horovitz 1898–1955', in Altman, A. (ed.), *Between East and West: Essays Dedicated to the Memory of Béla Horovitz*, London: East and West Library, 1958, pp. 3–8

Parry, L., *William Morris and the Arts and Crafts Movement: A Source Book*, London: Studio Editions, 1989

Paucker, P., *New Borders: The Working Life of Elizabeth Friedlander*, Oldham: Incline Press, 1998

— 'Two Typographer-calligraphers: Berthold Wolpe and Elizabeth Friedlander', in Brinson, C., Dove, R., et al. (eds.), *Keine Klage über England? Deutsche und österreichische Exilerfahrungen in Großbritannien*, Munich: iudicium, 1998, pp. 200–14

Peaker, C., *The Democratisation of the Art Book during World War II*, unpublished MA dissertation, University of London, 1997

Perloff, M., *The Vienna Paradox: A Memoir*, New York: New Directions Publishing Corporation, 2004

Philby, R., et al., *The Private Life of Kim Philby: The Moscow Years*, London: St Ermin's Press, 1999

Pick, H., *Guilty Victim – Austria from the Holocaust to Haider*, London and New York: I. B. Tauris, 2000

Piper, E., and Raab, B., *90 Jahre Piper: Die Geschichte des Verlags von der Gründung bis heute*, Munich and Zurich: Piper, 1994

Plant, M., *The English Book Trade: An Economic History of the Making and Sale of Books*, London: George Allen and Unwin, 1973

Rainbird, G., *The Rainbird Archive: An Autobiographical Bibliography*, London: Rainbird, 1985

Rand, P., and Him, G., 'Hans Schleger "Zero"', *Graphis: International Journal of Graphic Art and Applied Art*, vol. 32, no. 188, 1976–77, pp. 518–21

Randle, J., *Hellmuth Weissenborn, Engraver: With an Autobiographical Introduction by the Author*, Andoversford: The Whittington Press & The Acorn Press, 1983

— 'Hellmuth Weissenborn', *Matrix: A Review for Printers and Bibliophiles*, no. 2, Winter 1982, [between pp. 80 and 81]

Read, H., *Henry Moore, Sculptor*, London: Zwemmer, 1934

— 'Literature for Connoisseurs', *The Burlington Magazine for Connoisseurs*, vol. lxxii, no. 419, February 1938, p. 97

Rennhofer, M., *Koloman Moser: Master of Viennese Modernism*, London: Thames & Hudson, 2002

Rennie, P., 'Children's Illustrated Books of the 1940s', *Antique Collectors' Club*, October 2005, pp. 26–31

— 'Illustrated Books of the 1940s for Grown-ups', *Antique Collectors' Club*, February 2006, pp. 38–43

— 'Modern Illustrated Cookery Books', *Antique Collectors' Club*, June 2006, pp. 16–21

— '20th Century Guides', *Antique Collectors' Club*, May 2007, pp. 18–23

Ridler, C., *Out-house Publishing*, Oxford: Oxford Polytechnic Press, 1976

Riedl, J. (ed.), *Wien, Stadt der Juden: Die Welt der Tante Jolesch*, Vienna: Zsolnay Verlag, 2004

Ritchie, J. M., *German Exiles: British Perspectives*, New York, Washington DC, etc: Peter Lang, 1997

— (ed.), *German-speaking Exiles in Great Britain, Yearbook of the Research Centre for German and Austrian Exile Studies*, vol. 3, 2001

Röder, W., and Strauss, H., (eds.), *Biographisches Handbuch der deutschsprachigen Emigration nach 1933*, vols. 1–3, Munich/London: Saur, 1980–83

Röder, W., *Die deutschen sozialistischen Exilgruppen in Grossbritannien: Ein Beitrag zur Geschichte des Widerstandes gegen den Nationalsozialismus*, Hanover: Verlag für Literatur und Zeitgeschehen, 1968

Rose, J. and Anderson, P. (eds.), *British Library Publishing Houses 1881–1965*, Dictionary of Literary Biography, vol. 112, Florence, KY: Gale Cengage, 1991

Rosen, M., *The Wicked Tricks of Till Owlyglass*, London: Walker Books, 1990

Rosenthal, T., 'Walter and Eva Neurath: Their Books Married Words with Pictures', LOGOS, *Forum of the World Book Community*, vol. 15, no. 1, 2004, pp. 12–19

Roth, J., *Briefe 1911–1939*, ed. Kesten, H., Cologne and Berlin: Kiepenheuer & Witsch, 1970

Salter, R., *Fritz Kredel: Das buchkünstlerische Werk in Deutschland und Amerika*, Rudolstadt: Burgart-Presse, 2003

Saumarez Smith, C., 'Old Master', *The Guardian*, 2 December 2006, p. 22

Saur, K.-G. (ed.), *Aus Alten Börsenblättern: Ein Anzeigerquerschnitt für den deutschen Buchhandel 1834–1945*, Munich and Pullach: Verlag Dokumentation, 1968

Schauer, G., 'The Art of the Book in Germany', in K. Day (ed.), *Book Typography in Europe and the United States of America*, London: Ernest Benn Ltd, 1966

Schleger, P., *Zero, Hans Schleger: A Life in Design*, Aldershot: Lund Humphries, 2001

Schmoller, H., 'Der Schrift verschrieben: Berthold Wolpe und sein Werk', *Philobiblion*, vol. 25, no. 1, February 1981, pp. 9–27

— 'The Paperback Revolution', in Briggs, Asa (ed.), *Essays in the History of Publishing in Celebration of the 250th Anniversary of the House of Longman, 1724–1974*, London: Longman, 1974, pp. 283–318

Schorske, C., *Fin-de-siècle Vienna: Politics and Culture*, Cambridge: Cambridge University Press, 1987

Schürer, O., *Prag: Kultur, Kunst, Geschichte*, Munich: G. W. D. Callwey, 1935

Schwab-Felisch, H., 'Bücher bei Ullstein', in Freyburg, W. J., and Wallenberg, H., (eds.), *Hundert Jahre Ullstein 1877–1977, in vier Bänden*, Frankfurt am Main, Berlin and Vienna: Ullstein, 1977, pp. 179–216

Schwarz, F., 'Kulturarbeit in den englischen Internierungscamps', in Krug, H., and Nungesser, M., (eds.), *Kunst im Exil in Großbritannien 1933–1945*, Berlin: Frölich & Kaufmann, 1986, pp. 283–88

Seaton, M., 'A Family Affair', *Daily Telegraph Magazine*, 5 June 1999, pp. 50–53

Secrest, M., *Kenneth Clark: A Biography*, London: Weidenfeld & Nicolson, 1984

Sereny, G., *The German Trauma*, London: Allen Lane, The Penguin Press, 2000

Seyfert, M., 'His Majesty's Most Loyal Internees: The Internment and Deportation of German and Austrian Refugees as "Enemy Aliens", Historical, Cultural and Literary Aspects', in Hirschfeld, G. (ed.), *Exile in Great Britain: Refugees from Hitler's Germany*, Leamington Spa: Berg for the German Historical Institute, 1984, pp. 195–217

Sherman, A., *Island Refuge: Britain and Refugees from the Third Reich 1933–1939*, London: Frank Cass, 1994

Simon, O., *Introduction to Typography*, Harmondsworth: Pelican Books, 1945

— *Printer and Playground: An Autobiography*, London: Faber and Faber, 1956

Smith, M., *Station X: Decoding Nazi Secrets*, New York: TV Books, 1998

Snowman, D., *The Hitler Emigrés: The Cultural Impact on Britain of Refugees from Nazism*, London: Chatto & Windus, 2002

von Soldenhoff, R. (ed.), *Carl von Ossietzky 1889–1938: Ein Lebensbild, 'Von mir ist weiter nichts zu sagen'*, Weinheim and Berlin: Quadriga, 1988

Spivey, N., 'A Short History of the Phaidon Press 1923–1998', in Holman, V. (ed.), *Visual Resources: An International Journal of Documentation, Special Issue on The Early History of the Phaidon Press 1923–1967*, vol. 15, no. 3, 1999, pp. 279–379

Stent, R., *A Bespattered Page: The Internment of His Majesty's Most Loyal Enemy Aliens*, London: André Deutsch, 1980

Sternfeld, W., and Tiedemann, E. (eds.), *Deutsche Exil-Literatur 1933–1945: eine Bio-Bibliografie*, Heidelberg: Verlag Lambert Schneider, 1970

Strobl, G., *The Germanic Isle: Nazi Perceptions of Britain*, Cambridge: Cambridge University Press, 2000

Strubel, A., *The People of the Book: Jews in German Publishing 1871–1933*, New York: Leo Baeck Institute, 1990

Tanner, H., and Hanff, D., *Out of Nazi Germany: An Account of the Life of Dietrich Hanff*, London: Impact Books, 1995

Taylor, A. J. P., *English History 1914–1945*, Oxford: Book Club Associates, 1977

— *The Second World War: An Illustrated History*, Harmondsworth: Penguin Books, 1975

Thomas, A. (ed.), *Beauty of Another Order: Science and Photography*, New Haven and London: Yale University Press, 1997

Thompson, B., *Schnitzler's Vienna: Image of a Society*, London and New York: Routledge, 1990

Thompson, P., *The Voice of the Past: Oral History*, Oxford and New York: Oxford University Press, 1978

— *The Work of William Morris*, Oxford and New York: Oxford University Press, 1991

Timms, E., and Hughes, J. (eds.), *Intellectual Migration and Cultural Transformation: Refugees from National Socialism in the English-speaking world*, Vienna and New York: Springer, 2003

Trapp, F., '"Emigrantenliteratur" – eine Provokation für die Fachwissenschaft: Der Fall Walter A. Berendsohn', in Koch, E., and Trapp, F. (eds.), *Exil: Forschung, Erkenntnisse, Ergebnisse*, no. 2, 2007, pp. 5–20

Tschichold, J., *An Illustrated History of Writing and Lettering*, London: A. Zwemmer, 1946

Uhlman, F., *The Making of an Englishman*, London: Victor Gollancz, 1960

Ullstein, H., *The Rise and Fall of the House of Ullstein*, London: Nicholson and Watson, 1944

Unwin, P., *The Publishing Unwins*, London: Heinemann, 1972

Unwin, S., *The Truth about a Publisher*, London: Allen and Unwin, 1960

Van der Post, L., *Jung and the Story of our Time*, London: Vintage, 1976

Vaux Halliday, N., *More than a Bookshop: Zwemmer's and Art in the 20th Century*, London: Philip Wilson, 1991

Vinzent, J., 'Muteness as Utterance of a Forced Reality – Jack Bilbo's Modern Art Gallery (1941–1948)', in Behr, S. and Malet, M. (eds.), *Arts in Exile in Britain 1933–1945: Yearbook of the Research Centre for German and Austrian Exile Studies*, vol. 6, 2004, pp. 301–37

Vicenzi, O., *Permanente SchulDeform: die Zerstörung der humanistischen Schulbildung in Österreich, eine Dokumentation*, Vienna, Freiburg and Basle: Herder, 1989

Walter, H.-A., *Deutsche Exilliteratur 1933–1950*. vol. 1: *Die Vorgeschichte des Exils und seine erste Phase*. Part 1: *Die Mentalität der Weimardeutschen; Die 'Politisierung' der Intellektuellen*, Stuttgart and Weimar: J. B. Metzler, 1972; vol. 2: *Europäisches Appeasement und übersee-ische Asylpraxis*. Part 1: *Asylpraxis und Lebensbedingungen in Europa*, Stuttgart: J.

B. Metzlersche Verlagsbuchhandlung, 1984; vol. 3: *Internierung, Flucht und Lebensbedingungen im Zweiten Weltkrieg*, Stuttgart: J. B. Metzlersche Verlagsbuchhandlung, 1988; vol. 4: *Exilpresse*, Stuttgart: J. B. Metzlersche Verlagsbuchhandlung, 1974

Walter, H., *Doch das Zeugnis lebt fort: Der jüdische Beitrag zu unserem Leben*, Berlin and Frankfurt am Main: Verlag Annelore Leber, 1965

Walzer, T., *Unser Wien: die Arisierung von Österreich*, Vienna: Aufbau Verlag, 2001

Warburg, F., *All Authors are Equal*, London: Hutchinson, 1973

— *An Occupation for a Gentleman*, London: Hutchinson, 1959

Wasserstein, B., *Britain and the Jews of Europe, 1939–1945*, London: Institute of Jewish Affairs, 1979

Weidenfeld, G., *Remembering My Good Friends: An Autobiography*, London: HarperCollins Publishers, 1994

Weidle, B. (ed.), *Kurt Wolff: Ein Literat und ein Gentleman*, Bonn: Weidle Verlag, 2007

Weidle, B., and Seeber, U., *Anna Mahler: Ich bin in mir zu Hause*, Bonn: Weidle Verlag, 2004

Weissenborn, H., 'Mein Leben in London', *Illustration 63: Zeitschrift für die Buchillustration*, vol. 17, no. 2, 1980, pp. 51–54

Wendland, H., 'Der Illustrator und Pressendrucker Hellmuth Weissenborn', *Illustration 63: Zeitschrift für die Buchillustration*, vol. 14, no. 3, 1977, pp. 75–77

Wendland, U., *Biographisches Handbuch Deutschsprachiger Kunsthistoriker im Exil: Leben und Werk der unter dem Nationalsozialismus verfolgten und vertriebenen Wissenschaftler*, Part 1: A–K, Part 2: L–Z, Munich: K. G. Saur, 1991

Westphal, U., 'German, Czech and Austrian Jews in English Publishing', in Mosse, W., Hirschfeld, G., et al. (eds), *Second Chance: Two Centuries of German-speaking Jews in the United Kingdom*, Tübingen: J. C. B. Mohr, 1991, pp. 195–208

Whitford, F., *Bauhaus*, London: Thames & Hudson, 1984

Willett, J., 'The Emigration and the Arts', in Hirschfeld, G. (ed.), *Exile in Great Britain: Refugees from Hitler's Germany*, Leamington Spa: Berg, 1984, pp. 183–204

— *The Weimar Years,* London: Thames & Hudson, 1984

Wilson, F., *In the Margins of Chaos: Recollections of Relief Work in and between Three Wars*, London: John Murray, 1944

Wilson, H., 'Notes by the Way', *The Bookseller*, no. 1693, 12 May 1938, pp. 34–35

Winckler, J., 'Gespräch mit Wolfgang Suschitzky, Fotograf und Kameramann', in Krohn, C.-D., Rotermund, E., et al. (eds.), *Film und Fotografie: Exilforschung: Ein Internationales Jahrbuch*, vol. 21, 2003, pp. 254–80

Winder, R., *Bloody Foreigners: The Story of Immigration to Britain*, London: Little, Brown, 2004

Windisch, A., *Professor Dr L. C. Walter Tiemann*, Mainz: Gutenberg Gesellschaft, 1953

Wishmann, S., *Jugendstil, Art Nouveau: Floral and Functional Forms*, Boston: Little, Brown and Co., 1984

Wistrich, R., *The Jews of Vienna in the Age of Franz Joseph*, Oxford and Portland, Oregon: The Litman Library of Jewish Civilisation, 1990

Wittmann, R., *Geschichte des deutschen Buchhandels: Ein Überblick*, Munich: C. H. Beck, 1991

Wuttke, D., 'Die Emigration der Kulturwissenschaftlichen Bibliothek Warburg und die Anfänge des Universitätsfachs Kunstgeschichte in Großbritannien', in Krug, H. and Nungesser, M. (eds.), *Kunst im Exil in Großbritannien 1933–1945*, Berlin: Frölich & Kaufmann, 1986, pp. 209–16

Wyland-Herzfelde, G., *Glück gehabt: Erinnerungen*, Munich: DTV, 2003

Ziegler, P., *London at War 1939–1945*, London: Pimlico, 2002

Zühlsdorff, V., *Hitler's Exiles: The German Cultural Resistance in America and Europe*, London and New York: Continuum, 2004

Zweig, S., *Die Welt von gestern: Erinnerungen eines Europäers*, London and Stockholm: Hamish Hamilton and G. Bermann Fischer, 1941

Index

Numbers in italics refer to illustrations

A Book of Roses 136, *136*, 153
Abrams, Harry 164
Acorn Press 121
Adams, George (Teltscher) 141, *141*, 177
Adenauer, Konrad 96
Adler, Kurt 26
Adprint 9, 123, 72, 112, 151–2, 164, 168,
   197–8, 203
  'Britain in Pictures' 76, 110, 123, 154–5,
    159–60, 164, 168, 171, 197, 203, 204
  W. Foges founds 16–18, 150–1
  'The New Democracy' 157–8
  rise and fall of 150–61
Albatross Books 114, 115
Aldor, Francis 203
Aldus Books 160
Allert de Lange 53
Altmann, Lotte 73
Amadeus Quartet 90
Anschluss 22, 23, 48, 55, 57–63, 66
Anselm, Felix 18
Antal, Friedrich 41, 169
anti-Semitism
  and German-Jewish identity 31
  in Britain 66–7
  Nazi persecution 16, 49–55
Arnheim, Rudolf 217
Arntz, Gerd 158
The Art Book 143, *143*, 187
Arts and Crafts movement 100–1, 210–11
Atrium 200
Auerbach, Frank 215

Bacon, Francis 215
Baker, John 45
Barlach, Ernst 35
Barrett, Erica 150
Bates, Eric 188, *188*
Batsford 44–5
Batsford, Harry 45
Bauhaus 38, 52, 107, 112
Baum, Vicki 52
Bayer, Herbert 83, 107
Beazley, John 203
Bell, Clive 83
Bell, Quentin 211
Ben-Gurion, David 150, *150*
Benson, Patrick 217
Berenson, Bernard 40
Bergengruen, Werner 167
Berger-Hamerschlag, Margarete 210–11
  Journey into a Fog 144, *144*

Betjeman, John 37–8, 155–6, 167
Bilbo, Jack 84
Bing, Gertrud 28, 42
Birkbeck College, London 215–16
Black, Leon 188
Blaue Reiter Almanach 36
'Die Blauen Bücher' series 137, 137, 154–5
Bloch, Raymond, The Etruscans 142, 142
Blunt, Anthony 39, 40, 42–3, 82, 87, 90, 94
Blunt, Wilfred 82, 84–5
Boase, Tom 93, 208
Bodley Head 115
Boehm, Margaret 71
Bonham-Carter, Victor 57
book art 100–23
book design 145, 174–80
   L. Goldscheider 13–15
   Piper Verlag 36
book illustration and illustrators 117–23,
   198–9
book packaging, invention of 21–2
The Bookseller 26, 44, 45, 77, 159, 167, 178,
   179, 180
Borenius, Tancred 76
Börsenverein des Deutschen
   Buchhandels 26, 34
Brandt, Bill 153
Brandt, Rolf 117, 177
Braun, Ernie 115–16, 158
Britain, art and culture before World
War II 36–45
'Britain in Pictures' 76, 110, 123, 154–5,
   159–60, 164, 168, 171, 197, 203, 204
Britten, Benjamin 92
Brown, Margaret 216
Brown, Tim 209
Browne, Anthony 218
Buchtal, Hugo 87
BUGRA (International Exhibition for the
   Book Trade and Graphic Arts) 36, 100
Burgess, Anthony 168–9
Burlington Magazine 39, 41, 76, 169

Cambridge University Press 45
Caraffi, A. J. 215
Carr, David 214–15
Carriline, Ian 188, 188
Cassirer, Bruno 35
Cassirer, Paul 35
Cassou, Jean, Raoul Dufy 200
Century 187–8

Ceram, C.W., A Picture History
   of Archaeology 142, 142
Chamberlain, Neville 67
Charteris, Martin 58
Chittock, John 128
Cižek, Franz 30, 84, 210
Clark, Kenneth 39–42, 43, 68, 70, 74,
   82, 169, 200, 215
Cobden-Sanderson, Thomas James 102
Cohn, Leonie 170
Cole, Henry 38
Collins, William ('Billy') 197–8
Connolly, Cyril 179
Cook, Brian 45
Cook, G. H. 166
Cook, Olive, English Parish Churches 166
Cooper, Douglas 185, 185
Copplestone, Trewin 202
Corvin, Michael 121
Cosman, Milein 32–3, 35, 109
Courtauld Institute 42, 93, 208
Craker, Trevor 188, 188
Cranach Press 102
Cumberlege, G. F. J. 85
Curwen Press 103, 110, 111
Czigany, Magda 210

Dachinger, Hugo 72
Dehio, George 35–6
Deutsch, André 172, 204
Deutsche Dorfkirchen 137, 137
Diederich, Eugen 101
Dolfuss, Engelbert 59
Dorling Kindersley 161, 203
Dorling, Christopher 203
Double Crown Club 106, 109

Eckersley, Tom 177
Edser, Michael 213
Ehmke, F. H. 101
Ehrlich, Bettina 152
Einstein, Albert, Out of My Later Years 165
Einzig, Susan 117, 210
Elon, Amos 33
Elsevier 186, 216
Encyclopaedia Britannica Company 186
Enoch, Kurt 114
Epstein, Jason 196
Epstein, Mitch 216
Esslin, Martin 29
Ettlinger, Leopold 86

Faber, Geoffrey 75
FAMA 200
Fanthorpe, U. A. 66
Feibusch, Hans 109
Feltrinelli, Giangiacomo 170, *170*
Feuchtwang, Eva see Neurath, Eva
Feuchtwang, Stephan 22, 23, 168, 190
Feuchtwang, Wilhelm 23, 72, 164
Fischer, Bermann / Fischer Verlag 53
Fischer, Harry 9, 21–2, 72–3
Fischer, Samuel 33–4
Fischer, Wolfgang 21–2
Fletcher, Alan 187
Focal Press 127–28, 145, 216, 218
Foges, Peter 16, 18, 161
Foges, Wolfgang 20, 150, *150*, 208
  early career 16–19, *17*
  founds Adprint 9, 17–19, 150–61
  King Penguins 153
  Der Neuen Jugend 17–18, 126
  and W. Neurath 151, 159–60, 190
  and G. Rainbird 197
Foyle, Christopher 171
Foyle, William A. 60, 157
Foyle, William Richard ('Dick') 157
Frank, Otto 59, 93
Freud, Sigmund 16, 18, 27, 51, 208
Frick, Wilhelm / Frick Verlag 21–2
Friedell, Egon 16
Friedenthal, Richard 121
Friedlaender, Walter 43
Friedlander, Elisabeth 78, 109, 110, 111,
  118, 122, 123, 156
  cover design, *Brandenburg Concertos*
  110, 133, *133*
Friedländer, Max 35
Fry, Charles 45
Fry, Roger 40, 83
Futura 104, 107
Future Books 160

Gallimard, Claude 170, *170*
Games, Abram 108, 177
Geiringer, Alfred 58
Geiringer, Blanka 14
Geiringer, Erich 59
Geiringer, Fritzi 59
Geller, Uri 160
George Allen & Unwin 59, 88–90
Georg-Müller Verlag 34–35
German-Jewish publishers:
  flight of 55–63

persecution of 49–55
rise of 31–4
Gilchrist & Co., Leeds 164
Gill, Eric 15, 102, 103
Gleichschaltung 50–2
Glenconnor, Lord 157
Goldscheider, Blanka 62
Goldscheider, Gabriela (Gaby) 14, *14*,
  59, 61, 63, 93, 186
Goldscheider, Ludwig 9, 12, 13–16, *13*,
  27, 29, 89, 92, 145, 186
  book design, passion for 13–15
  emigrates to Britain 55, 58–63, 69–74
  finances 95
  'Josephs Klage' 48
  Michelangelo 135, *135*
  revisits Austria 96–7
Goldstein, Julius 105
Gollancz, Victor 44
Gombrich, Ernst 30, 31, 48, *48*, 68, 77, 151,
  170, 185, *185*
  advises T. Schüller 77, 86–7
  Caricature 136, *136*, 154
  legacy 208–9
  Neurath memorial lecture 215–16
  Story of Art 9, 15, 88, 90–4, 130, *130*, 186,
  187, 192, 208–9
  Weltgeschichte (*Little History of the World*)
  21, 91, 130, *130*, 192
Gombrich, Leonie 90, 192
Göring, Hermann 53
Grafe, Innozenz 69–71, *69*, *69*, 186
Grigson, Geoffrey, Flowers of the Meadow
  118, 134, *134*
Gropius, Walter 83, 170
Grundmann 177
Guggenheim, Samuel 105
Guttmann, Peter 175
Guttmann, Werner 110, 174–7, 188, *188*

Halberstam, Edith 119
Hall, Michael 168, 174
Halliday, Vaux 83
Hamburger, Michael 201
Hamilton, Hamish 110
Hamlyn 174, 213
Hamlyn, Paul (né Paul Hamburger)
  176, 201–2
Hammond, Alice 69, 70, 184, 191
Hanff, Dietrich 118
Harling, Robert 82, 205, 215
Harrap, Alice (née Kun) 150–1, 156, 157
Harrap, Ian 172

Harrap, Paull 157
Harrap, Walter 75, 172
Harvey, John 166
Haskell, Francis 216
Hausamann, S. 180
Hauser, Heinrich 53
Havinder, Ashley 83
Heartfield, John (né Helmut
    Herzfelde) 107–8, 153
Heinemann, William 196, 205
Hendry, Philip 94
Henrion, F. H. K. (né H. F. Kohn) 108,
    112–13, 177, 210
Herzfelde, Wieland 107
Herzl, Theodor 55
Him, George (né Jacob Himmelfarb)
    112–13, 210
Hinrichsen, Klaus 212, 223
Hitler, Adolf 49, 50
Hobsbawm, Eric 215
Hockney, David 191, *191*
My Early Years, jacket design 141, *141*, 178
Hoffmann, Edith 204
Hoffmann, Josef 27
Hofmannsthal, Hugo von 15, 27
Holroyd-Reece, John (Hermann Riess) 114
Horovitz, Béla 9, 12, *12*, 40, 93, *93*, 146, *146*,
    172, 184, *184*
    death 185, 186
    education 12–13, 20, 29
    emigrates to Britain 58–62
    influence on other publishers 202, 203
    Phaidon Verlag 12–16, 54
    religious observance 13–14, 31, 50
    and Joseph Roth 190
    settles in London 69–74
    Skira, admiration for 145–6
    and Thames & Hudson 190–2
    and Stanley Unwin 59–62, 88, 105
    war years 71–4
Horovitz, Elly see under Miller,
    Elly Horovitz
Horovitz, Hannah 13, 62
Horovitz, Joseph 13, 29, 62, 70, 90, 191
Horovitz, Lotte Beller 13, 61, 184, *184*,
    185, *185*
Howe, Ellic 78
Huntley, Simon 188, *188*
Hürlimann, Martin, English Cathedrals
    140, *140*, 164–6
Hutchinson, George 113
Huyghe, R., Art Treasures of the Louvre 167

IBA (International Book Exhibition) 100
ICI 111
Insel Verlag 33, 102, 103, 104, 106, 113, 153
Das kleine Blumenbuch 105, 118, 132, *132*
Isherwood, Christopher 28
Isle of Man internment camps 71–3, 113,
    121, 155, 156, 158, 164, 203, 212, 223
Isotype 28, 50, 129, 139, *139*, 157–9

jacket design 107–9, 176–8
Jaffé, Max 32
Janus Press 102
Jarrold of Norwich 164, 171–4
Jarrold, John 164, 171–4
Jäschke, Richard 82
Jewishness, German-speaking refugees 31
Jewish refugee book artists in Britain
    109–13
Jewish Refugees' Committee 57
Johnson, Hugh 203
Johnston, Edward 102
Juda, Elspeth 111
Juda, Hans 111
Jugendstil 101–2
Jung, Carl, influence on Eva Neurath 169

Kaine, Constance Neurath see under
    Neurath, Constance
Kaine, John 189, *189*
Kandinsky, Wassily 41
Kassemoff-Cohen, Wolf 121, 213
Kästner, Erich 117, 127, 200, 217
Kelmscott Press 101, 106
Kent, Charles and William 172
Kerenyi, Karl, Gods of the Greeks 165
Kerr, Alfred 77
Kerr, Judith 77
Kerr, Michael 77
Kessler, Harry Graf 102
Khrushchev, Nikita 17, *17*
Kiepenheuer, Gustav 53
Kiepenheuer und Witsch 96
Kindersley, Peter 203
King, Mervyn 9
Kinross, Robin 110, 187
Kippenberg, Anton 102, 103
KK Awards 216–17
Das kleine Blumenbuch 105, 118, 132, *132*
Kleitsch, Klaus 145
Klimt, Gustav 15, 27
Knapp, Wilhelm 128, 145
Koch, Rudolf 102, 104–6, 109, 118

Kokoschka, Oskar 38
  Walter Neurath 19, *19*
Kola, Richard 32
Kramer, Jakob 41
Kraszna-Krausz, Andor ('KK') 127–8,
  145, 216–18, 222
Kredel, Fritz 105, 106, 199
Kris, Ernst 209
Kurz, Hilde Schüller 41, 68, *68*, 85, 150,
  151–2, 155, 156, 192
Kurz, Otto 42, 68, 77, 86–7, 152, 156, 192

Lafitte, F. The Internment of Aliens 115,
  133, *133*
Landauer, Walter 53
Landshoff, Fritz 53
Lane, Allen 108, 113–17, 153–4, 201
K. Langewiesche, 'Blauen Bücher' 154–5
Lanston, Tolbert 111
Lanyi, Richard 32
Latham, Charles 45
Leipzig Academy for Graphic Arts
  and Book Design 103, 113, 119, 123
  manual (1912) 144, *144*, 211
Leppmann, Franz 52
Lethbridge, T.C., Boats and Boatmen 167
Levai, Kurt (later Frank Lloyd) 73
Lévy, Albert 62
Lewis, Jeremy 108, 115
Lewitt (Le Witt), Jan 113
Lissitsky, El 107
Lloyd, Frank (né Kurt Levai) 73
Lorant, Stefan 117, 126, 199
Lukács, Paul 17, 18
Lynd, Sylvia, English Children 138, *138*

Macaulay, Rose 155
Macdonald, Lesley 119
MacKirdy, Cailean 213
McLean, Ruari 103, 109, 171, 197–9
Macpherson, Kenneth and Bryher 83–4
Mahler, J. 93
Malik Verlag 107
Mann, Heinrich 53
Mann, Thomas 33, 168
Mardersteig, Hans 114
Marées, Hans von 36
Margesson, Frank 58
Maschler, Kurt 200, 217–18
Maschler, Tom 200, 217
Matheson, Hilde 154
Meidner, Ludwig 109

Meynell, Francis 78, 105–6, 109, 110, 114
Midgely, Peter (né Fleischmann) 212
Midgley, John 204
Miller, C. Douglas 128, 145
Miller, Elly Horovitz 13, 14, 93, *93*, 110,
  172, 174, 185–6, *185*, 186, *189*, 190
  Gombrich's *Story of Art* 90, 91
  life in Vienna and flight to Britain
    15, 58–9, 62, 73–4, 88
Miller, Harvey 13, 185, *185*, 186
Mitchell Beazley 161, 202–3
Mitchell, James 203
Moberley Pool 76
Moholy-Nagy, László 83, 107, 170
Moholy-Nagy, Lucia 111
Mommsen, Theodor 16
Mondadori 157
Monotype Corporation 111
Moore, Henry 37, 82, 83
Moore, Patrick 203
Mordaunt, Elinor 117
Morison, Stanley 102–3, 105, 109, 111,
  114, 185
Morris, William 100–1, 102, 103, 104,
  106, 210–11
Morrison & Gibb 175
Moser, Claus 30
Moser, Kolomon 27
Mosley, Oswald 67
Mowl, Timothy 37
Müller, Artur 189, *189*
Müller, Hans Alexander 119
Münz, Ludwig, Rembrandt 166–7
Musarion Press 69, 73

Nash, Paul 170
Neue Sachlichkeit 126–7
Neue Welt 18
Der Neuen Jugend 17–18, 126
Neurath, Constance (Connie) 20, 30–1,
  58, 153, 168, 188, *188*, 189, *189*, 190
Neurath, Eva (née Itzig, previously
  Feuchtwang) 165, *165*, 188, *188*, 214
  at Adprint 72, 156, 159, 164
  chances on Hürlimann photographs
    197–8
  early life 22–3
  and Jungian analysis 71, 169
  meets and married Walter Neurath
    156, 165
  Neurath memorial lecture 216

and Thames & Hudson 9, 159, 164,
167–9, 173, 175, 190
Neurath, Marianne 20, 22, 165
Neurath, Marie Reidemeister 156, 157–9
Neurath, Otto 28, 50, 156, 157–9
Neurath, Thomas 20, 30–1, 177, 178, 188,
188, 189–90, *189*, 191, *191*, 214
Neurath, Walter 17, 165, *165*, 170, *170*
art collection 38
at Adprint 72, 151, 153, 155, 159, 164
book packaging, invention of 21–2
commitment to young people 20,
208, 214
death 178–9
and designers 177
education and early career 19–22, 31, 32
emigrates to Britain 58, 72
as father of international publishing
196–7
Kokoschka drawing of 19, *19*
influence on other publishers 202,
203, 205
and Jarrold of Norwich 171–4
memorial lectures 215–16
and Thames & Hudson 9, 123, 145,
159–60, 164
Neurath, Wilhelm 50
Nicolson, Ben 37, 87
Nicolson, Nigel 204–5
Nkrumah, Kwame 160
Nonesuch Press 105, 109
Norrie, Ian 43
Novalis 129, *129*

Octopus 202
Oppé, A. p. 90
Osborn, Max 35
Ould Hermon 59
Oxenbury, Helen 218
Oxford University Press 84–7

Pächt, Otto 86
Panofsky, Erwin 41, 169
paperback, evolution of 113–17, 153–4
Parker, K. T. 90
Parrish, Max 123, 152, 159
Parrish, Mona 159
Pearson 203
Pelican Press 109
Penguin Books 44, 52, 76, 103, 108,
111, 112, 113–17, 172

Brandenburg Concertos, cover design,
110, 133, *133*
The Internment of Aliens, cover 133, *133*
King Penguins 136, *136*, 153–4
Pevsner, Nikolaus 37–8, 42, 86, 118, 154,
156, 210, 215
Phaidon Verlag 31, 54, 60
foundation 12–16
'Phaidon Drucke' 15, 129, *129*
Novalis 129, *129*
S. Unwin and 60–2
Phaidon:
championed by K. Clark 40
and George Allen & Unwin 88–90
E. H. Gombrich's *Story of Art* 9, 90–94
foundation 9, 12
jacket design 143, *143*
later developments 184–8
and Thames & Hudson 190–2
Van Gogh 33, *131*, *131*
photography 126–8, 145–6, 171–4, 199
Picture Post 123, 126, 145, 159, 199
Piper, John 153, 155–6
Piper, Richard / Piper Verlag 36
Poeschel, Karl Ernst 102–3
Pollock, Jackson 209
Pope-Henessey, John 90, 216
Praeger, Frederick Amos 186
Press of the Woolly Whale 106
Prestel 213
Priestley, J. B. 75–6
British Women Go to War 164
Propyläen Kunstgeschichte 34–6, 52
Publishers' Association 75
Puffin Books 117
Purnell, buys Adprint 157
Puyfelde, Leon van 90

Querido 53

Rainbird, George 197–9
Rathbone, Eleanor 57
Read, Herbert 19, 40, 43, 83, 91, 170, *170*, 175
A Concise History of Modern Painting 180
and Thames & Hudson 169–71
Read, Ludo 170
Reclam 113
refugee women, role of 156–7
Reinhardt, Max 14, 108
Religious Society of Friends 57, 95
Renner, Paul 36, 104, 107, 116
RIKOLA 32

Robertson, Bryan 214
Rosen, Michael 218
Rosenberg, Ruth 35, 52–3, 123, 152,
    156, 159, 168
Rosenthal, Tom 215
Roth, Joseph 15, 53, 190
Rotha, Paul 84, 152, 158
Rothenstein, Elizabeth 200
Rothenstein, Lucy 14, 14
Ruskin, John 38, 40
Russell, Bertrans 17, 17
Rutherston, Albert 83

Sackville-West, Vita 155
Sadler, Michael 41
Salfeld, Marianne 108
Salles, George 170, 170
Samuel Fischer Verlag 31, 34
Saumarez Smith, Charles 208–9, 215
Saxl, Fritz 42
Schaaf, Larry J. 217
Schapiro, Meyer 216
Scheu, Albert 20
Schiele, Egon 19, 27
    Neurath collection of drawings
        30, 32, 58
Schiff, Otto 57
Schlagman, Richard 186–8, 191
Schleger, Hans 112, 210
Schlosser, Julius von 87
Schmitz, Oscar Adolf 37
Schmoller, Hans Peter 108, 110–11,
    116–17, 122
Schnitzler, Arthur 15, 16, 23, 27
Schocken, Salman 55–6
Schoenberg, Arnold 208
Scholem, Siegfried 110
Schotten, Shalom 141, 141, 176–8
Schubring, Paul 35
Schüller, Erwin 85
Schüller, Hilde see under Kurz, Hilde
Schüller, Theodore ('Teddy') 29, 41, 84–7,
    86, 90, 91, 208
Schupf, Jacques 88
Schuschnigg, Kurt 59
Schwimmer, Max 119
Schwitter [Swiss blockmaker] 146, 146
Schwitters, Kurt 72
Seaton, Matt 19
Segher, Anna 53
Seliger, Max 119
Senior, Elizabeth 154

Seymour, John 203
Shand, James 199
Sieff, Israel 204–5
Simon, Oliver 82, 110, 111, 114, 116–17
Simons, Anna 102
Simpkin Marshall 74, 75
Simpson, Esther 77
Sims, F. J. 26
Skira 145–6, 200
Skira, Albert 83
Smollett, Peter (né Smolka) 17
Society for the Protection of Science
    and Learning 57, 77
Spectator 43
Spender, Humphrey 126
Spender, Michael 126
Spender, Stephen 126
Steiner-Prag, Hugo 100, 119
Stemmer, Arthur 19
Stenning, H. J. 70, 73
Steyrermühl Verlag 20–1, 22
Stone, Irvine 96
Stonor, Oliver 156
Strubel, Abigail 34
Suhrkamp, Peter 53
Summerson Committee 214
Suschitzky, Wolf 123, 126, 152, 153
Swinburne, Algernon 13

Tal, E. P. 54
Talbot-Klič process 135
Tanner, Robin 118
Taschen 213–14
Tate, Henry 38
Tauchnitz 114, 115
Taylor, A. J. P. 37
Taylor, Stephen, Battle for Health
    139, 139, 153
Taylor, Wendy 214
Te Neues 213
Thames & Hudson 152
    and democratization of art 179–81
    foundation and early years 9, 164–80
    How to Understand Modern Art 179
    jacket design 140–2, 140–2, 176–8
    and Jarrold of Norwich 164, 171–4
    later developments 188–92
    and Phaidon 190–2
    prizes awarded by 214–18
    'World of Art' 171, 179, 180
Theresianum Gymnasium, Vienna 29, 29
Tiemann, Walter 119

Tietze, Hans, Treasures of the Great
  National Galleries 179
Times Literary Supplement 93–4, 166,
  180, 208
Tisdall, Hans 199
Toynbee, Philip 204
Trier, Walter 117–18, 218
Tschichold, Jan 51–2, 105, 107,
  111, 116, 122, 154, 199
Tucholsky, Kurt 33, 53
Tudor Hart, Edith 123, 152
typography 103–7, 122, 199

Uhlman, Fred 36–7, 84
Ullmann, Elisabeth 156
Ullstein Verlag 34–5, 52–3, 117, 152
Ullstein, Herman 52
Ullstein, Louis 85
Ullstein, Rudolf 34
Unamuno, Miguel de 16
Ungar, Fritz 9, 12, 29, 61, 96
Unger, Hans 108–9
Unwin, Philip 88
Unwin, Stanley 59–62, 73, 74, 88,
  105, 94, 116, 172, 200
Unwin, T. Fisher 59
Upjohn, E. 93

Verlag Neuer Graphik 32
Vienna, cultural life before World War II
  15–16, 27–31

Wagner, Richard 100
Walker, Emery 102
Walter de Gruyter & Co. 35–6
Warburg Institute 41–2, 43, 87
Warburg Institute 209
Warburg, Aby 40, 42
Warburg, Frederic 76
Wedgwood, Josiah 57
Wegner, Christian 114
Wegner, Fritz 218
Wegner, Zoltan 153
Weidenfeld & Nicolson 173
Weidenfeld, George 28, 77, 165, *165*,
  204–5, 216
Weight, Carel 212
Weingert, P. 93
Weiss, E. R. 78, 104, 110
Weiss, Rudolf Emil 36

Weissenborn, Hellmuth 72, 78, 100, 111
  career 119–22, 222
  designs and illustrations 120, *120*,
    122, 123, 165, 212–13, *212*, 222
Werkbund 101
Whittington Press 121
Wiener Werkstätte 16, 27
Wilczynski, Katerina 152
William Collins 151
Wilson, Harold 204
Wilson, Hubert ('Petrel') 26
Wind, Edgar 42
Windsor Castle, catalogue
  raisonée 89–90
Witsch, J. C. 96
Wittkower, Margot 43
Wittkower, Rudolf 43, 77, 87
Wittman, R. 33
Wolpe, Berthold 15, 78, 105, 106, 117,
  122, 199, 210
Woolf, Virginia 37, 155
Würthle & Son 32

Yale University Press 192

Zweig, Stefan 15, 27, 29, 49, 73
Zwemmer, Anton 39, 82–4
Zwemmer's 39, 82–4, 94, 126, 201

Picture Credits

The author is grateful to the following for permission to reproduce photographs, and to copyright holders of books and images illustrated herein:

Erica Barrett fig. 8
Raymond Berger pl. 26
Peter Foges figs 4, 15
Fondation Oskar Kokoschka,
    Vevey/2012, Pro Litteris fig. 5
Leonie Gombrich fig. 7, pl. 2
Sandra Gonzalez fig. 2
Denise Grafe fig. 9
HarperCollins Publishers pl. 16
Hochschule für Grafik und
    Buchkunst, Leipzig pl. 27
Isotype Archive, Department
    of Typography & Graphic
    Communication, University
    of Reading pl. 18
Constance Kaine figs 16, 17, 21, 22, 23
Langewiesche Verlag pl. 15
Elly Miller figs 1, 3, 12, 14, 18, 19, 20
Penguin Group pls 7, 8, 9, 10, 13, 14
Phaidon Press Ltd. pls 1, 3, 4, 11,
    12, 24, 25
John Randall fig. 13
Andrew Schuller figs 6, 11
Jane Applebee Stokes fig. 24
Suhrkamp Verlag pls 5, 6
Thames & Hudson pls 19, 20, 21, 22, 23

Phaidon Press Limited
Regent's Wharf
All Saints Street
London N1 9PA

Phaidon Press Inc.
65 Bleecker Street
New York, NY 10012

www.phaidon.com

First published 2014
© 2014 Phaidon Press Ltd

ISBN 978 0 7148 6702 1

A CIP catalogue record for this book
is available from the British Library.

Designed by John Morgan studio

Printed in China